Problems of
a sociology of knowledge

International Library of Sociology

Founded by Karl Mannheim

Editor: John Rex, University of Warwick

Arbor Scientiae
Arbor Vitae

A catalogue of the books available in the **International Library of Sociology** and other series of Social Science books published by Routledge & Kegan Paul will be found at the end of this volume.

Problems of
a sociology of knowledge

Max Scheler

Translated by
Manfred S. Frings

Edited and with an introduction by Kenneth W. Stikkers

Routledge & Kegan Paul

London, Boston and Henley

This translation first published in 1980
by Routledge & Kegan Paul Ltd
39 Store Street, London WC1E 7DD,
9 Park Street, Boston, Mass. 02108, USA and
Broadway House, Newtown Road
Henley-on-Thames, Oxon RG9 1EN
Set in Monophoto Times New Roman
and printed in Great Britain by
Thomson Litho Ltd, East Kilbride, Scotland
Translated from the German edition published by
Francke Verlag, Bern 1960
Copyright Introduction Kenneth W. Stikkers 1980

British Library Cataloguing in Publication Data

Scheler, Max
Problems of a sociology of knowledge.—
(International library of sociology).
1. Knowledge, Sociology of
I. Title   II. Series
301.2'1   BD175   79-40119

ISBN 0 7100 0302 1

Contents

Translator's note

Max Scheler's 'Probleme einer Soziologie des Wissens' originally appeared as the introductory essay to the anthology *Versuche zu einer Soziologie des Wissens,* which he edited (Munich: Duncker & Humblot, 1924), pp. 1–146. The work later appeared, slightly changed and expanded, as part of Scheler's *Die Wissensformen und die Gesellschaft* (Leipzig: Der Neue Geist Verlag, 1926), pp. 1–229. The present translation of this text is taken from the 2nd edition of the *Wissensformen und die Gesellschaft,* edited by Maria Scheler, volume 8 of Scheler's *Gesammelte Werke* (Bern: A. Francke Verlag, 1960), pp. 16–190. Corrections made for the forthcoming 3rd edition of the *Wissensformen und die Gesellschaft* have been included in this translation.

Throughout the text the German term *'Geist'* has been rendered as 'mind,' except for particular instances where it had to be translated by 'spirit.' The primary context of Scheler's use of 'mind' is in speaking of the 'group-mind.' By contrast 'spirit' is used in connection with *'Drang'* (vital urge), i.e. in a metaphysical, not sociological, context.

DePaul University   M.S.F.
Chicago
November 1978

Introduction

Kenneth W. Stikkers

In every historical age a certain set of concerns and problems are experienced more deeply than others by those living in that age and lie most closely to its vital center, nagging at its heart, trying its people's souls, and hindering, to a greater or lesser degree, its life flow. These concerns are those that express themselves again and again through the intellectuals of the age—the artists, writers, and philosophers—as well as in the thinking of the masses.

For Western civilization in the twentieth century particularly profound has been the experience of social fragmentation and isolation. Social scientists, for example, have described our modern society as a 'lonely crowd', noting that ironically as people have been increasingly enmassed into cities and have become geographically closer together, the psychic bonds that hold people together in communal solidarity—in families, neighborhoods, nations, etc.—have steadily dissolved.[1] And while in pre-industrial ages social situation and cultural heritage provided one with a sense of place in the universe, a context of meaning, a sense of identity, in the modern age one frequently sees one's social relations and heritage as sources of deception and corruption and forms of enslavement. Society is often pictured as a giant bureaucratic-technological machine, which is thoroughly antithetical to man's true nature and which squeezes the last ounce of life from the human spirit for its own sinister, inhuman, and always very foggy purposes. (George Orwell's *1984* is, of course, a prime example of this portrayal.) Work in modern society, as described by Karl Marx, for example, is experienced not as an expression of one's identity but as a force that alienates man from himself, an activity imposed upon man not by natural necessity but by dictatorial institutional forces which bear the names of corporations.[2] One's nation is often as much a source of embarrassment as it is a source of pride. And, most

1

peculiarly, the family, long viewed in traditional communities as the positive core of one's identity, is today seen, especially by psychology, as the primary source of prejudices, deceptions, and neuroses of all sorts, as something to be gotten away from. (Indeed, one is almost led to believe that we would all have happy, healthy personalities if only we had no parents!) All these things, so familiar to us, are indicative of the prevalent experience of social fragmentation and isolation.

And if meaning, in general, resides in one's felt connection with something greater than one's self, a larger whole, a more feeling part of a *context*, be it social, religious, or whatever—then this social fragmentation must be seen as coincidental with a breakdown of experienced life context and a loss of meaning, i.e. with the rise of nihilism. Indeed, just as every age has had for itself an image of man, a representation of what it means to be human— e.g. the Greek hero, the rational man of the Enlightenment—the image we have of man in our age seems to resemble a cubist painting—viz. fragmented, distorted, confused or, more frighten- ingly, the figure in Eduard Munch's *The Scream*: throughout the literature and art of the twentieth century man is portrayed as a being who is internally screaming, screaming so violently that the entire world seems to vibrate—and yet, strangely enough, no one seems to hear, certainly no god. And such artistic portrayals of modern man are confirmed by the social scientists: according to every stress indicator known—heart attacks, suicides, alcoholism, violent crimes, drug usage, etc.—the concrete, experienced quality of life—not the abstract quality of life measured by gross national product and per capita income statistics—has steadily declined as the modern technological age has progressed, despite generally increasing affluence.[3] Indeed, far from being one concern among many, the experience of loss of meaning is one that engulfs our entire being. As Max Scheler so well observed, 'man is more of a problem to himself at the present time than ever before in all recorded history.'[4] Never before has the ancient dictum 'Know thyself' seemed so impossible. Twentieth-century man, unlike those before him, really does not know who he is or what his place is in the order of the cosmos: he is a being in search of his own meaning.

It was to such an age, in which the human context of things is experienced as hopelessly fragmented and the search for meaning reaches desperation, that the German philosopher Max Scheler (1874-1928) spoke. He, like Oswald Spengler,[5] Edmund Husserl,[6] Martin Heidegger,[7] Jose Ortega y Gasset,[8] Nicolai Berdyaev,[9] and so many others of his day, pointed to the 'crisis' of Western civilization. But among his contemporaries he stood out as a man of great vision, possessing enormous intellectual strength that enabled him to see beyond the impending crisis and prevailing pessimism of our age. As Heidegger wrote, Scheler was 'the strongest philosophical force in Germany, nay, in all Europe—and even in all contemporary philosophy':[10] for a whole generation of thinkers Max Scheler was a beacon of light which pierced the darkness of nihilism.

It has therefore been at a great loss to the English-speaking world that Scheler has remained in relative obscurity and his works have gone so long untranslated. The present translation of his *Problems of a Sociology of Knowledge* thus makes available Scheler's most significant work in sociological theory.[11] And it, together with his *Ressentiment,*[12] *Ethics,*[13] and *The Nature of Sympathy,*[14] which have already appeared in translation, now offers English-speaking people a significant view of this thinker's penetrating insights into the nature of human association, insights which are so badly needed in our times.

It is not then the purpose of this introduction to interpret the *Sociology of Knowledge* for the reader, for surely a great work is fully capable of speaking well enough for itself. But rather our intent is to place the work in the context of Scheler's thought as a whole by focusing upon what we consider Scheler's major contributions to sociological theory: 1 phenomenological sociology, or phenomenology of community, 2 value sociology, and 3 the sociology of knowledge.

1 Phenomenological sociology; phenomenology of community

In recent years there has been significant interest in the applications of 'phenomenology' to sociology. Many of these attempts at 'phenomenological sociology' represent sound scholarship and extremely creative and suggestive lines of thinking—the works of Alfred Schutz and Jürgen Habermas, for example. But the bulk of such writings merely claim as 'phenomenological' any 'descriptive' sociology and attempt to disguise as genuine 'phenomenological insights' all sorts of subjective biases and prejudices. In general, these misguided efforts lack any sort of reductive method—which is the heart of any genuine phenomenology—for leading to legitimate phenomenological insights into essences and separating these insights from unfounded assertions. All this has been to the dismay of the more empirical, scientific sociologists— and rightly so—and to the chagrin and detriment of legitimate and more rigorous phenomenology.

Scheler can properly be credited with being the father of phenomenological sociology, from whom thinkers like Schutz and

Habermas have gained their fundamental insights. And he offered the first significant alternative approach to sociology since August Comte's conception of that discipline as a positive science.

Comte defined Positivism as the 'science of facts,' and by 'facts' he meant, of course, empirical sense data.[15] Hence, ever since, and even more so today, sociologists have been obsessed with establishing their discipline as a genuine positive science. Indeed, at the beginning of virtually every introductory text in sociology one finds a fairly lengthy attempt to convince the reader that that discipline is truly a science.

But a number of contemporary thinkers, including those of the existential-phenomenological tradition in Germany and France, William James in America, and R. G. Collingwood in England, have criticized as misguided this effort to make all pursuits of knowledge part of one universal positive science.

Edmund Husserl, for example, saw positivism as a prime manifestation of the 'crisis' of Western civilization. Enamored by the extraordinary successes of Western science in the seventeenth, eighteenth, and nineteenth centuries, twentieth-century man has now sought to extend its principles so that virtually every realm of human existence, including that of spirit, i.e. every realm of human subjectivity, has, in the name of science, been naturalized, reduced to an objective material nature within the forms of spatio-temporality and made to conform to the laws of that presumed objective nature, e.g. the laws of cause and effect.[16] And in so far as science commits itself to the goal of providing *causal* explanations for events,[17] it already from the beginning commits itself, quite uncritically, to such a naturalization of human subjectivity. Thus, for example, the human mind, upon the generally accepted authority of experimental, behavioralist psychology, has been reduced to a physical brain, which functions not upon the principles of reason but upon the laws of bio-chemistry; emotions, feelings of sympathy and compassion, experiences of beauty, all inner experiences of conscience, and all sensitivities to questions of ethics, justice, and human dignity are similarly reduced to bodily states within a physical environment. And modern psychology offers us abundant advice on the subject of human sexuality but, in general, is strikingly silent on the subject of personal love. Husserl called such an objectivistic, positive science 'naive' because it 'holds what it calls the objective world to be the totality of what is, without paying any attention to the fact that no objective science can do justice to the subjectivity that achieves [i.e. thinks] science.'[18]

In America William James voiced similar criticisms of modern science. He was appalled by its insensitivity to moral issues and its tendency to breed ethical apathy. He wrote in 1896:[19]

> When one turns to the magnificent edifice of the physical
> sciences, and sees how it was reared, what thousands of
> disinterested moral lives of men lie buried in its mere
> foundations; what patience and postponement, what choking
> down of preference, what submission to the icy laws of outer
> fact are wrought into its very stones and mortar; how absolutely
> impersonal it stands in its vast augustness...

James suggested that just as we look back upon former ages and
laugh at what appear to us as silly beliefs and errors, so too future
generations will look back in disbelief at our modern science's
refusal to recognize the realm of spirit, of human subjectivity, as in
any way significant:[20]

> this systematic denial on science's part of the personality as a
> condition of events, this rigorous belief that in its own essential
> and innermost nature our world is a strictly impersonal world,
> may conceivably, as the whirlgig of time goes around, prove to
> be the very defect that our descendents will be most surprised at
> in our boasted science, the omission that to their eyes will most
> tend to make it look perspectiveless and short.

Science's insistence that human subjectivity constantly be made to
conform to the impersonalism of its objective laws and principles,
James claimed, constituted 'intellectual imperialism'. It was for this
reason that James denounced psychology—the discipline that he
himself had once worked so hard to establish as a legitimate
science—as 'that nasty business', adding that 'all that one cares to
know lies outside it.'[21]

And in England, R. G. Collingwood, like Husserl and James,
described modern science as the domination of the abstract,
general, and objective over the concrete, particular, and subjective
and therefore saw it as a force that alienated man from himself and
obscured him from, rather than aided him in, his search for self-
understanding. 'Abstractive by its own chosen nature', Collingwood wrote in 1924, science[22]

> throws the object outside the subject in the form of law, a
> universal, over against its own instances; and therefore when it
> tries to return upon itself it can only study, not itself, but the
> abstract law of its own operations regarded as something
> objective and not subjective, not itself but some alien
> determinant of itself. This alien determinant, which it calls
> nature or the objective world, is in reality a pure fiction of the
> hypostalized or abstract universal.

5

Despite their different traditions and orientations, Husserl, James, and Collingwood, among others, all observed that as modern science has progressed and increasingly dominated Western life, modern man has become increasingly unable to address those questions that burn most deeply in the human heart, questions of meaning.

Indeed, the issue at stake in these criticisms of modern science is not that of whether science is 'correct' or 'incorrect' in its descriptions of our world. Rather, the issue is, as Edmund Husserl so well pointed out in his chilling commentary on modern life, *The Crisis of European Science and Transcendental Phenomenology*, whether or not man can even live with such a one-sided view of himself, whereby his entire spiritual life is denied as not verifiable according to the principles of scientific objectivity.[23] Natural science's conception of human life as a complex of bio-chemico-physical processes, for example, may have been adequate and even necessary for the development of modern medical technology and all the benefits of improved health care it may have brought us, but it has virtually nothing to say about the *meaning* of that life to which it attends. This silence regarding questions of meaning is in no way an inherent 'defect' of science, but when science, enamored by its own successes within the realm of physical nature, attempts to encompass all other realms of human existence and claims the final word in all matters, then it acts as a censor of any discussion touching upon those issues closest to the human heart and becomes a positive barrier to man's self-understanding and search for meaning.

In general, the behavioral and social sciences have been particularly obsessed with modeling themselves after the natural sciences—e.g. witness their concern with scientific method, experimentation, and statistical data. And to the extent that they, in the name of positive science, have come to monopolize discussions focusing upon human relations, they have tended to stifle discussion of the most meaningful issues and have left a void that man's spiritual nature yearns to fill: the image of the human person presented to us through the generally accepted authority of the social sciences is one that we cannot recognize as that of the concrete beings we are. Modern psychology tells us that we as individuals are repertoires of behavior determined, through physical laws of cause and effect, by bio-chemical processes and material environmental factors and, as such, possess no imma-terial, spiritual side, or soul.[24] But we do not recognize such an individual as the dear friend—the concrete, living, breathing *person*—with whom we share, over a glass of wine or beer, our greatest hopes and joys, who comforts us in our darkest hours of despair, and with whom we share our innermost feelings and secrets. Nor does social science's description of human relations in the language of roles and institutions, structures and functions, and its attempt to quantify such relations and subject them to statistical laws, present a recognizeable image of those essentially qualitative relations we enjoy with friends and family members, with whom we share a very special psychic bond which gives us a privileged access to those persons' innermost lives. Such descriptions may be adequate for the more superficial transactions of business and law, but they fail sadly in helping us to understand those deeper, more meaningful inter-*personal* relations characterized by sympathy and love. And to the extent that modern business and politics have adopted this image of man as their model (e.g. the adoption of behaviorist psychology by managerial and marketing sciences) they have created institutions in which the human spirit is stifled and we as persons do not feel at home.[25]

Scheler was strikingly aware of the narrow limits of a sociology that tried to make itself a strict positive science, as Comte conceived it. And so his analysis of human groupings began, not with the study of objective institutional structures and functions and of the roles of those within such institutions, but with a careful phenomenological investigation into those subjective, experiential, psychic bonds that unite unique, individual *persons* in feelings of love and sympathy.[26] In offering such a radically new foundation for the study of interpersonal relations, Scheler, while acting as the Director of the Institute for Social Scientific Research at the University of Cologne from 1921 until his death in 1928, was at the forefront of an entirely new and exciting movement among European social thinkers, whose significance has been recognized by only a few philosophers and social scientists of the Anglo-American tradition.

Foundational to Scheler's analysis of interpersonal relations is the distinction made by Ferdinand Tönnies[27] between society (*Gesellschaft*) and community (*Gemeinschaft*). 'Society' designated for Tönnies not human association in general, as the term is commonly used today, but specifically those types of groupings held together by objective structural, organizational (even bureaucratic) bonds, bonds which are primarily contractual in nature, such as those operative in business and politics. A community, on the other hand, is a human group held together by highly subjective, felt bonds of solidarity, for example, the bonds of blood that hold together a family or tribe. Society is basically additive; that is, it is an aggregation of relatively autonomous individuals and equal to the sum of its parts. Community, though, is basically organic and more than the sum of its members. As Tönnies explains,[28]

7

the Gemeinschaft among people is stronger and more alive; it is the lasting and genuine form of living together. In contrast to Gemeinschaft, Gesellschaft is transitory and superficial. Accordingly, Gemeinschaft should be understood as a living organism, Gesellschaft as a mechanical aggregate and artifact.

To the extent, then, that community is based in co-feelings, co-experiences, and organic principles, it is a 'natural' form of association; while to the extent that society is based upon organizational structures created through mechanistic principles of human reason, it is an 'artificial' form of association.

In his *Ressentiment* Scheler, too, sharply distinguishes these group types from one another and from a third group type not considered by Tönnies, the mass:

> In fact, 'society' is not the inclusive concept, designating all the 'communities' which are united by blood, tradition, and history. On the contrary, it is only the *remnant,* the *rubbish* left by the inner *decomposition* of communities. Whenever the unity of communal life can no longer prevail, whenever it becomes unable to assimilate the individuals and develop them into its living organs, we get a 'society'—a unity based on mere contractual agreement. When the 'contract' and its validity cease to exist, the result is the completely unorganized 'mass', unified by nothing more than momentary sensory stimuli and mutual contagion.

And Scheler characterizes modern life, of course, as primarily societal, rather than communal.[29]

The implications of Tönnies's analysis were for Scheler enormous. To begin with, modern sociology, by insisting that *all* forms of human association be examined in terms of their structure, function, and other sorts of objective (i.e. external) characteristics, looks at communal groupings through societal eyes, distorting their distinctively organic bonds to make them fit into a societal frame of reference. That is to say, sociology has been amazingly naive in regard to its own *societal* presuppositions. But, moreover, if sociology is indeed, as Comte defined it, a positive science which studies only empirical fact, then sociology, by definition, is absolutely incapable of ever penetrating into those inner, highly subjective, felt bonds which hold us together in the deepest and most meaningful of interpersonal relations, those relationships that are essentially communal in nature, and must restrict itself to describing only those more objective, structural—e.g. contractual—bonds holding individuals together in societal groups, i.e. institutions. And in so far as empirical science focuses upon *particular* facts, or data, making the individual primary and the whole secondary, it cannot comprehend the organic *unity* of a community: as the physicist Werner Heisenberg so well stated, 'If harmony in a society [viz. community, in Tönnies's sense] of the unity behind the multitude of phenomena, the language of the poets may be more important than that of the scientists.'[30] Thus, a method other than that of positive science, which sociology has adopted as its own, is required for us to gain insight into communal life. Such a method we might term a phenomenology of community.

Scheler's notion of phenomenology, contrary to the claims of much secondary literature, was developed quite independently of Husserl's and must be understood on its own terms.[31] (Indeed, attempted critiques of Scheler often badly miss the mark because they try to interpret and criticize Scheler from the standpoint of Husserlian phenomenology.[32]) While for Husserl phenomenology is a reflexive act that cuts across the normal flow of *consciousness* to reveal and delineate its eidetic, or essential, structures, i.e. its intentional nature, as the subjective condition for the possibility of all thinking whatsoever, especially science, phenomenology for Scheler is an *'attitude'* based in a 'psychic technique', a specific act of spirit, that blocks the normal flow of vital drive, of *life*, to reveal its growing, striving, becoming tendencies, on the one side, and the givenness of the world as resistance, on the other—a technique which Scheler saw already in Eastern Buddhism, a major source for his thinking. Scheler emphasized that phenomenology is *not* a method because

A method is a goal-directed procedure of *thinking about* facts,
for example, induction or deduction. In phenomenology,
however, it is a matter, first, of new facts themselves, before they
have been fixed by logic, and second, of a procedure of *seeing*.[33]

Conceived as such, phenomenology is not foundational for all philosophy (i.e. 'pre-philosophical') as it is for Husserl, but is a technique that provides us with insights of a special kind and occupies a much more modest position.

Moreover, while for Husserl the phenomena of dator consciousness are constituted within the polarities of noesis and noema, for Scheler the reality of the world is given within the polarities of vital drive (*Drang*), tending towards increasing spiritualization, and resistance. In his *Metaphysik* Scheler denied the sharp distinction commonly made between living and non-living things, arguing that a vital growing, becoming tendency permeates all nature and could be found already even in the pulsations of sub-atomic particles.[34] This vital urge is not random or chaotic in its movements, but rather, in its striving towards increasing spiritualization, it projects, like a cone of light from an automobile headlight, its own possibility, its own *ability-to-be*, ahead of itself as a phantasmic image.[35] Vital drive seeks out those object correlates in the world that most adequately fulfill its interests. And what is experienced as 'real' as existing, can be so experienced only in-so-far as it presents itself against a world-context which withstands or *resists* vital drive's coming-to-be: such is Scheler's understanding of the meaning of being-in-the-world. The experience of reality is constituted within the co-relation of vital drive and world resistance, and this experience of resistance is prior to the perception of the whatness (*Sosein*) and existence (*Dasein*) of things as well as the cognition of essences (*Wesen*). As Scheler writes, 'We comprehend, therefore, in the order of givenness, the being-*real* [*Realsein*] of an indefinite something *prior to* its *what*ness [*Sosein*].'[36] In short, where there is no *tension* between drives and the resistance of the world, there is no reality given to life. (The world itself may, of course, continue to exist without such a tension, but we would have no way of ever knowing.) Hence, Scheler is in full agreement with Heraclitus's claim that 'Strife [*polemos*] fathers all things.'[37] It was the very lack of any notion of resistance that Scheler found most objectionable in Heidegger's *Sein und Zeit*[38] and of which he was also critical in the phenomenologies of Hegel and Husserl[39]—i.e. there is no resistance factor in Dasein's way of being-in-the-world, in the unfolding of Spirit in history, nor in transcendental subjectivity, respectively. We might imagine a world like the one envisioned in the German fairy tale 'The Land of Cockaigne,' portrayed by the sixteenth-century Flemish painter Pieter Bruegel the Elder, where every human desire—be it appetitive, sexual, or power based—is immediately fulfilled: such a world must be an imaginary world, an unreal world, precisely because it is a world where there is no strife, no resistance to vital drive.

So, too, in a utopia where there is perfect harmony, there would be no social reality, no social group given whatsoever—that is to say, no experience of being-with one another—for that group. *Social* reality, like all other realms of being, rests upon strife: this is the metaphysical foundation for all social theories that identify the 'natural state' of man as one of conflict (e.g. Thomas Hobbes and various other 'social contract' theorists). But such theories confuse the metaphysical principle of strife (*polemos*) with the political state of war, projecting onto the latter their insights into the former. Indeed, no utopia or social ideal (e.g. the ideal of peace[40]) can ever become completely realized: rather, it can be real only in-so-far as it is in the process of becoming, struggling for existence against the resistance of the world.

Except for rare moments, human existence *suffers* from lack of vital fulfillment—i.e. suffering is co-constituted with reality in vital drive's encounter with the resistance of the world. In this sense suffering is the subjective correlate of the 'real' in experiences of resistance. Thus the task of all thinking—philosophical, religious, scientific, etc.—is, according to Scheler, to eliminate this suffering,[41] and this means to make the world less real. There are basically two techniques for this, two major traditions in world history.

The first technique is manifest in the Western heroic attitude: vital drive, expressing itself either in brute strength or in rationality, seeks to rise up and overcome the resistance of the world, just as the Western (e.g. Greek) hero seeks to overcome his enemies and all other barriers that stand in his way. In the realm of knowledge this attitude is expressed in the rationalistic attempt of Western science to conquer reality conceptually, to bring it under the rule of abstraction and logic, principles and laws, viz. to technologize it. And by so conceptualizing and abstracting the world, the Western mind has sought to overcome the suffering within human existence and in so doing make the world less real.

The second technique, found mainly in Eastern mysticisms, e.g. Buddhism and Taoism, but also in the West, e.g. in Christianity, is the psychic technique of non-resistance. Such a technique seeks to block or 'dissolve' the vital urge (i.e. the will) and thereby cancel, as much as possible, the world's resistance. All phenomenologies, whether they be Husserlian, Heideggerian, or Schelerian, are based, more or less, upon such an attitude; this for Scheler is the heart of the phenomenological reduction and bracketing process. The technique of non-resistance puts out of action the reality of the world by nullifying its resistance, puts aside its *ontic* claims, makes it unreal, and lets essences come forth and show themselves. It is a technique for letting the world *ontologically* and essentially *be*. Moreover, such a showing of essences can only take place in the absence of drive impulses and sense perception, i.e. in the absence of resistance. It is a technique that does not seek knowledge—as long as knowledge is understood in terms of a certain mastery over things through conceptualization—but in allowing insight into essences it brings forth wisdom, in-so-far as wisdom has at its heart a sense of humility and recognition that being overflows the categories of thought and thus can never be completely tamed by reason. (Indeed, what phenomenologist ever speaks of phenomenological 'knowledge'?) In the same way Socrates at times describes wisdom as 'not knowing', i.e. not pretending to possess or have mastered truth: rather than offering a counter-position, or resistance, Socrates, by blocking his own drive for mastery,

11

allowed a position to come forth, stand, and show *itself* (according to the *Logos*) to be either true or false. Hence, one might argue that such a technique of gaining insight into essences through non-resistance is more consistent with the original understanding of philosophy as 'love of wisdom' than those techniques connected with modern science, whose aim is knowledge (*scire* = to know) and mastery of the world, both conceptually and technologically.

While both techniques aim at de-realization of the world there are important differences, then, in the ways this is done. First, the technique of overcoming the resistance of the world does not allow the essences of that world to show through as does the technique of non-resistance: the former seeks to control the world and not to gain insight into its essences. Second, the technique of overcoming the resistance of the world at the same time seeks to overcome the suffering of the world, but it is in no way concerned with understanding the meaning of that suffering. Modern medical technology, as an example of that technique, might be able to relieve the suffering of the child who is ill, and even save his life, but it has nothing to say to the mother of that child about the meaning of his suffering should he die. Modern medicine may prolong human life but cannot address the meaning of that life. And if indeed suffering is at the foundation of all experiences of reality, as Scheler contends, then the technique of control is incapable of addressing any question of meaning whatsoever. The physicist Werner Heisenberg was able to reduce the world to a 'world formula', and the philosopher of science Carl G. Hempel may represent biological life with the formula: $Lx \equiv Dx \cdot Mx \cdot Rx$, whereby Lx = living organism, Dx = definitive boundary, Mx = metabolic function, and Rx = reproductive function.[42] But such formalizations of the world and life carry no meaning. The technique of overcoming resistance, in its effort to control the world, *formalizes* that world, i.e. constructs a network of concepts and abstractions in which it seeks to 'catch' the world, and thereby shuts off and drains all essences and meanings from it: it is a technique that may, in some instances, successfully de-realize the world and overcome its suffering but in so doing leaves a yawning void for the human spirit that only a non-scientific mode of thinking can fill.

So now after elucidating Scheler's phenomenology in general, we can begin to understand what a phenomenological sociology entails. It is *not* an effort to collect and systematize data about social existence (Scheler emphasizes this at the very beginning of the *Sociology of Knowledge*), nor does it seek to formalize and make abstract that existence in terms of structures, functions, roles, etc. Rather, it seeks insights into the concrete experiences of persons living-with one another in groups, into their co-feelings and co-thinking. It examines not the objective, external structures of the group but the inner, subjective psychic bonds which unite persons in sympathy and love. Applying, now, Scheler's phenomenological attitude, such insights are gained not by maintaining an objective, critical distance in relation to the group, a stance which gives the observer the illusion that he is intellectually comprehending, i.e. dominating, that group; for indeed, to claim such comprehension implies a position of domination, a position of looking down upon the group as though from above. Rather, it is a sympathetic entering-into the inner life of a group by blocking one's own vital interests and thereby nullifying social resistance, always recognizing that complete dissolution of resistance is impossible and that some social distantiation will always remain. One allows himself to be overcome by and taken up into the co-living and co-thinking of the group and views that group not in terms of his own societal frame of reference but, as much as possible, within the terms of the group itself.

Such a technique thus resembles that of the 'participant observer.' But unlike a phenomenological sociology, this latter technique still clings to its 'objective' standpoint, i.e. its societal standpoint (for what is objectivity but itself a subjective demand of societal life). And like the technique of the participant observer, phenomenology recognizes that the more one is taken up into a group, i.e. the more he becomes part of that group, the less able he is to describe that group. But because its goal is essential insight rather than conceptual knowledge, phenomenological sociology does not see this as a shortcoming of its technique as does the more scientific sociologist with regard to the participant observer.[43]

II Value sociology

First and foremost Max Scheler was a philosopher of *value*: the question of value permeates the entirety of his writings. Thus his phenomenology must be understood not only in terms of vital drive and resistance but also as a phenomenology of value: that is to say, prior to all other intentional acts, whether they be acts of consciousness (as in the phenomenology of Husserl) or acts of the lived body (e.g. Merleau-Ponty), are intentional acts of value-ception, or value feelings. The center of experience, then, is not any transcendental subjectivity, nor a body-subject, nor a *Dasein* who raises the question of the meaning of Being. Rather, experience is centered in the one through whose acts all values manifest themselves, that is, in the *person*: the person, through his acts, is, for Scheler, the bearer of all values. Hence, Scheler's phenomenological sociology in general and sociology of knowledge in particular must be seen in the light of his focus upon value and philosophy of the person.

While the tendency of twentieth-century philosophy and social science has been toward increasing relativism (both cultural and individualistic) in all matters, especially those touching upon value, Scheler courageously argued against such a tendency and sought to show, through a thorough phenomenological analysis of concrete moral acts, that organic drive-life, in its process of be-coming and tendency towards increasing spiritualization, strives to realize itself according to an *absolute hierarchy of values,* which he calls the 'ordo amoris,' or 'order of the heart'; that is to say, vital drive is always value-intended. Such a hierarchy can never be completely comprehended by the mind, for, like Blaise Pascal, Scheler maintains that 'the heart has its own reasons' which the mind cannot understand: 'The heart possesses a strict analogue of logic of its own domain that it does not borrow from the logic of the understanding.'[44] Rather, we can gain only occasional and fragmented glimpses into such an order of values through our deepest experiences of conscience.

Scheler thus offered his own very tentative delineation of five value spheres, or value ranks, in this hierarchy. At the bottom is the sphere of sensible values, ranging from the agreeable to the disagreeable, from the pleasureable to the painful. Next is the value sphere of utility, ranging from the useful to the useless and including the practical, the efficient, and the economical. Third is the value sphere of biological life, ranging from the noble to the vulgar and including health and disease, strength and weakness. Fourth is the sphere of spiritual values, and there are three types of such values: aesthetic values (viz. the beautiful), the value of justice (as grounded in feelings of right and wrong), and the value of the pure cognition of Truth (as it is sought by philosophy, for example). Fifth is the sphere of the Absolute, ranging from the Holy to the Unholy.

Scheler arrives at such an approximation of the hierarchy of values through a phenomenological analysis of concrete moral acts; that is to say, the order of values shows itself to us in such acts rather than in rational thought. A moral act occurs when a person *prefers* the contents of one value sphere over that of another. The higher values reveal themselves as those which are preferred over lower values in acts presenting themselves to conscience as morally good; conversely lower values are preferred to higher values in acts presenting themselves as morally evil. For example, when reading Plato's *Phaedo* one experiences the life of Socrates as a moral life, the value of philosophical truth (belonging

14

to the sphere of spiritual values) presents itself as a higher value than the value of biological life which Socrates sacrificed for the former. And our feelings of moral disgust at one who ruins his health by engaging in excesses of bodily pleasure reveals such pleasure to be a lower value than life. Stated more generally, in concrete moral acts the higher values show themselves as those for which lower values *ought* to be sacrificed: e.g. the value of biological life shows itself to conscience in moral acts as that *for which* pleasure *ought* to be sacrificed and as that *which ought* to be sacrificed for spiritual values (as in the case of Socrates) or for the value of the Holy (as in the case of the religious martyr).

Because the coming-to-be of vital urge takes place always in terms of value, intentional acts are not merely acts of 'consciousness of' but are also always relative to some particular value. Prior to all acts of perception and thinking are intentional acts of *value*-feeling: all perceiving and thinking is value-intended, i.e. aimed at a particular value (e.g. the acquisition of pleasure, utility, the preservation of life, art, salvation). Prior to their appearances as specific 'thises' and 'thats' the objects of experience present themselves to vital urge as either interesting or uninteresting, fulfilling or unfulfilling: as Scheler states, 'Everything which we perceive must, before we perceive it, in some way address and interest our vital drives.'[45] Those things that provide adequate contents for our value-feelings we find vitally interesting and thus become part of the 'real'; those things that provide inadequate contents for and fail to address our vital interests become part of the 'unreal'. Only secondarily do objects become individualized and acquire specific characteristics. Using Scheler's analogy of the automobile headlights, we might imagine ourselves driving down a dark road when suddenly 'something' appears before us: before we determine whether it is a deer or a cloud of smoke or a tree or a person, it appears merely as 'something' of which we *ought* to be cautious. Or, we might imagine ourselves in a crowded airport waiting for a loved one to arrive. The thousands of people passing by are 'seen' only as 'not-the-one-for-whom-we-are-looking'—i.e. they are not really seen at all; they are not 'real' to us. Suddenly we spot the one whom we have anxiously awaited and our looking ends: our value intentionality is fulfilled, and we only then realize, 'This is Mary,' or 'This is Father'.

Hence, under no circumstances should one interpret the hierarchy of values as a formal, rationalistic *criterion,* or pre-established set of principles, for deductively determining ethical behavior. For if, indeed, value-feeling *precedes* all perception and thinking, then the givenness of values in moral acts is *prior to* their being intellectually grasped and articulated. Ethical behavior can

15

never be the result of one's determination and apprehension of formalized ethical principles (as in Kant) but is the result solely of the ethical character, or value comportment, of the individual person. We do not choose our values; rather, values choose us. At best, thought can only very slightly and subtly steer a given value-feeling toward appropriate object correlates. But reason can never provide values themselves: thought without a felt value, without emotive cognition, is impotent. Moreover, Scheler radically shifts the paradigmatic location of the moral ought from the rational mind, which objectively observes and judges a given act from a distance, as it were, to the inner, solemn experience of 'pangs of conscience', which occur when one's personal striving towards spiritualization of drive through realization of higher values, has missed its mark: it is in this intense, negative experience that the 'proper' order of values most clearly reveals itself to the human heart.

The apparent relativity of values, which modern social sciences accept so uncritically, arises from the fact that different cultures and groups assign different contents (objects and acts) to the different value spheres. For example, one group might view the horse as a work animal and thus assign it to the value sphere of utility, while another group might see the horse as a sacred animal and thus assign it to the value sphere of the Holy. So, while the *contents* of the value spheres may be relative, the hierarchical order of the spheres remains absolute.

Scheler suggested several characteristics that distinguish the higher value ranks from the lower,[46] two of which are of direct relevance to our understanding of his value sociology.

First, the higher the value the less dependent it is upon material goods and the more holistic and less quantifiable its contents tend to be. And the lower the value the more dependent it is upon material goods and the more divisible and quantifiable its contents tend to be. For example, the Holy is essentially immaterial, indivisible, uncompromising, and non-quantifiable; it is an absolute unity, or One. While at the other end of the spectrum the value of pleasure readily lends itself to division and quantification and is essentially material. We can divide up a bottle of wine, but we cannot compromise God. The value of half a loaf of bread is approximately half that of a whole loaf, but half of a Rembrandt painting is not worth half of the whole work.

Second, the higher a value the deeper and more enduring is the fulfillment that it yields. Thus. bodily pleasure endures only as long as there is physical stimulation, and it leaves the individual longing for additional pleasure and deeper satisfaction, i.e. longing for a more ultimate experience. The feeling of bliss corresponding to the value of the Holy, by contrast, endures despite the experience of disvalues at a lower level: the divine bliss of the saint is undisturbed by bodily pain and earthly unhappiness. Moreover, the feeling of bliss leaves one wholly satisfied and desirous of nothing more.

Within every individual person, inscribed in the heart, the entire spectrum of values is present. But for each individual one particular value stands out as dominant, thereby dictating that person's own order of preferences among the values, an order which may coincide or conflict with the ideal hierarchy. And it is this particular order of value preferences, one's *ethos*, that forms the core, or essence, of one's personality. Thus one gains the most profound insight into the personhood of another when one catches a glimpse, e.g. through phenomenological method, into the ethos of that individual, an insight which empirical science, because it is concerned solely with the objective and external, cannot provide. As Scheler writes, '*Whoever has the* **ordo amoris** *of a man has the man himself*. He has for the man as a moral subject what the crystalization formula is for a crystal. He sees through him as far as one possibly can'.[47] Therefore, corresponding to each of the value spheres is an ideal person type, for each of which historical examples can be found. And these ideal person types are, from lowest to highest: the bon-vivant, the leader of civilization (businessman, politician, inventor, etc.; e.g. John D. Rockefeller, Napoleon, Thomas A. Edison). the hero (e.g. Ulysses), the genius (e.g. Beethoven), and the saint (e.g. Christ, Buddha).

While value is the heart of our individual and unique *intimate* selves, it is also at the same time the core of our *collective* selves. That is, simultaneously with any particular value-feeling, a person immediately experiences himself in psychic unity with others who share that value-feeling: values are essentially *co-given*. Moreover, one is *aware* of the co-givenness of values *prior to* their givenness to his intimate self. Thus Scheler maintains that the 'we' (collective self) is prior to the 'I' (intimate self). The co-givenness of values, then, is the very foundation for the possibility of our collective existence. Therefore, every human association, like every individual person, has at its core a particular ethos, which can only be glimpsed phenomenologically. 'Whether I am investigating the innermost essence of an individual, a historical era, a family, a people, a nation, or any other sociohistorical group,' Scheler claims, 'I will know and understand it most profoundly when I have discerned the system of its concrete value-assessments and value-preference, whatever organization this system has. I call this system the ethos of any such subject.'[48] It is this identification of value, ethos, as the heart of any group that is perhaps Scheler's

17

most significant contribution to sociological theory.

For each value sphere in Scheler's hierarchy, there is a corresponding ideal group type, just as there is a corresponding ideal person type, which may have historical manifestations. Correlative to the value of the Holy is the community of the Church, a community of saints and believers—not to be confused with the church as an institution—or, as Scheler sometimes terms it, the community of love (*Liebesgemeinschaft*). Correlative to spiritual values is the cultural community (*Geistesgemeinschaft*), or community of intellectuals. The cultural community consists not so much of a physical congregation of scholars and artists as it does of the co-feelings shared by those who seek Truth, Beauty, and Justice, although, of course, it may have concrete, historical manifestations, such as the Academy of Plato or the university as it may have existed before being taken over by the bureaucrats with their utilitarian values. Correlative to life values is the life-community (*Lebensgemeinschaft*) whose cohesive force is the bonds of blood and which is represented by the family, the tribe, and the nation. Correlative to values of utility is society, characterized by contractual and institutional relationships—e.g. business and the state—which perpetuate themselves often at the expense of life, spiritual, and religious values. And, finally, correlative to the value of sensual pleasure is the mass or herd.

Because higher values are characterized by unity and the lower values by fragmentation, groups bound together by shared feelings of higher values are more closely united psychically than groups bound by shared feelings of lower values: the former's feelings of togetherness are stronger than the latter's. Thus, for example, religious wars are always fought with the greatest intensity because of the uncompromising nature of the Holy which is at stake and the degree of value unity within the opposing groups. On the other hand, the mass is the most fragmented of groups since each member merely seeks to maximize his own pleasure and it is unified, as we noted above, 'by nothing more than momentary sensory stimuli and mutual contagions.' Groups held together by higher values tend to be more enduring than groups held together by lower values. The great religions continue to exist while nations rise and fall, and nations of peoples outlast the particular states that they form. And, moreover, in so far as higher values are also more deeply satisfying than lower values, collective life centered around higher values will be more satisfying than collective life centered around lower values. Hence, the lower the value comportment of a group the greater is its tendency to emphasize, and even glorify, the autonomous individual, as we find in modern society.

Because it is at the level of society that a group is *primarily* fragmented and atomistic, viz. equal to the sum of its individual members, while all forms of genuine community are primarily organic, viz. greater than the sum of their parts and hence much more closely united than society, Schler accepts Tönnies's distinction between society and community as the most fundamental between group types. But going beyond Tönnies, Scheler's analysis of human associations in terms of ethos and his identification of value as the heart of any group provided a much deeper foundation for such a distinction and also enabled him to distinguish distinct types of community which Tönnies did not see.

The best known application of Scheler's value sociology is his theory of *ressentiment*, which provides numerous penetrating insights into the nature of social conflicts and has provided the foundation for several studies of such conflicts.[49] Scheler gets his clue from Friedrich Nietzsche, who, in his *Genealogy of Morals,* accuses Christianity of being a *ressentiment*-laden religion. Christianity, Nietzsche claimed, is a 'slave morality': it elevates everything that is of negative value into something of positive value and thereby distorts the 'natural' order of values.[50]

Weakness is to be made a *merit*. . . and impotence, inability to retaliate, is to become 'goodness'; timorous lowliness becomes 'humility'; submission to those whom one hates is 'obedience' (obedience toward the one whom they say decrees this submission,—they call him God). The inoffensiveness of the weak, even the cowardice in which he is rich, his unavoidable obligation to wait at the door acquires a good name, as 'patience', it is also called virtue; the inability to avenge oneself is supposed to be a voluntary renunciation of revenge, sometimes it is even called forgiveness ('for *they* know not what they do—we alone know what *they* do'!). They also speak of 'love for one's enemies',—and they sweat while doing so.

Scheler defended Christianity against Nietzsche's attacks, arguing that Nietzsche misunderstood Christianity and that he confused Christianity as it has developed historically with the essence of Christianity. But, Scheler suggests, in his theory of *ressentiment* Nietzsche has provided the kernel of a profound understanding of modern life: that is, modern life is fundamentally resentful.

In general, *ressentiment* is a disposition of the whole person rooted in weakness. As Scheler explains,[51]

Ressentiment is a self-poisoning of the mind which has quite definite causes and consequences. It is a lasting mental attitude, caused by the systematic repression of certain emotions and

19

affects which, as such, are normal components of human nature. Their repression leads to the constant tendency to indulge in certain kinds of value delusions and corresponding value judgments. The emotions and affects primarily concerned are revenge, hatred, malice, envy, the impulse to detract, and spite.

Ressentiment is based in the tendency to compare oneself to others[52] and can be of two sorts. The first type is based upon a disvalue and the inability to realize a particular felt positive value. An individual (or group) who lacks the contents of a particular felt value sphere is resentful, viz. envious, of another who possesses such contents. The *ressentiment* of the rich by the poor, of the haves by the have-nots, is a prime example. The second type is rooted much more deeply in a basic value weakness, in the inability to feel a particular value. It is *ressentiment* by one whose own ethos is centered around a relatively lower value for one whose ethos is centered around a relatively higher value: the former secretly and subconsciously realizes, because the absolute hierarchy of values is inscribed in every man's heart, his own value weakness, which he can never volitionally overcome. Indeed, the first form of *ressentiment* can be the cause of the second. The primary effect of *ressentiment,* then, is *'value delusion',* as Scheler describes:[53]

> To relieve the tension (between his factual ethos and the absolute hierarchy of values), the common man seeks a feeling of superiority or equality, and he attains his purpose by an illusory *devaluation* of the other man's qualities or by a specific 'blindness' to these qualities. But secondly—and here lies the main achievement of *ressentiment*—he falsifies the *values themselves* which could bestow excellence on any possible objects of comparison. . . when we feel unable to attain certain values, *value blindness* or *value delusion* may set in. Lowering all values to the level of one's own factual desire or ability . . . contriving an illusory hierarchy of values in accordance with one's personal goals and wishes—that is by no means the way in which a normal and meaningful value consciousness is realized. It is, on the contrary, the chief source of value blindness, of value delusion and illusion.

Value delusion expresses itself in two ways. First, one can turn that which is secretly desired, but which he is unable to attain, into an object of disvalue by ridiculing it, defacing it, or destroying it. For example, the victim of unrequited love may grow to hate, or perhaps even kill, the one he loved. A poor person may express his frustrations through acts of vandalism against those institutions that he feels are the cause of his condition. A person may ridicule an idea (philosophical, religious, etc.) that he may be unable to understand but which he secretly recognizes to be of value.

The second expression of *ressentiment*'s value delusion is often the more sinister because it is the more subtle and more difficult to recognize: an individual may drag down to his own level a value that he secretly recognizes to be higher than his own factual value comportment, making the higher value accountable to his own value sphere, and elevating his own ethos, sometimes absolutizing it. For example, an individual whose own factual value comportment is utilitarian may secretly recognize other values to be higher than his own. This individual may therefore drag down such things as education and art (things that are fundamentally spiritual) to the level of utility. He will not deny the value of education and art, make them objects of disvalue, as in the first expression of value delusion; instead, he will make such things accountable to utility values. He will insist that education be evaluated in terms of its usefulness for a particular profession; he will equate it with training and the provision of skills. He may view art objects strictly as economic investments rather than as things of beauty or sources of new insights. Or, such an individual may view religion as a source of profit. We are disgusted by such acts because we recognize in our hearts the perversion of values that is taking place.

Scheler describes various types of value delusion and offers numerous examples of *ressentiment* in modern life. 'But the most *profound* perversion of the hierarchy of values', he contends, 'is the *subordination of vital values to utility values,* which gains force as modern morality develops.'[54] Such a distortion of values Scheler calls the 'ethos of industrialism.'[55] According to such an ethos, 'life itself—the sheer *existence* of an individual, a race, a nation—must be justified by its *usefulness* for a *wider* community. It is not enough if this life in itself contains higher values than usefulness can represent—its existence must be "earned",' e.g. economically. This sacrifice of life for the sake of utility takes place at several different levels. For example, modern morality dictates that one give up his vital spontaneity and creativity for the sake of control (e.g. self-control) and bureaucratic efficiency (this we often define as maturity!). Or, life is treated as a commodity, e.g. by the businessman who reduces the life of his employees to the commodity of 'labor', treating them like the machines they operate, and whose only concern is with the usefulness of that life for production. But in the more extreme instance, just as *all* human groups have something for which they deem it worthy to die (e.g. religion, one's nation, etc.), the modern age justifies thousands of deaths each year, through automobile accidents, factory accidents, and mining disasters, by suggesting that these deaths are the 'price of progress.' The deterioration of the environment at the hands of modern industry and the harmful effects this has on human health are similarly justified. And so each year thousands of lives are sacrificed on the altar of absolutized utility.

One should not construe Scheler's comments as a blanketed condemnation of technology as such; it does not represent for Scheler any disvalue. On the contrary, within the ideal order of values, technology and utility values in general have their own proper place. But when utility values dominate over values of life, spirit, and the Holy, the hierarchy of values has become seriously perverted. This, indeed, appears to be the case in modern society. As Scheler so pointedly observed in concluding his indictment of the modern technological ethos:[56]

> With the development of modern civilization, *nature* (which man had tried to reduce to a mechanism for the purpose of ruling it) and *objects* have become *man's lord and master*, and *the machine* has come to dominate *life*. The 'objects' have progressively grown in vigor and intelligence, in size and beauty—while man, who created them, has more and more become a cog in his own machine. . .
>
> If we consider the transvaluation of the relation between tool and organ in its totality, we must conclude that the spirit of modern civilization does not constitute 'progress' (as Spencer thought), but a *decline* in the evolution of mankind. It represents the rule of the weak over the strong, of the intelligent over the noble, the rule of mere quantity over quality. It is a phenomenon of decadence, as is proved by the fact that everywhere it implies a *weakening of man's central, guiding forces* as against the anarchy of automatic impulses. The mere means are developed and the goals are forgotten. And that precisely is decadence!

Scheler's value sociology thus has at best an ambivalent relationship to Marxist sociology. On the one hand, Scheler reinforces Marx's criticisms of capitalist society: indeed, Scheler's attacks on bourgeois life are much more radical than anything Marx could devise because they go far beyond the political and economic manifestations of that ethos and penetrate straight to its value core and fundamental value weakness and delusion. In this regard Marxists have tended to applaud Scheler. But, on the other hand, if Marxism's aim is to offer the most radical critique of capitalism possible, then, from a Schelerian standpoint, it falls dismally short of its goal because it accepts quite uncritically, i.e. as materially conditioned, the entire utilitarian ethos which underlies capitalism. For Scheler, Marxism was just one more societal ideology along with capitalism, and the antagonism between the two systems is not fundamental but simply over how utilitarian values can best be realized (not so different from the competition between corporations for a particular market).

And in general Scheler was critical of contemporary sociology which has tended to see all groups through the eyes of societal values, those of utility. For example, the tendency to analyze all groups in terms of structure and efficient relationships among members reflects the general societal tendency to see all things in terms of practical effects. Structural analyses in themselves leave the value core of a group—its ethos—untouched and are significant only in so far as a group's structure (e.g. its institutional arrangements) can be related to this core.

III The sociology of knowledge

In general, the sociology of knowledge takes as its point of departure the sociological nature of all human knowledge. For Scheler in particular the fundamental principle of the sociology of knowledge is that 'the *forms* [viz., not the contents] of mental acts, through which knowledge is gained, are always, *by necessity, co-*conditioned sociologically, i.e. by the structure of society.' It describes the sociological conditions that in part determine what constitutes 'knowledge' for a group and the laws by which knowledge distributes itself within that group. It traces the selection of what a group considers *worth* knowing, on the basis of its prevailing constellation of values and interests, viz. on the basis of its *ethos.* And in so far as its task is not merely to describe the external, objective structures of knowledge within a group but also to gain essential insight into the *group mind*, the *co*-thinking of the group, the sociology of knowledge cannot rest upon the methods of positive science but readily lends itself to phenomenological viewing.

It was Wilhelm Jerusalem who first spoke of a 'sociology of cognition' (*Soziologie des Erkenntnis*) in a 1909 article.[57] Scheler immediately recognized the significance and profound implications of the essay and reprinted it in the first issue of his journal, *Kölner Vierteljahrshefte für Sozialwissenschaften (Cologne Quarterly for Social Sciences)*.[58] Major thinkers prior to Jerusalem who hinted at the ideas that later became part of the sociology of knowledge, and thus helped lay the foundation for this area of study, were Karl Marx,[59] Wilhelm Dilthey,[60] Max Weber,[61] Emile Durkheim,[62] and Charles Sanders Peirce.[63] But it was Scheler who in the present work offered the first systematic treatment of the discipline.[64]

The sociology of knowledge is a major part of the sociology of culture. And in so far as its aim is a comprehensive viewing of all that passes for knowledge within various groups, it is foundational to and provides the broad context for all more specialized studies of culture, such as the sociology and philosophy of religion, language, education, and science, intellectual history (history of ideas), etc. It is foundational, too, for metaphysics, and so Scheler saw the *Sociology of Knowledge* along with his essay on American pragmatism, *Erkenntnis und Arbeit* (*Cognition and Work*), as together forming a propaedeutic for his *Metaphysik*, and claimed the latter was not understandable without the former two.[65]

It is in regard to this connection between the *Sociology of Knowledge* and *Erkenntnis und Arbeit* that Scheler's relationship to American Pragmatism is significant. Scheler's main source of information on American Pragmatism was Jerusalem, who was a close acquaintance of William James, the major proponent of Pragmatism in Germany, and the translator of James's *Pragmatism* and *Pluralistic Universe* into German. James, particularly his *Pluralistic Universe*, greatly influenced Jerusalem's sociology of cognition. After reading this work, Jerusalem wrote to James:[66]

> What has struck me most is the compenetration and
> interpretation of our mental events (we say in German
> 'Erlebnisse') and his [Bergson's] conception of 'pure drives'.
>
> To place myself inside the events has been the main purpose
> of my psychology of knowledge. Not only the sensational place
> of events but truly the process of thinking gets another aspect
> when considered from within.
>
> That Life exceeds Logic, as you formulate it, that is one of my
> fundamental convictions.
>
> I hope to send you, in a few weeks, an article where the
> outlines of my future sociology of knowledge are given. I am
> very eager to hear what you think of this new way.

The above is the first appearance of the term 'sociology of knowledge' in English.

Although quite critical of Pragmatism at times, Scheler sided with it and Bergson against the Hegelianism of his day.[67] He was a great admirer of James, especially of the humility James displayed as a thinker, and based much of his own analysis of 'The Idea of Peace and Pacifism' upon James's insights in 'The Moral Equivalent of War.'[68] Moreover, Scheler identified as the genius of American Pragmatism its insight that knowledge *neither precedes* our experience of things (*ideae ante res*), as in Platonic idealism, *nor follows from* experience and is based upon the correspondence of a proposition with an objective world (*ideae post res*), as claimed by empiricists (e.g. Aristotle). Rather, for Scheler American

24

Pragmatism provided the first significant alternative to the idealist and empiricist traditions in suggesting that knowledge resides *in* concrete human acts (*ideae cum rebus*) where it becomes *functionalized*. Several thinkers have noted the influence of Peirce and James upon Scheler's phenomenology and sociology,[69] but no systematic study of this has yet appeared.

Surely Scheler's thought would have provided greater depth for the American pragmatic school of sociology, centered at the University of Chicago. George Herbert Mead and Albion Small were among the first American sociologists to recognize the significance of Scheler's phenomenological sociology and sociology of knowledge, and they may have been the ones responsible for inviting Scheler to the University of Chicago, an invitation Scheler accepted but later was unable to honor due to increasing malfunction of his heart. Small, for example, said of the *Sociology of Knowledge*:[70]

> This book deserves to rank and to function among the principle orientation-monuments for all sociologists. It affords an outlook for the widest survey of the area of the adventure to which sociological pioneering is committed. . . While it is true that sociology must deal with 'pauperism, prostitution, and plumbing', it is all the more true that sociology must take part in explaining the highest, widest, and deepest reaches of the human mind. No previous methodological treatise has done as much to impress this fact as the volume before us. . .
>
> Obviously the methodology thus contemplated is in direct antithesis with prevailing sociological tendencies in the United States. Unless we are willing, however, to assume that wisdom begins and ends with us, here is a challenge which we cannot afford to decline. Perhaps the synthesis next in order is perception that all positive or 'scientific' knowledge, as we call it, must eventually recognize its accountability to all the relativities which a valid epistemology discovers.
>
> At all events, this book opens up vistas of social relations compared with which our sociological searchings thus far have been parochial.

Like Small, the philosopher Paul Schilpp also noted that Scheler provided a comprehensive view of culture from which American sociology and social philosophy could greatly benefit, and he was the first to bring Scheler's thought to America.[71] Alfred Schutz made a significant effort to bring Scheler's phenomenology and sociology together with James's Pragmatism.[72] He and Howard Becker, who because of his interest in sympathy as the foundation for social life traveled to Germany to study with Scheler, did much to acquaint American social thinkers with Scheler and sparked some interest in him in the early 1940s.[73] And while their works show no references to Scheler, the thought of Charles Horton Cooley,[74] Robert E. Park,[75] Ralph Barton Perry,[76] and John Dewey[77] also share some of the concerns of the sociology of knowledge. But on the whole these connections between Scheler and American Pragmatism have gone unexplored.[78]

What interest in Scheler's thought did exist in America was severely undermined by an unfortunate 1942 article by V. J. McGill, which appeared as part of a 'Symposium on the Significance of Max Scheler for Philosophy and Social Science' in the journal *Philosophy and Phenomenological Research*.[79] In his paper McGill charged that Scheler's thought was an anticipation of Nazi doctrine—a charge which seems ridiculous in the light of the fact that Scheler was among the first in Germany to warn of the coming of fascism (as we see already in the *Sociology of Knowledge*) and one of the first to be placed on the Nazi index of banned books (which is the main reason for his fall into relative obscurity during the late 1930s and 1940s). McGill's article, combined with a general suspicion in America and England of anything German, was sufficient to frighten away many scholars who otherwise may have taken interest in Scheler.[80]

The most important implication of Scheler's value sociology for the sociology of knowledge is this: if, indeed, the essence of a group is its ethos and this ethos is prior to and determines all other sociological factors, then what constitutes knowledge for a group, what a group considers *worth* knowing, as well as what it considers trivial, will likewise be dictated by that group's ethos. In short, value is prior to and determines knowledge.[81]

Scheler never clearly delineated the correlations between ideal group types and the types of knowledge present within those groups, but he did offer some suggestions along these lines by delineating three distinct types of knowledge:[82] 1 knowledge of salvation, 2 cultural knowledge, or knowledge of pure essences, and 3 knowledge that produces effects. Knowledge of salvation is that belonging to the community of the Church: within such a community the only things worth knowing are those that lead to salvation (e.g. knowledge of revelation); all other concerns appear trivial. Knowledge of pure essences is that found within a cultural community: it is knowledge of Truth, Beauty, and Justice, knowledge that is 'unbiased' by individual perspectives and concerns and that transcends particular historical and social circumstances, viz. knowledge of what is eternal. Knowledge of effects is societal knowledge: it is knowledge that can be used for

practical purposes, knowledge that leads to control and manipulation of things, i.e. the knowledge of technology.

The 'objective hierarchy' among these forms of knowledge
'exactly corresponds to the [objective hierarchy of] value modalities.'[83] It is not a hierarchy of exclusion but rather one in which
the higher grows out of and incorporates the lower, while at the
same time the lower is dependent upon the higher.[84] Scheler
describes the forms of knowledge and this developmental process
in this way:[85]

> knowledge of control which, in a practical way, serves the
> transformation of the world and all achievements by which we
> can change it and leads us to the next highest purpose,
> 'knowledge of culture'. This knowledge enables us to enlarge
> and unfold the being and circumstance of our spiritual person
> into a *microcosm* as we try, in the manner appropriate to our
> unique individuality, to partake in the totality of the world, or,
> at least, in its essential structural patterns. From 'knowledge of
> culture' our path leads to 'knowledge of salvation'. That is the
> knowledge by which the nucleus of our person seeks to partake
> in ultimate being and the *very* source of all things. . .

While Scheler does not himself delineate those forms of
knowledge corresponding to the life community and the mass, we
might extrapolate such forms. Knowledge for the life community
expresses itself in heritage, tradition, and 'folk wisdom', passed
down uncritically and by word of mouth, from generation to
generation. It is knowledge of the mythic origins of the
community, its heroes and moments of glory. The wise men of the
life community tend to be the elderly because they are the ones
who are most familiar with such traditions and represent the
blood-ties which bind the community together. And knowledge for
the mass is entirely sense knowledge.

Scheler's *Sociology of Knowledge*, then, is in large part a
response to Marx and Comte. As we have already noted above,
Scheler was critical of Marxism's exclusively economic presuppositions and tendency to reduce, as does capitalism, all forms
of human association to utilitarian, economic functions. And he
was critical, too, of Comte's theory of three stages wherein Comte
suggested that science is an overcoming of the illusory knowledge
of religion and metaphysics. To the contrary, Scheler suggests that
science is rooted in metaphysical and religious knowledge and can
never pull free of its foundations.

Knowledge for groups of lower value comportments, because of
the divisibiility of the contents of such values and fragmentary
nature of such groups, tends to become increasingly individual,

27

private, and relative. Knowledge for the mass, therefore, is entirely private and non-communicable.[86] And societal knowledge is *primarily* individual and private; dialogue is extremely difficult in a societal setting. Societal knowledge tends to be atomistic: it focuses upon the 'atoms' of empirical data, or 'facts', which can be quantified and subject to statistical analyses, and over-arching theoretical issues are of only secondary interest. Thus, societal man tends to become weighted down with large quantities of data but becomes increasingly unable to comprehend the general context or meaning of that data and separate what is important from what is trivial: when knowledge becomes quantifiable all bits, or atoms, of information become equal in importance. The more meaningful an issue, the less collective agreement there tends to be in society. And societal man, because in society the bonds of trust are weak, retreats from genuine dialogue, which may bring about some common understanding, into the opinions of his own autonomous self, a self that is fortified and guarded at all costs; thoughts become the private possession of such a self.

Surely what Scheler describes in this regard is all too familiar to us. The modern West, with its obsession with gaining knowledge of control, offers a paradigm of societal knowledge.[87] And Francis Bacon's maxim that 'Knowledge is power' was one of the first announcements of the coming of the societal age in which we find ourselves. A major dictum of modern morality is that one must always be in perfect control of his own autonomous self. Indeed, maturity is generally defined in terms of such control, and insanity, in terms of lack of control. Modern man drives, controls, and manipulates, rather than lives in, his body in much the same way he drives his automobile. And modern education, confusing itself with technical training, aims at developing such control, thereby producing human fuel for society's technological and bureaucratic machinery rather than cultivating free personal spirit.

The retreat from genuine dialogue is seen not only among the masses but also in the advocacy system of settling disputes, whether they be in law, philosophy, or whatever. One view is played off against another, and each autonomous thinker is more interested in establishing the 'superiority' or 'correctness' of his own private position (often to improve his stance politically within his profession) than in arriving at some higher truth, than in following the *Logos*: reason is not so much a vehicle for seeking wisdom as it is a weapon for defeating one's opponents. The societal thinker is a specialist, a technician of knowledge and ideas, who finds himself isolated within the confines of his own area of specialization, a kingdom over which he seeks absolute control. Thus he is able to say more and more about less and less (until he says everything about nothing!) but finds himself increasingly speaking to no one but himself. The modern age is indeed, as Scheler so pointedly noted, the age of the 'lonely thinker'.

Ressentiment, along with its value deception and value blindness, can infect knowledge. The value-weak individual, or group, may be blind to, refuse to see, entire realms of knowledge—e.g. tradition, metaphysical and religious knowledge,etc.—denounce these types of knowledge as myth, prejudice, and sources of deception (e.g. Comte), or drag them down to his own factual level of cognition. Such detraction of higher forms of knowledge is certainly the case in modern society, where knowledge is increasingly evaluated in terms of its practical effects. This is all too familiar to those of us in the humanities, who are constantly made to justify our studies in terms of utilitarian values (e.g. vocational and economic useful-ness), as when it is asked, 'What does one *do* with philosophy?' Or, what is not empirically verifiable, in accord with the model of science, and aims for higher truths than what is available empirically, is often casually dismissed as 'nonsense'.[88] Philosophy based upon language analysis is a prime example of such value delusion: unable to gain insight into knowledge of essences and salvation, language philosophers suggest that philosophical ques-tions can be eliminated merely by making language more efficient and for this purpose set themselves up as the 'technicians of language'. Meaning in language is equated with language's use and effects (e.g. Wittgenstein).

We see, too, within the *Sociology of Knowledge* Scheler's ability to see beyond the immediacy of our age, with all its confusion and pessimism, and place it into a broader context of human history. Mankind in the twentieth century, Scheler prophesied, is entering a new era, an era which he termed the 'World-Age of Adjustment'.[89] Such an age is characterized by a coming together of vital and spiritual principles, tending towards a harmonious integration of these two forces in a new person type. Along with this tendency is the convergence of the major world cultures— as witnessed already in the internationalization of the sciences, the development of global communication networks, and the relative ease of world travel—and the reversal of East-West polarities, that is, an exchange of techniques for eliminating suffering. And, the movement towards adjustment means also an adjustment of male and female principles: Western society, long dominated by male heroic values, will find new meaning in those values that it has so long repressed as 'feminine', as evidenced by the rise of the 'feminist movement'.[90]

Scheler based his view of the World-Age of Adjustment upon a unique theory of human drives. History, he suggested, acts itself out

29

not only as temporal processes that are affected by the mind, but more fundamentally as pre-temporal 'phase laws' (which are not to be confused with 'laws of history', such as the dialectical thesis and antithesis between capitalist and proletarian classes). The drive-conditioned phase laws are not linear or progressive but rather are similar to vertical phase motions in nature, whereby each phase corresponds roughly to a culture, race, nation, etc. The most important aspect of the phase laws is the pre-temporal shift in the predominance of three main drives: the drives of procreation, power, and nutrition. (We say 'pre-temporal' because history is a function of these shifts and not vice versa.) Their respective predominance reflects itself in large stretches, or periods, of historical time. In the first period the procreative drive dominated over the other two drives and served to preserve the blood of genealogical groups in prehistoric time and the age of myth. Later this predominance shifted to the power drive, a shift reflected in the gradual increase of power groups, power states, and power cultures and in an 'organization mind'. The future World-Age of Adjustment is conditioned by a shift to the predominance of the nutritive drive. Such an age will be marked by a growing concern with the business of things and world rather than with the domination over men, as evidenced already today by the growing concern over food shortages and economization of natural resources. Future history will likely be less dramatic and even 'unhistorical'. It will truly be an 'Age of Economy', in the original meaning of this term, viz. the age of the human 'household', and hence an age in which men will be less inclined to invest in power struggles and have less tendency towards war.

The *Sociology of Knowledge,* then, is itself an expression of the World-Age of Adjustment: it provides a broad framework in which the various forms of human knowledge might come together in global understanding. It suggests to us vast new possibilities of human knowledge and new levels of human self-understanding, both personal and collective. And, moreover, it contains what is so lacking in the philosophies of our century, a vision beyond the limits of our narrow scientific-technological mentality. The present work represents a significant segment of Scheler's life-long effort to penetrate beyond the social fragmentation and nihilism of our age, a herculean task which he pursued relentlessly and courageously.

De Paul University   K.W.S.
Chicago
November 1978

Part one

The essence and concept of a sociology of culture

1 Cultural sociology: sociology of real factors, and the hierarchical laws governing the effectiveness of ideal and real factors

The following studies pursue a limited goal. They are an attempt to point out the *unity* of a *sociology of knowledge* as a *part of the sociology of culture,* and, above all, to develop systematically the problems of such a science. They do not pretend to solve any of these problems conclusively but only to discuss in detail the directions in which their solutions seem to lie for the author. They attempt to bring about some systematic unity in the rhapsodic and disordered mass of problems at hand, some of which have already been taken up in detail by science and others only half met or barely suspected, problems posed by the fundamental fact of the *social nature* of all knowledge and of its preservation and transmission, its methodical expansion and progress. The relationship of the sociology of knowledge to the theory of the origin and validity of knowledge (epistemology and logic), to the genetic and psychological studies of knowledge as it evolves from brutes to man, from child to adult, from primitive to civilized man, from stage to stage within mature cultures (developmental psychology), to the positive history of the various kinds of knowledge, to the metaphysics of knowledge, to the rest of the sociology of culture (sociology of religion, art, law, etc.), and to the sociology of real factors (sociology of blood groups, power groups, economic groups, and their changing 'institutions')—all this must necessarily be touched upon.

In establishing the overall concept of 'sociology' *two criteria* will serve us here. First, this science deals not with individual facts and events (in time—history) but with *rules, types* (average types and logical-ideal types), and, where possible, *laws*. Second, sociology analyzes the whole gamut of the (predominantly) human content of life, subjective and objective, whatever it may be called, and it investigates this content descriptively as well as causally according

33

to its *factual* determination only, not its 'lawful' or ideal determinacy according to which the content of life is supposed to be. It investigates this content through the temporally successive or simultaneous *forms of association and relation* that exist among men in experiencing, willing, behaving, understanding, action and reaction, as well as in a real and causal way, that is, a way that does not have to belong to the consciousness-of-something of the person involved.[1]

The principal divisions of sociology, which we merely introduce here without further analysis, can be arranged according to the following points of view: 1 *Essential* considerations, in contrast to the investigation of *contingent* facts, i.e. a pure *a priori*[2] sociology in contrast to an *empirical*-inductive sociology. 2 The simultaneous and successive connection and relationship among men and groups, that is, sociological *statics* and *dynamics* (Comte). Sociological dynamics differs from all philosophies of history in its exclusion of objectively viewed goals, values, and norms and consequently in its strictly causal and (artificially) value-free position. Of course, it does not exclude taking into account values, ideals, and the like as psychological and historical causal factors. 3 The investigation of the *predominantly spiritually* conditioned activity, valuation, and behavior of man, directed toward spiritual or '*ideal*' goals, and the investigation of activity, valuation, and behavior resulting *predominantly* from *drives* (drives toward propagation, nourishment, power), which at the same time are directed toward the *real* alterations of such realities according to their social determinacy.

This 'predominant' intention—for every human act is at once spiritual and determined by drives—and more precisely, the intention *ultimately* directed toward the ideal or the real goal, is that according to which we have to distinguish between a *sociology of culture* and a *sociology of real factors*. Certainly the experimental physicist, the painter, and the musician also change reality when they perform an experiment, paint, play music, or compose. They do this, however, to reach an ideal goal only, for example, to acquire knowledge of nature or to obtain for themselves and others an aesthetically worthy meaning for intuitive understanding and appreciation. And surely, on the other hand, the business administrator, as well as the simple industrial worker of lowest qualification, man in general as a producing and consuming being, and any worker whose end and goal is to change realities (for example, the practical technician as distinct from the scholar and technologist), the prominent statesman as well as the voter in an election, still deal with a great many preparatory and especially intellectual activities directed toward the ideal realm. But they do so only for the sake of a real objective, i.e. for the sake of effecting a change in reality. On the one hand, the activity terminates in the ideal realm, on the other, in the real world. We reject as fatuous forms of spiritualism all theories that try to delimit the foundations of economics without going back to the hunger drive, that delimit the foundations of the state and state-like structures without reference to the drive for power, and that delimit marriage without reference to the sex drive. It is senseless to maintain that economics has nothing to do with the drive for nutrition and the feeding of men because there are publishing houses and art shops, because one can buy and sell books and buttercups, and because even animals have a drive for nutrition and nourish themselves *without* economics. It is senseless to maintain that therefore economics is intellectually and rationally conditioned and finalized in exactly the same sense as are art, philosophy, science, etc. This is simply not so! Without the nutritive drive and the objective goal that it serves biologically, viz. nourishment, there would be no economics — and no publishing houses or art shops either. Without the drive for power there would be no state, no political culture, no law laid down by the state, no matter what affairs it may deal with. The only thing correct about the above thesis is that without mind and its normative regulation there would be no economics, no state, etc. *Therefore, a spiritual theory of man is a necessary presupposition for cultural sociology, and an instinct-drive theory of man is a necessary presupposition for the sociology of real factors.*[3]

This division of sociology into cultural sociology and the sociology of real factors, the sociology of the *super*structure and *sub*structure of human life, is, of course, a division which sets up two extreme poles between which there are a great many intermediate *transitions*, for example, technology, which depends for its growth on economic and political-juridical factors as well as on scientific ones, or, in contrast to a 'pure' art, a purposive, utilitarian kind of art, conditioned by the values and ideals of those in power, say, a religious ruling class. But to characterize *typologically* and determine by specific rules a sociologically conditioned event with reference to these two poles and to establish by specific rule what in this event is conditioned, on the one hand, by the *autonomous self-development of mind,* such as by the logical-rational development of law or by the immanent logic of religious history, etc., and, on the other hand, by the determination of sociological *real factors,* which are factors of the particular institutions and *their* own causality — this is, indeed, a main task of sociology. But without the above-mentioned distinction between the sociology of culture and the sociology of real factors this task cannot be accomplished.

True, this division is not only 'methodologically' but also *ontologically* grounded; but it is for the intrinsic end of sociology a provisional division to the extent that sociology's ultimate and proper task consists in examining the kinds and the orderly sequence of the *reciprocal effects* of ideal *and* real factors as well as of the spiritual and drive factors that determine the contents of human life, which is always socially conditioned by nature. Indeed, I see that the highest goal of all non-descriptive and non-classificatory sociology, that is, of all *causal sociology,* is knowledge of a first *law of sequential order*—not in the same sense of a mere temporal succession of events in human history (which was Comte's false and senseless ideal, senseless because the history of man passes only *once*)—*governing the realization of ideal and real factors of determination* for all life-contents belonging to human groups, factors 'sociologically' conditioned, viz. through re-lationships among men, various kinds of relationships, and human groupings. This sociology treats not *only* the phase-rules that pertain to the relationships and forms of economy, power, and reproduction (to name the most important divisions of real factors) belonging to different groups and cultures in their temporal coming-to-be, or of religion, metaphysics, science, art, and law in their temporal coming-to-be as 'ideal factors'. Important as this descriptive task may be as a preliminary undertaking, this sociology also treats something altogether different, namely, the *law of order governing the realization of ideal and real factors* out of which results, at every point of time within the historical-temporal passage of human social processes, the undivided totality of the life of the group. This is not a law of completed, temporally successive events, but a law of the *possible* dynamic *coming-to-be* of any completed event in the order of temporal efficacy.

Such a law, which I sought for years and which I believe I have found in principle without being able to give its full demonstration here,[4] would have a number of characteristics that can be accurately described.

1 First of all, this law defines the *principal kind of effective interdependence* within whose scope ideal and real factors, the objective spiritual and real conditions of life and their subjective human correlate, i.e. their particular 'spiritual' and 'drive' structures, work out their effects upon the potential movement of social-historical being and activity upon preservation and change. Our thesis is as follows:

Mind, in the subjective and objective sense as well as in the individual or collective sense, determines only and exclusively the particular *quality* of a certain *cultural* content that may *come* to exist. Mind as such has in itself *no original trace* of 'power' or 'efficacy' to bring this content into *existence*. Mind may be called a 'determining factor' but not a 'realizing factor' of possible cultural developments. Within the above-mentioned scope the *negative* factors, or *selective* real factors of what is always *possible* through understandable motivation, are always the *real, drive-conditioned factors of life,* that is, the peculiar combination of real factors: the constellation of powers, the factors of economic production, the factors of the qualitative and quantitative conditions of populations, as well as geographical and geopolitical factors that may in each and every case be given. The 'purer' mind is, the less potent it is in its dynamic effect upon society and history.[5] This is the great common element of truth in all skeptical, pessimistic, and naturalistic conceptions of history, economic as well as racial, power-political as well as geopolitical. Only to the extent that 'ideas' of any kind are *united* with interests, drives, and collective drives or 'tendencies', as we call the latter, do ideas *indirectly* acquire the power or the possibility of being realized, for example, religious or scientific ideas. The *positive*, realizing factor of a purely cultural content is always the *free act* and the free will of a 'small number' of *persons,* primarily the leading persons, model persons, and pioneers, who in turn, by virtue of the well-known law of psychic contagion, of deliberate and non-deliberate imitation (copying), are followed by a 'large number', a majority. It is in this way that a culture 'spreads'.[6]

Quite different is the relationship of determination between existing ideal and real factors and their subjective correlates in men (spiritual and drive structures) with respect to *newly emerging real factors*, such as a new international allocation of political powers, the economic relations of production, racial miscegenation, and racial tension. The *latitude* for their objective and real 'becoming possible' is determined in existence and nature not by ideal factors at all but *only* by the particular makeup of *real factors that were previously given*. With respect to these (precisely the inverse of the previous case) everything that we call 'mind' has only a *negative, 'guiding'* (i.e. restraining or non-restraining) *casual* role, in principle, *only* a negative role for realization and, therefore, *no quality-determining* role whatsoever. Human mind—of the individual as well as the collective person—and the will can do but one thing: restrain or not-restrain (release) that which, by reason of a strictly autonomous and real causality or development, blind to meanings (conscious-wise), wants to come into existence. If mind sets up qualitative goals and goals for transforming real factors, goals that are not at least within the latitude of the causal relationships peculiar to these real factors, it bites on granite and its 'utopia' fades away into nothing. What is called a planned economy, or a 'constitution for world politics', or a planned, legal eugenics and racial selection is a utopia of this kind.

On the other hand, it is always an errant venture to try to derive *univocally* the positive meaning and value-content of an existing religion, art, philosophy, science, or juridical system only from real conditions of life such as kinship, economy, power-politics, or geopolitics. Only that which has *not* come into existence out of the *latitude* of the autonomous law of meaning inherent in the qualitative determination[7] of the history of religion, law, and mind—even though from the viewpoint of intellectual history its *potential* might have been realized as readily as what actually occurred—only this 'explains' the status of real conditions and the existing combination of real factors. Raphael needs a brush—his ideas and his artistic visions do not create it; he needs politically and socially powerful patrons to employ him to exalt *their* ideals: otherwise he cannot act out his own genius. Luther needed the interests of dukes, cities, territorial lords leaning toward particularism, and the rising bourgeoisie; without these factors nothing would have come out of the dissemination of the doctrine of the '*spiritus sanctus internus*' reading of the Bible and of '*sola fides*'.

Just as we reject all naturalistic sociological interpretations of the becoming of culture's *meaning-content,* we must also reject, on the basis of a pure sociology of culture, any theory (reminiscent, for example, of Hegel) that holds that the course of cultural history is a *purely* spiritual process, one determined by its own *logical sense*. Without the negatively selecting forces of the *real* conditions and without the *free* voluntary causality of 'leading' *persons*—though, of course, this freedom refers only to the 'if' or 'if not' of the action, *never* to the 'what' of logical meaning—absolutely nothing is effected by purely spiritually determining factors, even on the basis of the purest intellectual culture. And nothing at all, of course, is effected in the field of the realities with which the sociology of real factors deals. These realities follow their strictly *necessary* course with respect to existence, quality, and value (therefore, also, with respect to so-called 'progress' or 'regress'), a course that is 'blind' from the viewpoint of the notions of value and meaning belonging to the subjective *human* mind—their own course of *fate*.[8] Only one sovereign, changeless privilege remains for man: to be able through his mind 'to reckon', and not, however, to calculate, the future with a sort of *expectation* that remains hypothetical and probable; furthermore, to be able through his will to *restrain* temporality and to ward off something coming into existence, or to accelerate or slow down something else in its *temporal succession and measure* (*not,* however, in the *order of time,* which is predetermined and unchangeable), as a catalyst does for a process of chemical synthesis.

In the spiritual-cultural sphere there is, therefore, potentially 'freedom' and autonomy of events with respect to quality, meaning, and value—yet in their practical expression these can always *be suspended* through the causality of the 'substructure' proper to it; '*liberté modifiable*' ('suspendable') one might call it.

Conversely in the field of real factors there is only that '*fatalité modifiable*', which Comte aptly and correctly discussed.

In the former case the real circumstances have a suspending effect on that which is being realized from among the spiritual potentialities.

In the latter case mind has a suspending effect, in the sense of temporal displacement, upon that which corresponds to the fate of historical tendencies.

2 A second characteristic of the law of causal factors is that it includes and joins in a unified way *three* dynamic and static modes and relations:

(a) the relations of the *ideal factors with one another*: α static, β dynamic, and γ those such that the actual 'situations', the 'statics', present themselves as the result, as the relative momentary representation, of the dynamic, that is, as the stratification of older and newer power-effects (every concrete culture is stratification);

(b) the relations of the individual *kinds of real factors with one another*—again from the three viewpoints above; and

(c) the relations of the three chief groups of *real* factors with the various kinds of *ideal* factors—of course within the scope of the universal laws of ideal and real factors already defined and described.

In every age and everywhere we have to do with human society, we confront some kind of '*objective spirit*',[9] viz. a *meaning* incorporated in some material or reproducible psycho-physical activity, such as tools, works of art, language, writing, institutions, morals, customs, rites, and ceremonies. Exactly corresponding to this subjectively, we encounter a *changing structure of the 'mind' of the group,* a group-mind possessing a more or less binding significance and power for the individual, or at least experienced as 'obliging'. *Is there now an order* by which these objective meaning-contents of culture and the spiritual structure of acts—in which such contents constitute, 'maintain', as well as alter themselves—mutually *establish* themselves *according to laws*? What is the *genetic* relationship between myth and religion, myth and metaphysics, myth and science, saga or legend and history, religion and art, art and philosophy, mysticism and religion, art and science, philosophy and science, and the realm of current values and the theoretically 'assumed' existence and quality of the world? The simultaneous relationships of meaning and the relationships of becoming (motivations) between these objective structures of meaning are extremely numerous, and each requires extensive special study. One might lean to the opinion here that surely all these should somehow be 'mutually' dependent and reciprocally motivating—but there is no *lawful order* of foundation among them. We are of the opposite opinion, without being in the position to prove this in detail.

There are *essential* dependencies among the ideal factors, not merely contingent, existential dependencies in their being and becoming—difficult as it may be to discover them. There are such dependencies as, for example, among religion, metaphysics, and positive science, between philosophy and positive science, between technology and positive science, between religion and art. These correspond exactly to the *order of the origin and to the structural order* ('foundation') *of the acts given with the nature of human mind:* for example, comprehension of values and of being and evaluation, or value-preference, on the one hand, and willing and doing, on the other, perception or representation of objects and being moved by drive impulses with a determined direction (as a condition for such perceptions), practical impulses of will and of movement and goal-free impulses of expression, thinking and speaking—all these build upon each other not 'first this way, then that way', but according to the strict laws of their own nature.[10] In a universal *essential theory of human mind* are to be anchored ultimately all the factual dependencies of objective cultural contents that we empirically find. Whoever speaks of random 'reciprocal effects' is in error.

But within this quite universal and formal framework for these laws of spiritual acts, in general, there are changing, incipient, and transient *special structures and special functional organizations of group-minds.* To discover them is the first goal of anyone setting out to acquire a descriptive knowledge of any particular historical group-culture, studied from all sides and according to all kinds of values and goods. Apart from these universal essential laws of mind—which are not at all laws of 'one' real mind, of one real group or one individual being—*mind exists beforehand only in a concrete multiplicity* of endless manifold groups and cultures. To speak of some kind of *factual* 'unity of human nature' as a presupposition of history and sociology is, therefore, useless and even harmful. A *common* law of structure and style permeates only the living cultural elements of *one* group, permeates the religion and art, science and law, of *one* concrete culture. To work out these laws for each group in the chief phases of its development is one of the highest goals that the discipline of the history of mind can set for itself.[11] We reject, therefore, the notion that there is a certain *fixed*, 'inborn' functional apparatus of reason, given in all men from the beginning—the idol of the Enlightenment as well as of Kant. We reject it as a presupposition of sociology, as we also reject the theory of the monophyletic origin of man which is usually connected with it. Spiritual unity, as well as the blood kinship of all races, may be the *end* of all history—and all history is in fact also the history of the levelling of blood—*but a point of departure* for [historical] events and a presupposition for sociology it certainly is *not*.[12] Rather, the platform from which all sociology has to start is the *pluralism* of groups and cultural forms.

We can still '*understand*' in principle, though not concretely, the coming into existence of spiritual structures assumed to be relatively 'original'; i.e. we can understand how in general the spiritual structures that are carried forward by tradition, *if* they have an origin, can and must originate from an amorphous mind, that is to say, through a gradual '*functionalization*'[13] of the genuine grasp of ideas and their association with contingent things. This 'functionalization' is first performed by pioneers and subsequently carried on by the masses along with and after the pioneers, not, however, externally 'imitated', as are bodily movements and deeds. To that extent the spiritual and rational apparatuses of every great cultural unit and every cultural period, *notwithstanding their multiplicity and diversity*, can be partially and inadequately *true and ontically valid* (although, of course, they need not be so). For they all arise from the grasp of the *one* ontic ordered realm of ideas and values through which this 'contingent' real world passes. Thus we escape a philosophical *relativism*, to which, for example, Spengler falls victim, despite our assuming a multiplicity of rational organizations. We do not, however, escape this kind of relativism by denying or restricting, as is presently done by cheap extremist philosophers of value, the clearly recognizable fact of relativism, even with respect to rational organizations themselves, and therefore do not avoid falling into an equally cheap 'Europeanism' or a similar viewpoint, which is taken by treating *one* culture only as the 'platform' supposedly valid for all men and all history. We do not escape relativism either, as E. Troeltsch strangely enough wishes to do,[14] by 'affirming' our European platform with a mere 'postulate', viz. a '*sic volo, sic jubeo*', in spite of our knowledge of its relativity. On the contrary, we avoid relativism, as Einstein's theory does on its own basis, by lifting up the *absolute realm of ideas and values* corresponding to the essential idea of man far above *factual* historical value systems, for example, by viewing all orders of goods, ends, and norms of human society in ethics, religion, law, and art as simply relative and as conditioned by a historical and sociological standpoint, preserving nothing but the *idea* of the eternal objective *Logos*. To penetrate the boundless mystery of that *Logos* in terms of an *essential and necessary history of mind* is the prerogative not of *one* nation, *one* cultural unit, one or even all past ages of culture, but it is the prerogative *only of all of them together*, including those of the future, in the *solidarity* of spatial and temporal *cooperation* among the irreplaceable (because individual), unique subjects of the culture.

In concrete and particular cases we can no more explain the presumably 'original' spiritual structures of groups than we can explain from the psychic functions of man's animal ancestors 'mind' as such, when considered as a *basic presupposition* of human history or of man himself (his 'idea').[15] At best we can only show how one *structure* developed *from another* in terms of their inherent laws of sense and understandability, as, for example, in the sequence of Western styles of art or forms of religion.

In sharp contrast to this development of *spiritual structures* according to laws governing the transition from one level of development to another stands the phenomenon of the *accumulation of works,* which corresponds only to *one* spiritual structure and to one cultural unit in time and place. Since we assume a true and *genuine genesis* of all subjectively functional *a priori* structures of human mind—not their constancy, as Kant does—we must definitely reject all theories that see in the history of man *only* an accumulation of *achievements* and works, rather than a *development* and transformation *of the spiritual faculties* of man, which is first of all a development or transformation of his *a priori*, subjective apparatus of thinking and evaluation. Since we unconditionally reject every culturally significant inheritance of received psychic attributes so-called (along with Weismann, the recent scientific theory of heredity, and now also Bumke),[16] it is certainly our opinion that the psycho-physical human organism has not chaged essentially in historical time, unless in terms of the already presupposed influence of culture itself. We reject, therefore, the theory that is manifest in the whole of Spencer's sociology, that the spiritual structures could be acquired by the so-called 'species' and then handed down through heredity to the individual. But Weismann's conclusion, that the whole history of culture is therefore only accumulation, we find not at all valid. Weismann presupposed, as did Spencer, that not only the vital-psychic element, which we share essentially with the higher primates—this we also affirm—but also 'mind' and 'reason' in man is *univocally* conditioned by man's psychophysical system. This, however, we deny.[17] We maintain rather that for sociology, psychology, biology, and history human mind is simply a *presupposition* to be accepted, and that mind poses a problem of at most a metaphysical and religious order, and not of the order of positive empirical science.

If this is the case, however, then mind itself, including its power—and all that is not just the sum of the achievements of mind at a certain stage of its development by virtue of the changing conditions of blood relations and milieu—*really and truly unfolds itself.* This development can signify progress and growth as well as regression and decline of mind, but, in every case, it signifies a change in mind's *own constitution.* The following types of change come under consideration in this respect: changes in the form of thinking and attitude, as in the transition from *'mentalité primitive'*, recently described by Lévy-Bruhl, to a civilized condition of human thought which then follows the principles of contradiction and identity; changes in the *forms* of *ethos* as forms of *value*-preference itself, i.e. not merely changes in the esteem for *goods* that stem from one and the same basic law of value-preference or ethos; changes in the feeling for styles and artistic sentiment itself (which since Riegl are assumed in the history of art); changes from the early Western organismic world-view, which extended into the thirteenth century, to the mechanistic world-view; changes from the predominant grouping of men according to clans without state authority to the age of 'political society' and the state, or from a predominantly 'life-communal' to a predominantly 'societal' group form; or changes from a largely magical form of technology to a largely positive one—these changes are of an entirely *different order* of magnitude (not of just different magnitude) than, for example, those of 'practical morality' adapting a form of ethos to changing historical circumstances[18] (such as the adaption of the Christian ethos to the economic and social conditions of late antiquity, the Middle Ages, and modern times), or changes only within the expanse of a primarily organismic world-view. For the sociology of the dynamics of knowledge nothing is more important than this difference: whether the *forms* of thinking about, evaluating, and viewing the world *themselves* underlie a particular change, or if only their *application* to the quantitatively and inductively expanded materials of experience are subject to change. A definite and precise criteriology of this difference is still to be developed.

Moreover, a universal phenomenon of all spiritual development is a process clearly seen already by Herbert Spencer, viz. the *differentiation and integration of the spheres of culture* and the

43

spiritual acts and value-experiences that underlie them. It is reflected most strikingly in the gradual separation of the leader and pioneer types of groups from the intellectual professions: for example, the magician, physician, priest, technician, philosopher (sage), scholar, researcher, etc. However, in applying this principle of differentiation and integration it is of basic importance that these levels of differentiation be set in *correct order*. It is especially because the levels are falsely assigned that gross errors occur. For example, one must acknowledge that religious, metaphysical, and positive knowledge, or, as we can also say, knowledge of salvation or of redemption, knowledge of culture, and practical knowledge, or knowledge for control of nature, from *their very origin* differentiated themselves from the rudiments of natural- and historical-*mythical* thinking and viewing—'the dream of the awakening of the people'—and that they then took a largely distinct line of development. Comte already took the mythical for religion, for instance, and did not see the fact that in the modern age of the West religion by no means *yields* to metaphysics in importance but is only *differentiated* from it more clearly than it was in the Middle Ages, and that also positive science and metaphysics are more sharply distinguished from each other— already by the fact that the sciences now emerge as an *endless process* whereas metaphysics appears as a personally bound and closed *'system'*. And because of Comte's confusion there arose the basically false theory of the so-called 'law of the three stages', that is, the theory that metaphysical essence-thinking 'developed' out of religion, and scientific thought, in turn, out of metaphysics. Comte, therefore, took for a temporal stage of development what *de facto* was only a *differentiating* process of *mind*.[19] Or, out of the magic techniques over the powers of nature the *positive* technique of *control*, on the one hand, immediately and originally differentiates itself from the expressive technique of *religious cults* and the ritual technique of representing sacred events, on the other hand. If this is acknowledged, serious mistakes are avoided. Similarly, also art and crafts (tool technics) doubtlessly have a common point of departure in structures that express the activities of the soul and *at the same time* are carried out in such a way as to serve some continued useful end.[20] But if one so misconstrues the situation so as to derive art from work and technology (as, for example, G. Semper has done in his work on the development of style, and more recently C. Bücher in *Arbeit und Rhythmus*), or if one so misconstrues it so as to think that work and technology are derived from art, as the Romanticists did, and now quite rashly also Leo Frobenius, then serious errors are the result. Theories like that of Albert Lange, according to which metaphysics is 'poetry in

concepts', or the theory of Wilhelm Ostwald, who holds that art is
'the foreshadowing form of science', or the 'gnostic' error that
religion is essentially a degraded popular metaphysics in 'pictures'
for the masses (Spinoza, Hegel, E. von Hartmann, Schopenhauer,
etc.), or the converse error of both de Bonald and de Maistre that
metaphysics is only a subsequently rationalized folk-religion that
goes back to revelation through persons or to an original
revelation, or the theory that metaphysics is an illegitimately
rationalized prophecy of a religious or poetical kind which is
subsequently compressed into a system (the 'prophetic philosophy'
of Max Weber and Karl Jaspers); in general theories which
without further ado look upon one or two of the above-mentioned
three kinds of knowledge as 'dying out', on the basis of quite
particular levels of development within a narrowly confined
culture, such as that of late Western Europe—as Comte did when
he considered knowledge of salvation and metaphysics as dying
out, and as Dilthey did, but only with respect to 'metaphysical'
knowledge[21]—all these theories are serious errors of one and the
same kind. They arise from the faulty assessments of the
differentiating and integrating processes and especially of the
degree of originality contained in particular patterns of mind and,
moreover, from the fact that *certain secondary meshing and
mingling phenomena* belonging to the highest cultural forms are
taken for logical ideal types. Thus, for example, mysticism—a
general and strictly definable category of spiritual behavior,
namely, an ecstatic and immediate knowledge of identification in
intuition and feeling—*can* be found in a particular religion and its
dogma (Indian, Christian, Sufic, Jewish, Taoist mysticism) as well
as in philosophical metaphysics (for example, in Plotinus, Spinoza,
Schopenhauer, Schelling, Bergson); it can be found in a spiritualis-
tic as well as in a naturalistic Weltanschauung (for example, in the
intellectually cool mysticism of Plotinus and in the Dionysian
mysticism of entrancement), in a predominantly theoretical
disposition (as contemplative mysticism) as well as in a practical
one (practical ascetical mysticism and the belief that union results
from acts of will of a certain superior kind, as in Thomas à
Kempis). In all cases, mysticism 'itself' remains an independent
category of kinds of knowledge or of participation in a
presupposed absolute Something or Value that never proceeds
from *its own* source of knowledge—a participation that is always
(genetically) an entirely *uncreative, secondary, and belated*
phenomenon—a going back! If this is not seen, a common mistake
of ecclesiastical writers is the result, making orthodox Christian
mysticism *the* mysticism and ignoring its entirely supraconfessional
and even suprareligious nature. Others make it an independent

source of 'religious' knowledge,[22] or a source of 'metaphysical' knowledge, as in the 'intuitionism' of Schopenhauer or Bergson. The mixed forms of mysticism always presuppose the very existence of the *pure* type.

Closely allied to that part of the sociology of culture sketched above is a second part that treats the more or less organized *social forms of spiritual cooperation*. In every age the *three basic types* of knowledge first appear in social forms which correspond essentially to their highest intended ends. These types of knowledge are necessarily distinct according to the quality of their presupposed object. This is true for all the basic kinds of specifically spiritual, cultural activity. For the predominantly religious forms of *knowledge of salvation* there are *congregations, churches, sects,* loosely organized, 'floating' mystical groupings or directions of thought united only theologically. There are on the other hand 'schools of *wisdom*' and *educational* communities, in the ancient sense, which bind the teachings, research, and life-practices of their members into a union that spans life-communities and often even nations, and which all together recognize a 'system' of ideas and values that pertain to the whole world. Finally, there are *instructional and research organizations of the positive sciences,* based on the division of their proper objects and separation of work, and more or less connected with the organizations of technology and industry or with certain professional organizations, such as those of lawyers, physicians, and officials: 'scientific organizations' we call them. Similarly the arts develop their 'master schools'. Each of these forms develops dogmas, principles, and theories in formulas that rise above natural language to the level of 'cultural language', or that are expressed in 'artificial' systems of signs according to conventions of measurement and 'axioms' that they recognize in common.

The organizations of knowledge are, of course, to be distinguished from forms of instruction and 'schools' in which children of various age groups first *acquire* the average knowledge of the state of culture prevailing in the life-community about them (in their family, clan, state, nation, or cultural units). In such schools the average and socially necessary level of knowledge is *only handed down* from generation to generation, in a way that differs according to castes, estates, and classes. In relation to these *teaching and educational organizations* the groups named above represent a superstructure from which newly acquired knowledge very slowly filters down to the teaching staffs in the 'school-houses' of communities, cities, states, churches, etc.

Furthermore, the above-mentioned forms of knowledge-content are to be distinguished from what men have in common by virtue of belonging to a certain estate, profession, class, or party, i.e. from the *mixed* patterns of collective *interests* and (presumed) knowledge that we choose to gather under the inclusive title of '*prejudice*', the prejudices of estate, profession, class, and party. The peculiarity of this *pseudo*-knowledge is that those who have it in common remain *unaware* of both the collective root of interests behind this 'knowledge' and of the circumstance that only they as a group, and only by virtue of belonging to one of these groups, have this knowledge in common. If after becoming automatic and unconscious these systems of 'prejudice' try to justify themselves in conscious deliberation behind the aegis of religious, metaphysical, or positive-scientific thinking, o˙ by drawing on dogmas, principles, and theories originating in those higher organizations of knowledge, then we have those new mixed forms called '*ideologies*', of which the prime example in our modern history is Marxism, as a kind of 'ideology of the oppressed'. To subject the origin of *all* knowledge to the laws of the rise of ideologies is a specific thesis of the economic interpretation of history. 'Public opinion' serves here already as a certain filter-bed through which prejudices and ideologies are tempered[23] and which is a position held in common by the 'educated' of a group.[24]

The sociology of culture has to distinguish and define the forms of spiritual cooperation *according to an ideal typology*, and it has to seek out *phase-orders* within the completion of these forms and within each single cultural whole—phase-orders also with respect to the shifting of power-relations among these organizational forms of knowledge, for example, the relation of the Church to philosophy, the relations of both of these to science, etc. One must always consider the relation of the *content* of knowledge, such as the *content* of faith, whether dogmatically defined or not, to organizational *forms*. For example, the content of the Jewish religion of Yahweh necessitates its being a non-missionary religion of a chosen people and that one 'people' be its carrier. Thus the content of polytheistic and henotheistic forms of religion exclude universality (even as a *claim*). Likewise, the content of Plato's theory of ideas required to a great extent the form and organization of the Platonic Academy, and the organization of the Protestant churches and sects is determined primarily by the very *content* of faith, which can exist *only* in this and no other social form.[25] Thus also the object and method of positive science necessarily require the *international* form of cooperative exchange and organization. On the other hand, the content and even the risk of metaphysics demand a *cosmopolitan* form of cooperation of individually different, and irreplaceable, unique minds of peoples or their representatives. The most universal differences and, in order of magnitude, the *primary* differences in the possible organizational forms of knowledge are, however, those that are connected with the very types of socialization through which cultures run: the *essential forms* of human grouping, namely, the forms of the transient *masses*, the stable *life-community* (in the sense of F. Tönnies), *society*, and the *personalistic system of solidarity* among independent individuals responsible to themselves and to one another.[26] As will be pointed out, these differences are always simultaneously accompanied by differences in the *forms* of thinking and viewing. For example, the type of thinking in what is predominantly a stable life-community among historical groups must of necessity be primarily of the following kind: 1 It *preserves* and proves a traditional store of knowledge and truth. It does not pertain to research and discovery. Its vital logic and 'form of thought' will be an *'ars demonstrandi'*, not an *'ars inveniende'*, and *construendi*. 2 Its method must be predominantly ontological and dogmatic, not epistemological and critical. 3 Its 'form of thought' must be conceptually *realistic*—not nominalistic as in a society; but at the same time its form of thought no longer construes *words* themselves as *properties* and *powers* of things as did the men of the primitive tribes, where, according to Lévy-Bruhl's correct wording, all acquisition of knowledge rests upon a 'dialogue' of men with spirits and demons who express and divulge themselves in the phenomena of nature. 4 Its system of categories must be principally *organological*, i.e. oriented to the organism and then generalized to everything else. The world must be a kind of 'living being' for it, not a mechanism as it is for a society.

Despite the quite different paths that can be taken by the concrete history and structure of a spiritual culture, certain *phases of a very formal kind are sociologically prescribed,* from whose realm even that which is genuinely 'historical', i.e. the individual and non-repeating factors, cannot escape. Thus the medieval university (of Paris, Prague, Heidelberg, etc.) in its historical facticity and the modern university of the absolutist state in its dramatic transformation—first through the Reformation and Humanism, then in the Age of Absolutism, and finally through the era of liberalism following the French Revolution—is certainly something that can be described only *historically* as it developed within the various emerging nations. Yet, the fact that this university in its course structures and plan, which clearly reflect the dominating relations between theology, philosophy, and science in medieval society and in the medieval establishment, was not essentially a research institute where a living language was spoken, but an institute with a 'learned' tradition to be handed on in a dead language—this is not a historical but a *sociological* fact. We can, therefore, study this university in certain phases of Arabic, Jewish, and Chinese cultural history, such as the educational traditions of old China since the fall of the dynasty. Likewise the course of the so-called 'dispute about universals' in medieval philosophy[27] is a fact to be known only *historically*. However, that conceptual realism *itself* prevailed as a living *mode* of thought—not as a logical 'theory'—in the Middle Ages, while in the modern age the mode of thought is nominalistic, is again a *sociological* fact. That the *organological* categorial structure of the medieval world-view reveals the domination of Platonism and Aristoteleanism, and that *mechanical-technical* thought took over with Gilbert, Galileo, Ubaldis, Leonardo, Descartes, Hobbes, Huygens, Dalton, Kepler, and Newton, are *historical facts;* it is *not* a historical fact, however, that a kind of thinking that subordinated all reality, the inanimate world *and* the spiritual one, to forms of thought and being, which were primarily seen in the *living organism* ('form' and 'matter'), was replaced by a kind of thought that now sees in the 'motion of inanimate masses' and *its* laws forms to which, as soon as they are functionalized, even living, social, economic, spiritual, and political worlds are successively subordinated, or at least 'should' be subordinated. This is a *sociological* fact, inseparable from the replacement of the hand-tool by the machine, from the incipient transformation of community into society, from production for a free market (merchandise economy), from the disappearance of the vitalistic principle of solidarity in favor of an exclusively individual responsibility, and from the rise of the *principle of competition* in the ethos and desires of Western society. That, in an essentially *unending* process—an ideal totally alien to Aristotle and the Middle Ages—of methodic 'research', detached from identified persons and particular technical tasks, knowledge of nature should have been accumulated and *stocked* in order to be used at will, and that this 'positive' science should be more and more completely *cut off* from theology and philosophy, both of which at the beginning of the modern age appeared as *personally* bound, *closed systems*— these things were not possible without a simultaneous collapse of the medieval economy of demand and without the rise of the new spirit of principally unlimited gain in business (limited only by mutual competition); they were not possible without the new covetousness of the absolutist mercantile states, which, in contrast to the 'Christian West' under Pope and Emperor, from the 'European concert', held together by the principle of 'balance of power'.

A further task of general cultural sociology is the problem of determining to which essential *forms of change the cultural domains*—or certain components of cultural domains, such as *styles* and *techniques* in art—are subject, i.e. to which motions of

49

budding, blooming, and fading. The forms of change belonging to the various kinds of knowledge are only a special case of this larger, more comprehensive question concerning the sociological *dynamics* of culture.

It seems to me that this area breaks down into *several* large *complexes of questions*:

Is spiritual culture subject to the basic *mortality* of those predominantly *biological* collectives and units of descent that bore and produced that culture? And to what extent? Or, with what (non-measurable) degree of durability does one area of spiritual culture relate to another, i.e. religion as compared to philosophy and philosophy as compared to science, etc.? Let us call this problem the problem of *the extent of 'culture's capacity for surviving'* the groups that produced it. In what areas is culture merely a *one-time*, unrepeatable, vital and *psychic expression* (Spengler calls it 'physiognomy', mistakenly applying this form of change to all culture) of the collective soul belonging to the biological collectives that bear it, so that it necessarily disappears with collective biological existence, for example, with the hereditary races, peoples, and clans and their sociological real factors and conditional states?

Second, in what areas of values and things does there predominate that special kind of *'growth'* of culture, which—based on an *entirely* spiritual transference from people to people in time (tradition and acceptance)—both *preserves* the culture already acquired and surmounts and surpasses it in a new and living cultural synthesis—an 'uplifting' [*Aufheben*] in the double sense of Hegel—in such a way that (a) no living cultural meaning of a past period will thereby lose its value; and (b) not, indeed, the vitality and sense of a culture, but rather its origin remains attached, in a principally *irreplaceable* and *non-substitutive* manner, to certain *individual* subjects of culture in coexistence and through the course of time? In this form of motion, it is not only possible but also *desirable* to speak of a *suprabiological cooperation of cultural contents,* independent of the racial, political, and economic existence of peoples; for example, one should speak of the 'mind' of ancient culture, the 'mind' of Confucian ethics or of Buddhist art in the growth of a 'world' and universal culture—a cooperation that rests on the fact that an individual cultural subject (an age or cultural unit) is determined for only one individually specific 'cultural calling' to be effected through this particular subject. It is easy to see that in the special sphere of 'knowledge' only that knowledge can be found in this form of motion which, first, is independent of the quantum of inductive experience and is, therefore, *knowledge of essences*; second, has been *functionalized* in categorial structures; and, third, is 'accessible' only to *one* certain phase and to one definite concrete subject within the universal development of history. I call this form of motion *'cultural growth* through the interweaving and acceptance of available spiritual structures into a new structure', and I avoid the Hegelian expression, 'dialectic growth', used by E. Troeltsch, K. Mannheim, and others—albeit I grant that Hegel saw this form of growth as form, even though his *application* of this category in his philosophy of history was totally inadequate due to the narrowness of his European horizon, a narrowness which reaches the point of extreme naiveté. The fact *that* Hegel saw that form of growth is shown by his theory of a *development* of the categories—in contrast to Kant's theory of a static organization of reason, in marked contrast also to mere progress in reason's *application* to quantitatively expanding materials of experience. And it is also shown by Hegel's theory that only the transtemporal (though continuously disclosed in historical time) context of *all* historical cultures make up the total meaning of world history, and not some temporal, distant goal, a so-called 'end condition' of continuous 'progress', as in the positive systems such as those of Comte and Spencer. The deep truth expressed by Leopold v. Ranke, that every phase of culture is 'immediately near God', that every age and people has 'its own self' against whose ideal nature it is to be measured, and that there is no 'mediation of epochs through succeeding epochs', is an element—though only a partial element—of this idea of 'growth'. Let it be added that too little consideration has been given as yet to the thought of a possible *monopoly* and privilege, so to speak, of the early and youthful periods of particular cultures with respect to certain achievements and productions and certain irreplaceable kinds of knowledge, as well as of younger mankind in general as compared to the more mature mankind (especially with regard to knowledge of salvation and knowledge of form).[28]

Only the third form of motion is the one we term *cumulative progress* (or retrogression) in temporal *succession,* or what we term 'international cooperation' if it is of a simultaneous character. While religion, art, and philosophy in their supratechnical core mainly belong to the second form of motion, the *exact sciences,* in so far as they are based on numbers and measures, and, furthermore, the positive *techniques* for controlling nature and the techniques of social organization (in contrast to forms of political *art*) -in medicine, in contrast to the 'physician's art', all that is based on the progress of medical science and technique (surgery is the prime example)—are the chief substrates of possible cumulative progress. The difference between this form of motion and the second one is evident. It is here that we are concerned only with such goods as build upon one another cumulatively without necessitating a change in the *mode* of thought, in the ethos or in the spiritual structures themselves, so that each generation stands upon the results of the past; we are concerned, moreover, with value-goods that can be *handed down and accepted* continuously from age to age, from people to people, and in this acquisition or enhancement the members of any culture can in principle *replace* and *substitute* for one another, once the 'methods' have been discovered. This discovery, however, can be only the effect of a *special* historical, individualistic, spiritual structure, such as the unique structure of the late Western cultural situation with regard to our positive science and technology. The form of motion moves ever onward, continuing across any possible fall of nations, if I may say so, and, of course, right athwart the *expressive features of their soul*. It strides no less across the kinetic phases and syntheses of the second kind of culture, without friction, so to speak. The sequential form of time, in which this 'cosmos of civilization' (as Alfred Weber called it) advances, is found here as it is in the case of cultural growth. However, that *which* in 'progress' takes the place of the temporal sequence is here exclusively bound to the *quantum* of mankind's growing *fortuitous* experience, to the magnitude of the achievement at hand—and not to a positive individual 'cultural calling', not to an inner-qualitative, spiritual cultural determination of the concrete subjects. For this reason and no other, in sharp contrast to the second form of motion, a *devaluation* of the older state necessarily accompanies the 'progress' of its successor. There is, therefore, nothing here like a *trans*temporal interconnective sense to cultural contents, no 'cosmopolitan' cooperation in ever-new cultural syntheses, but there is a single, steady, potentially unlimited progress toward a *final goal*: (a) toward a world-image whose elements, selected according to the value of control and the will of a spiritual, vital subject to dominate over nature (living, social, inanimate), contain the epitome of all laws of the spatio-temporal coincidences of phenomena, a goal, therefore, that is independent of both psycho-vital nature and the spiritual-personal *individuality* of the bearer of culture, but which allows nature to be controlled for desired ends; (b) toward the aggregation of the necessary apparatus for this control (technology). Although this third form of motion surpasses all the others, in unity, continuity, and predictability of the stages of motion, universality, and general validity, in the positive increase of values, i.e. in its progressive character (as opposed to retrogression), in certainty and linearity, and in being principally unlimited, still the content and evaluation assigned to it are in turn conditioned by the content of *metaphysical* knowledge.

The problems so far touched upon concern only regular growth conditions that prevail *among the products of mind itself.* But the most profound and fruitful questions for the sociology of culture lie within a different problem area, an area marked out by the question: In what *lawful order* do the real *institutions,* corresponding objectively to the *drive structures* of the leading elite, have an effect on the production, preservation, advancement, or obstruction of that *ideal meaning-world,* which, at every point of time in the real history of events and situations, hovers *above* this history of realities and also out in *front* of the possible history of the future as a project, expectation, faith, or program? It is a cognitive possibility that we obtain only through human history, not at all through a cognition of nature or so-called natural history, a cognition that we, in human history, not only can conjecture and interpolate becoming processes from fixated processes that have already become, but we can also follow the coming-to-be of what has become by *reliving* the interests, efforts, plans, programs, projects, and unsuccessful 'experiments' from which this or that historical reality has sprung. This possibility always springs up as a minimal *fraction* of those ideas and desires, projects and plans, that precede the given realities, and it always has a *basically different* makeup than any group or individual who played, willed, knew, or expected a historical role. We are in a position to know clearly this immense quantitative and qualitative *difference* between potential spiritual history, i.e. history that is *possible* and *becoming* at every point of time, and *the* history, the event, work, and actual condition, that has *already occured.* We know this difference by virtue of the twofold source of knowledge: the reliving of plans, projects, and ideas, on the one hand, *and* all that which becomes known as actually having happened, on the other.

This *difference,* always and constantly present, between what is happening and what has happened, points to the place where the *real factors in the history of mind* and its ideal works *take effect,* sometimes blocking the realization of what was *logically* expected, sometimes disrupting its 'continuity of meaning', and sometimes promoting and 'extending' it. The basic error of *all naturalistic* explanations of history is that they ascribe to the real factors, which they set up as the decisive factors—be they race, geopolitical structure, or conditions of economic production—the role of determining *univocally* this ideal world of meaning as we find it incorporated in the works of mind and by which we bring matters to an understanding. Their error is that they assume they can 'explain' this ideal world from the world of *real* history. The contrary error of all ideological, *spiritual,* and *personalistic* interpretations of history, on the other hand, is no less grave in so

53

far as it supposes that one can understand the history of real data, of institutions, and of the conditions of the masses, directly or in a roundabout way, as a rectilinear extension of the history of *mind*.

We, however, say that with respect to the course of real history, human mind and will are capable only of *directing* and *guiding*[29] a fixed phase-order of events and situations that have their own laws, which come on automatically, and which are independent of the 'will' of man and *blind* to mind and value. Mind cannot do one bit more! Where ideas do not find forces, interests, passions, drives, and their 'business' objectified in institutions, they are utterly meaningless *in real history*—whatever the spiritual value of ideas may be. There is no such thing as the 'cunning of the idea' (Hegel), enabling an idea to come upon interests and affections from the rear, as it were, to 'make use' of them and hence master them. Conditions and events are quite indifferent to such 'cunning'! What Hegel called the 'cunning of the idea' is only a transfer of the liberal and static system of harmony of the eighteenth century to the dynamism of the sequence of historical periods. Thus the course of real history is completely *indifferent* to the logical requirements of spiritual production! But neither does the course of real history univocally determine the meaning and value of spiritual culture.[30] The course of real history releases, restricts, or limits only the mode and measure of the *effect* of spiritual powers. That *which* is effected, if it can be effected, is always incomparably too complex and rich to correspond to a 'univocal' determination by real factors. This implies that the history of real conditions and events can explain, according to laws of meaning, only the *difference* between *potential* achievements and what has *actually* been achieved in the history of mind. The *'fatilité modifiable'* of the history of real factors, therefore, does not at all determine the positive *meaning-content* of the works of mind, though it does hinder, release, delay, or hasten the development of the works and the *realization* of this meaning-content. To use an image, in a certain way it opens and closes the *sluices* of the spiritual stream.[31]

Nevertheless it must be recognized that in spite of this sovereign indifference of the real history of institutions, events, and conditions to spiritual history and to the demands of *its* inherent logic of meaning, the prevailing constellation of economy and political power and the qualitative and quantitative character and racial admixture of the populace do, beyond doubt, show certain *similarities of overall style* to contemporaneous spiritual culture— even though the masses (the 'large number') and the elite leadership (the 'small number') seldom make a good match. Still this state of affairs does not exist because one of these series shaped the other to its image, as is assumed by both the ideological-personalistic and the naturalistic-collectivistic theories of history. These 'agreements' arise rather from the fact that the higher spiritual structures of an epoch and group, by which the history of real factors is 'directed' or 'guided', and according to which, in the completely different area of the history of mind, the production of works takes place, are *one and the same* structures.

That the extent of the 'directing' and 'guiding' influences upon the sequence of real history in the course of a *relatively closed,* coherent cultural process is not always the same, is only mentioned here in passing. In the *three principal phases* of a culture—the aspiring and blossoming, youthful phase, fruition, and decline—the extent of the directing and guiding *decreases* markedly. As it decreases, the *collectivistic moment of fatality,* and with it man's sense of determinism, *increases,* and the real process of history becomes less amenable to direction and guidance. The final phase of such a process is the *massing of life.* Moreover, in this final phase the spiritual and ideal cultural content and the personal groups who represent and carry it detach themselves to an ever greater degree from the 'service' of directing and guiding the history of real factors, and they exist and live for their own sake. What had once been a causal factor—or *co*-factor—in real history (even if only in the service of direction and guidance) becomes increasingly an *end in itself,* a value in itself. *'L'art pour l'art', 'La science pour la science',* etc., are the slogans of such late periods. The individualist, living completely for himself and for his own field of occupation and its formation, for example, in 'dandyism', is one of its outstanding phenomena.

Still for cultural sociology the quite central question is this: Is there in the span of human history one *constant order, or an order that changes in a lawful way* with the order of phases pertaining to the courses run by relatively closed cultural units, an order followed by the real factors in executing that opening and closing of the sluices that we accepted as basic to their possible influences on the history of mind? This point is touched upon here because the years of controversy and opposition among the *three chief trends* in historical and sociological thought, which we can describe as *racial nativism, politicism,* and *economism*—an opposition which in the first place concerns the *sociology of real factors* —must also find expression in the history and *sociology of spiritual culture.* Gumplowicz, Gobineau, the Rankeans and neo-Rankeans, and the economism of Karl Marx represent one-sided lines of thought in this respect. All three together fall into the error of 'naturalism' when they replace the opening and closing of the sluices with an *univocal* determination of spiritual cultural contents. We have already rejected this kind of 'naturalism'. But their inner

55

opposition remains of course if we introduce our rule of universal dependency and ask: Which of the real factors in their particular forms close and open the 'sluices' for the realization of spiritual potencies in a *primary, secondary, or tertiary* way?

In answer I can only introduce here a series of theses whose complete grounding will be given elsewhere.[32]

An assumption—mostly tacit and unconscious—in this controversy between the sociological tendencies described above, seems to me to be that the independent variable among the three factors, blood, political power, and economics, remains *one and the same* throughout the whole course of history, or that—as the purely empiricist opportunists of methods assume—there is no firm order to the history-forming forces at all: things are just first one way and then another.

The earliest crack in this false assumption common to the disputing parties was made by the ethnologists. They discovered more and more clearly a large variety of *pre*-state, *pre*-political 'societies', namely, an immense era in which *family and blood ties* predominated. Ethnologists thus broke through the ancient and Christian prejudice, unfortunately still very widespread among historians and philosophers, that the 'state' is an essential condition of human nature. *Social life in general* is undoubtedly such an essential condition, as is the formal law of a 'great number' of followers and a 'small number' of leaders, a law that embraces even animal groups. Even the early stages of cultural peoples—not only the half and fully primitive races—the further we penetrate into their past, terminate in the *predominating* family and blood ties, and everywhere there were centuries of *conflict* in the beginning of the 'state', viz. first there was a more permanent warlord class, and then their youthful followers *opposed* the order of the clans and its multitudinous forms of organization and law, opposed its sanctuaries, opposed its morals, customs, ceremonies, and rites, opposed its world-image and its mentality, thus leaving this *pre*-political world of mankind in shambles—a world which in every respect rested upon the *primacy* and order of *blood* relations and age and *their own* socializing and history-forming powers. This fact is to be looked upon today as one of the most certain results of the investigations of primitive races.[33]

The second crack in this common assumption comes from a completely different source: *late Western history*. To my knowledge it was Werner Sombart's special service to historical sociology to have first pointed out in his disputes with Karl Marx, to whose views he was very close in his youth, that the *pre*-capitalistic world of Europe was certainly *not* determined by the primacy of economic factors, but by *another* law of history-generating processes existing between state and business, politics and economy, the power structure and the wealth of groups—and different from the way in which the capitalistic world has effected itself more and more forcefully in certain phases since its beginning. He saw that the economistic basis of history (in Marx's sense) does not apply even remotely to the *whole* history of the West, or to all mankind for that matter, or even apply up to the time of that mystical 'leap into freedom' of the socialistic society of the future which will eliminate all class struggles, but that this economism—once freed of the 'naturalistic' character that makes it a genuine economic 'materialism', according to which the economic conditions univocally explain the *content* of spiritual nature—is in fact approximately valid *for a narrowly limited epoch of late Western history,* and *only* Western history. After I had contributed some detail to this insight,[34] Sombart developed it in great style, especially in the second edition of his major work and the chapter entitled, '*Machtreichtum und Reichtumsmacht*'.

From these insights, it seems to me to follow that in the course of history there is *no constant* independent variable among the three chief groups of real factors: blood, power, or economics. There are, however, *laws ordering the respective primacies* in their repressing and releasing effects on the history of mind, i.e. there is a *different* law of order for particular *phases* in the historical course of a culture. Because of this, the opportunism popular among historians of the empirical and methodological schools is just as untenable as the false assumption common to the three lines of thought mentioned above, namely, the assumption that *one* of the factors is primary.

In years of work on the problems of sociological dynamics, primarily in real history itself rather than in its effect on the history of mind—which alone is under discussion here—I have sought to establish these ideas in several directions. In particular, I have sought to ground it in a theory of the *developmental order of human . drives.*[35] The result of these efforts is that certain *law of sequence* of which I have spoken. Its content is this:

In the course of any coherent cultural process relatively *closed* in space and time, *three* large phases are to be distinguished. It is presumed here without contest that nowhere is there *de facto* any such coherent course in one and the same biologically *unified* people. But an attempt will be made, by means of the abstract method of separating and comparing, to distinguish the *inner* autonomous causes, at least in the form of thought experiments, from the more or less 'catastrophic' causes of development occurring *externally*, such as wars, migrations, natural calamities, etc., so as to distinguish the actual causal factors in the course of

57

history. In this ideal presupposition there are the following phases for the course of events conditioned *only by inner* causes: 1 a phase in which *blood relationships* of every kind and the institutions rationally regulating *them* (rights of fathers and mothers, forms of marriage, exogamy and endogamy, clan groups, integration and segregation of races, together with the 'limits' set for them by law and custom) form the *independent variable* of events and determine at least primarily the *form* of groupings, i.e. determine the *latitude* for that which *can* happen through other causes of a real sort, such as political or economic ones; 2 a phase in which this effective primacy—understanding this word in the same limited sense of determining the latitude—passes over to the *political* power factors, primarily to the workings of the *state*; and 3 a phase in which *economics* holds the effective primacy and in which the 'economic factors' are the first to determine the conditions for real events, 'opening and closing the sluices' for the history of mind. In this way the old dispute among various conceptions and explanations of history would itself become *historically relativized*. It would, moreover, be brought into an inner relationship with all other phase orders, for example, the predominantly personally con-ditioned courses of history and those predominantly collectively conditioned, such as those pertaining to the most universal laws of groupings (horde, life-community, society, unification of personal solidarity among irreplaceable individuals in a 'collective person'), and finally also with the *inner construction principles of the world images of the groups* in these phases.

With regard to the first phase, it appears that a rule can now be established with considerable universality, viz. that all *high cultures* in their coming-to-be represent a non-additive cultural mixture of both predominantly indigenous *matriarchal*, animistic cultures and predominantly *patriarchal* ones of active personalities, entailing and fostering distant trade, and, furthermore, that those among them that show the richest and most varied historical life also show the *greatest racial stratification*—and that, out of this double stratification above, one of the strongest motivating forces for the birth of all high culture, with its separation of castes, estates, and classes and its division of labor, explains itself.[36] Only in these admixtures and stratifications are the dynamic opposition and tensions that discharge themselves in the birth of high cultures engendered. Family tensions, racial conflicts, and the unceasing settlement of these conflicts through political 'state power', which rises considerably precisely because of the increasing *leveling* of these conflicts, are the most important factors in the genesis of high cultures. That the primary causes for the distinctions in caste, estate, and class are by no means to be found in the differentiation of economic classes of ownership, as asserted by the Marxists and also C. Bücher, among others, who transfer a regularity of the third phase into the first phase, nor are they to be found in the separation of professions, which becomes hereditary, as G. Schmoller[37] was inclined to suppose, but that they can be found in the stratification of *races* on the basis of their inborn dynamic powers and, above all, on the basis of their urge for domination or submission—to have seen all this clearly seems to be the outstanding contribution of Gumplowicz to the sociology of real factors. As long as and wherever the views on religious and metaphysical fate are *different* in the higher and lower classes, and for men and women, with reference to views on mortality and immortality, or life after death,[38] or where the distribution of religious and metaphysical knowledge itself is ordered according to caste (for example, the 'holy books' are withheld from the Sudras in India), here also is a cultural effect of these facts of *race sociology*. Religious-metaphysical democracy has been throughout history the highest presupposition of every other kind of democracy and its progress, political as well as social and economic. It has always been, however, the blood-bonded *political* authority (usually in the form of monarchy) that, almost always with the help of relatively 'lower' strata, has given rise to that leveling of differences of blood, race, and clan, which paved the way for that *metaphysical*-democratic view—a type of thinking that became the chief *presupposition* and starting point for the entire development of the West, as far as we can survey it, in contrast to Asia. Apart from Russia, whose whole history is characterized by changes of alien rulers (Tartars, Swedes, Poles, Germans, Jews) who lorded it over the submission-happy racial conglomeration, the Western history of social orders and classes, from the very beginning, has been determined predominantly by political causes, so that the primary law governing the formation of social strata is more veiled than cleared by this feature of history alone. Only in the transition from late antiquity to the historical phase of the 'German and Romance peoples' (Ranke) does the *primacy of blood factors* appear again, but in connection with so many other inner 'reasons for the decline' of late ancient civilization that here also this primacy could be questioned, as Max Weber did in his agrarian history of Rome. For its part, the *political* principle of power, which secondarily leads to the formation of classes, remains the springboard and germ of all class divisions and, at the same time, regulates the latitude of *potential* economic configurations until the end of the absolutist and mercantilist era. Moreover, capitalism is, up to this point in time, primarily the instrument of *politically* derived powers and of powers not based on economics at all, however much the simultaneous economic development may have come to their aid. Only in the age of high capitalism (the age of coal) does there gradually dawn an era that can be described in a relative way as *predominantly 'economic'*—whose special laws of motion Marx not only exaggerated naturalistically into historical 'materialism' but also erroneously generalized for *all* of history. Only in this way could he make 'all' of previous history the outcome of economic conflicts between classes.[39]

Our law of the three phases of primary causality governing the real factors should not be taken as applying to three phases of a single, coherent universal history. This law—one course in the coherent historical process that, under the above restriction, never occurs empirically but is only internal—is valid only relatively for the smaller, not for the larger, group units, which are already meshed in a jointly destined historical process. Examples will clarify this. In the formation of the great 'national', political units, political power invariably preceded economic unification. Liberalism and free trade *follow* state capitalism in the absolutist-mercantile era. Even the German Customs Union is entirely of political origin and a political instrument.[40] Once the economic unity of business and trade has been prepared in this way for the unit 'nation', then within this unit—and only within it and not yet in the relation of the European nations toward one another—the *primacy of economics* gradually comes to the fore in all *intra*-national relations. In spite of this, however, the *political* power maintains its *primacy* within the larger unity of 'Europe', notwithstanding an incipient, so-called 'world'-economy, which is in fact only an interweaving of national economies. The changing economic motives of European alliance politics before the World War, especially the battles over markets outside Europe for the rapidly expanding population and industry of European society, should not cause us to overlook the fact that the highest positions of power as well as the goals of politics—quite distinct from the above motives—were not of economic origin at all but were first of all a residue from the age of European power-politics. Schumpeter's profound discussion of this question in his *Soziologie des Imperialismus* seems to me entirely excellent. The economic expansionism and imperialism of the greater European powers could never have led to the World War had not *political* and military power-complexes existed whose reality, nature, and mind originated in the pre-capitalistic era of power-politics in Europe, reaching back even to the feudal period. The rescue of economics that Schumpeter undertakes after his excellent refutation of the popular Marxist thesis that 'world capitalism' was the main cause of the World War,[41] when he remarks that the present political superstructure of the economic conditions of production would correspond to a much *older economic* phase than that of the present, is only quite artificial. A strange bargain! If economic conditions of production in the course of the entire period since the beginning of capitalistic economy—the 'dynamic' economy in Schumpeter's view—did not have within them the power to transform the political and juridical superstructures, then is not the whole economic thesis false?

I have tried—in what here I can only intimate and not develop in detail—not only to verify inductively the above 'law governing the order of causal factors', in this restricted sense, in the three phases of history, but also to make it understandable *deductively* according to a *'theory of the origin of human drives'*—which I have made basic to the sociology of real factors, in the same sense that the theory of mind is basic to cultural sociology—and, at the same time, according to the laws of *vital-psychic aging,* by which certain basic drives of man become predominant over others in the most important phases of aging. I understand here under basic drives those drive systems from which all special drives proceed, partly through the process of vital-psychic differentiation, partly through the association of the drive-impulses with spiritual interaction. The *sexual and reproductive* drives, serving primarily the species, the drive for *power,* serving both the individual and groups, and the *nutritive* drive, directed toward the preservation of the individual— all of which are objectivized only in institutions based upon the actuality of real sociological factors and, at the same time, appear in various ways as repressed or released in legal forms—show a *transformation,* to be sure, in the dynamic relationships of their dominance over or subordination to one another. This transformation will perhaps make, in the not-too-distant future, the phase-law governing the order and re-order of real historical causal factors in the three phases translucent as a simple *law of aging* of the peoples, who carry and underlie all cultures, i.e. as the law of a process that does not determine or concern in any way the ideal cultural sphere, which is in principle 'immortal', but rather touches it only secondarily—a sphere which, however, initially embraces *all real* factors and real institutions alike.[42]

We have to reject completely all those theories that, merely reviving the theses of the utopian rational socialism of the eighteenth century in the pseudo-form of historical 'evolutionism', assume the possibility that at any future point in history the relationship between ideal and real factors—which we have established above in its twofold form, namely, as the restraint or release of spiritual potencies by real factors and as the 'directing and guiding' of real history through the spiritual, personal

61

causality of the elite—could in principle ever be transformed *into its opposite,* viz. that both human *mind* and *ideal* factors could *positively govern* the *real* factors according to plan. The dream of Fichte, Hegel (the 'Age of Reason'), and, following them, Marx— who defers this into a future period of history in his theory of the 'leap into freedom' (in this theory he is a complete disciple of Hegel and his prejudice of the potential *'self-power* of the idea', derived from antiquity)—will remain for all time a mere dream. It is well to note that only against the background of a positive 'rule of reason' over real history—instead of the mere direction and guidance of a *temporally ordered* process that is in itself *fated*—could there arise the accusing caricature about man's history found in Marxism, or the patently 'messianic' theory of the historical 'call' of the proletariat to put an end to all class conflicts, and thus the doctrine of the cessation of the economically determined world of historical ideal structures. Our view is exactly opposite to that of Karl Marx, namely:

There is no constant in the effective primacy among real factors; among them there is an ordered variability. There is, however, a *basic relationship of the ideal factors to the real factors in general* (as we have described it above) that is strictly *constant* throughout the entire history of mankind and in no way permits an inversion or even an alteration.[43]

The manner, however, in which the three real factors, operating in different orders within their phases, work upon the realm of ideal factors, which take their course according to their own special laws, indicates to us an indubitable 'developmental progress'— though only in the restricted sense that the *discharge of the spiritual potencies* in the three phases of blood, politics, and economics becomes increasingly *richer and more diverse.* This progress, however, pertains only to the contrariless and value-free *fullness* of the discharge of the spiritual potencies—in no way does it pertain to the spiritual potencies as measured by pairs of values, such as 'true and false', 'good and evil', 'beautiful and ugly', etc. The realization of the spiritual potencies of the group is partly hindered and partly released by the institutional conditions of *all three* kinds of real factors. But this restraint and release is not of one and the same magnitude and power in the three phases of the different kinds of causal primacy. The restraint and selection that the spiritual potencies obtain by way of the real factors in periods and groups characterized principally by economics is the *least,* but the release of the potencies is the *greatest.* For spiritual production within the ideal succession of works, as well as for the direction and guidance of real sequences of history, realizes its spiritual potentiality itself all the more richly when *only economic* restraints, such as those contained in the conditions of production and ownership and the organization of work, make the first 'selection' in the realization of the potencies. But in the case where already *blood* ties and, furthermore, ties of clans or age groups directly or indirectly decide the discharge of spiritual potencies, the degree of restraint is *greatest*, and the possibility of their release, the smallest. *Power*-politics occupies a middle position. In its very highest stages of life, therefore, where the amount of *work* and the accumulation of possessions become more important factors in determining the possible discharge of any spiritual potencies, spiritual culture need not have the greatest positive 'value', but it is nevertheless always the *richest*, the most differentiated, the most colorful, and the most stratified. Furthermore, the energy, generally so meagerly imparted to human mind, that is directed into the course of real conditions, fated in their *order* and with respect to direction and guidance, is at its maximum here. Romantic sentiment and romantic thought, which Karl Marx took over far more than he knew—especially as it vented its bitter criticism against finance and 'liberalism'—will in vain play on the sentimental theme of 'soul' against 'mind', 'life and blood' against 'money and mind' (O. Spengler) and in vain try to tear apart this inseparable connection among economism, maximal freedom, and the discharge of mind. For it is the tragic fact, definitely rooted in a metaphysical field, we think, that 'death and birth' in the development of *real* historical and social situations is always fundamentally different from that in the development of fullness within the *ideal* realm of human culture.[44]

Part two

Sociology of knowledge

Let us now tie in the sociology of knowledge with the aforementioned framework of cultural sociology. It will not be too difficult to understand the problems of a sociology of knowledge — which is perhaps the most important part of a cultural sociology.

2   Formal problems

There are first of all a number of *formal problems* that bring the sociology of knowledge into close relationship with a theory of cognition and logic, on the one hand, and developmental psychology, on the other. All of these formal problems rest on *three possible basic relations* that knowledge has to society. First, the knowledge that the members of a group have of one another and the possibility of their mutual 'understanding' is not something that is added to a social group; rather, it is something that *co-constitutes* 'human society'. The data, however, that is collected in objectivating thinking (for example, the classification of races according to objective qualities such as color, shape of the head, and statistical data, such as the number of deaths in the city of Cologne in 1914) is *not* an object of sociology. Second, there belongs to a 'group' a knowledge of its own existence, no matter how vague this knowledge may be, and a knowledge of generally accepted *values and ends* (no class is, therefore, without a class-consciousness). All knowledge, especially general knowledge about the *same* objects, *determines,* somehow, the *nature* of the society in all its possible aspects. Finally, all knowledge, conversely, is co-determined also by the society and *its* specific structure.[1]

The first axioms of the sociology of knowledge

There are a number of principles, therefore, that are the *basic axioms* of the sociology of knowledge, principles which are little known in their full significance:
1 All human knowledge, in so far as man is a 'member' of a society in general, is not empirical but *'a priori'* knowledge. The genesis of such knowledge shows that it *precedes* levels of self-consciousness and consciousness of one's self-value. There is no 'I' without a 'we'. The 'we' is filled with contents prior to the 'I'.[2]

67

2 Empirical participation of a human being in the experience of his fellow human being realizes itself *in different manners*, depending upon the essential structure of the group. These 'manners' are to be understood in terms of *ideal types*. On the one pole of this participation there is *identification,* as we find it, for example, among primitives and masses, in hypnosis, or, in certain pathological states, in the relationship between mother and child.[3] The other pole is characterized by *conclusions based upon analogy* between body-gestures and particular contents of experience. In individualistic *society* the 'other's' life is comprehended by 'someone' exclusively in this fashion, for example, always in relation to the 'alien'. And the alien is also the one with whom a conscious *'contract'* is made. Whenever a legal contract binds subjects endowed with *will* a *mediate conclusion* is made between them in the realm of cognition.

Between these two forms of transmission among human beings there are several others that I wish only to enumerate here: first, the *co-experiencing* among human beings through *'contagion',* without knowledge of such co-experience; and second, the types of automatically *imitative* actions and expressions (which is a later phase) and the 'copying' of purposes. This copying is called *'tradition'* with respect to the generations of groups. Tradition is a concept to be distinguished sharply from all 'historical' knowledge; that is, tradition does not constitute the knowledge of history but rather the very possibility of history, i.e. the *historicality* of life. In sharp contrast to these two forms of transmission (which can be found already among higher animals) there is the subjective immediate *'understanding'* of others' experiences, according to laws of motivated experience and the objective understanding of meanings connected either with material things (works of art, documents, tools, inscriptions, etc.) or with reproduced actions that objectively 'mean' or 'name' something, for example, *'language'* when it is distinguished from *expressions* of mere inner states, no matter how rich, specialized, and differentiated such expressions may be. Twenty-two different expressions of affectations have been observed among anthropoid apes. Even if 1,000 of them, however, had been observed, there would not be any trace of language or 'naming functions'. Also, representation, for example, self-representation in dancing and singing or the representation of 'meaning' in objective material, as in hieroglyphics and art, or customs, mores, rites, cults, ceremonies, and descriptions of persons, are all understandable, objectified comportments that are *common to the group*. Types of understanding, including kinds of co-feelings distinct from contagions, are proper only to *human* society—animals do not have them.

So far we do not know sufficiently whether or not there are other forms of transmission besides the ones mentioned, including the specifically 'social' acts of *mind*, such as teaching and instructing, making and receiving announcements, making public and remaining silent, giving orders and obeying, having patience and forgiving, etc., i.e. whether or not there are forms of transmission beyond 'consciousness' and realized by heredity. It appears certain, however, that there is no 'innate' knowledge of specific objects but only more general or more specific innate *functions* for acquiring knowledge of a certain kind. It appears also to be certain that inherited 'aptitudes' and 'talents' are *originally different,* in both individuals and genealogical, racial groups, with regard to the acquisition of knowledge. Within *those* differences in social needs and effects of 'milieu', and not those differences in class disposition, there lies the ultimate ground for the qualitative character of the basic differences among castes, estates, and occupations within nations. According to scientific studies in heredity, *talent* is to be regarded as an accumulated hereditary factor, even if there is no heredity of acquired functions. This is also true with regard to psychic factors. But with regard to a *genius* things appear differently.[4] A genius does not appear by laws of heredity, but comes into existence like a 'meteor'. He is peculiarly independent of the accumulation of 'talents', whose heredity seems to follow Mendel's laws. There are no specific accomplishments necessary for a genius as there are for men with specific talents. Indeed, what characterizes the genius is that he can be separated, for the most part, from specific accomplishments. But it is through the combination of specific talents (musical, technical, etc.) that the genius also gives a specific direction to his accomplishments. What characterizes the genius is always a *love of something* [*Liebe zur Sache*] that reaches ecstatic devotion to ideas and values, a *surplus* of spirit beyond what is biologically significant, and beyond the originality of the work that was created according to no rules (Kant).

No matter how *thinking-, willing-, loving-, hating-,* etc., *'with-one-another'* genetically comes about, it is the foundation for two categories without which also a sociology of knowledge cannot do: the *group-soul* and the *group-mind.* These are not for us metaphysical entities that would substantially precede all living and experiencing with one another; rather, they are only the subject of psychic and mental contents which always *produce* themselves ever *anew* in experiences with others.[5] Group-soul and group-mind are never mere sums of the knowledge of individuals 'plus' a subsequent communication of this knowledge. Only for the individual's knowledge *of himself* and his nature does the

69

knowledge-with-one-another represent a limit; the less developed and more primitive a group is, the stronger is this limit. We denote as 'group-soul' the collective subject only of those psychic activities that are not 'spontaneous' but *'act themselves out'*, such as forms of expression or other automatic and semi-automatic, psycho-physical activities. We denote as the 'mind' of the group, on the other hand, the subject that constitutes itself through conscious *spontaneous acts* of co-experience, intentionally related to their objects. Thus, for example, myth, the artistically, individually unstructured fairy tales, 'natural' folk-language, folk-songs, folk-religion, customs, mores, and costumes rest on the group-*soul*. But the state, the law, refined speech, philosophy, art, science, and the 'public opinion' of a group rest predominantly on the group-*mind*. The group-soul 'has effects and grows' in all men, even when they are asleep, and its effects alone are 'organismic', in the romantic sense of the term. The group-soul is *impersonal* in its origins and anonymous. The group-mind, however, appears only in *personal representatives*. It is determined by personal leaders, model persons, and, in any case, by a 'small number' (v. Wieser), an 'elite' (Pareto), in its original contents, values, goals, and direction. The group-mind is the 'bearer' of its objects and cultural goods by way of its always new and spontaneous *acts*. Such objects and cultural goods would fall into nothingness were such acts not always *spontaneously acted out* anew. Every 'spiritual' possession of culture, therefore, is a continuous regeneration and re-acquisition; it is a *creatio continua*. The group-*soul* works in any group from 'below' to 'above'; the group-*mind*, from 'above' to 'below'.

The sociology of knowledge concerns itself primarily with the 'mind' of the group. It traces the laws and rhythms through which knowledge filters downward from the top of society (the knowledge of the elite) to find out how knowledge distributes itself in time among groups and social levels and how society regulates such distribution of knowledge—partially through institutions *that disseminate it,* such as schools and press, and partially through *restrictions,* such as secrets, indexes, censorship, and prohibitions that forbid particular castes,[6] estates, or classes to acquire certain kinds of knowledge.

3 A third principle of the sociology of knowledge, which at the same time is a principle of the theory of cognition, states that there is a *fixed law that orders* the origin of our knowledge of reality, i.e. our knowledge of what generally 'brings about effects', and orders the fulfillment of the individual spheres of knowledge, constant in human consciousness, and the correlative *spheres of objects*.[7]

Before we formulate the above law let us first enumerate the *spheres of being and of objects,* which are irreducible to one

70

another: (a) the *absolute* sphere of reality and value, of the Holy, (b) the sphere of the *with-world*, including its past and future, i.e. the world of society and history, or the world of what is the 'other'; (c) the sphere of the *outer and inner worlds*, as well as the sphere of one's own *lived body and its environment*; (d) the sphere of what is 'alive'; and (e) the sphere of what is *inanimate* and of what appears to be 'dead' in the *corporeal world*. To this date cognitional theory has tried to reduce these spheres to one another while the spheres' contents, of course, have continuously changed throughout history. (We cannot describe these tendencies in detail here.) Some, for example, have tried to reduce the inner world to the outer world (Condillac, Mach, Avenarius, and materialism); others have tried the opposite (Descartes, Berkeley, and Fichte). Some also have tried to reduce the sphere of the Absolute to the other spheres (for example, by establishing causal 'conclusions' regarding the nature and being of the Divine in general); some have tried to reduce the vital to the pregivenness of the inanimate world (as Descartes and Th. Lipps did in the 'empathy theory' of life). Some have tried to reduce the with-world to the pregivenness of one's *own* inner world *and* an outer corporeal world (theories of analogy to and empathy with the other's consciousness); some have tried to reduce the division between subject and object to a pregivenness of 'fellow men' into whom an environmental element, such as 'this tree', is 'introjected', only to be themselves introjected by an observer (Avenarius); some have tried to reduce one's own 'lived body' to a mere associative relationship between self-perception of one's own ego and organic sensations and one's own body as externally perceived. All such attempts are erroneous. The spheres mentioned are irreducible to one another and are, at the same time, *co-original* with every human consciousness. Yet it can be proved that there is an *essential order to their givenness and pregivenness* that remains constant in all human development. That is to say, one of these spheres, in any phase of development, is 'filled' already while another is not yet so filled. Furthermore, the reality of the objects that fill such spheres can be 'doubted', or they can be left 'undecided', provided the reality of other objects in other spheres *cannot* be so doubted or left undecided.

If we leave aside the place of the sphere of the Absolute in this order, the following basic proposition is valid for the purposes of our sociology of knowledge: the *'social' sphere of the 'with-world'* and the *'world of the historical past'* is *pregiven* to *all* other spheres in terms of a) reality, and b) general and specific contents. The 'thou' is the basic existential category of human thinking. Primitives, for example, see all natural phenomenon in terms of the 'thou'; all nature is for them a field of expression and a 'language' of spirits and demons behind natural appearances. Let me add some more equally important laws governing the pregivenness of the spheres: 1 The sphere of the outer world is *pre*given to the sphere of the inner world 2. The world appearing as 'animate' is *pre*given to the world appearing as 'dead', i.e. as '*non*-living'. 3 'The' outer world of co-subjects belonging to the with-world is always *pre*given to what 'I' as an individual have and 'know' of the outer world; the outer world of 'my' with-world is also pregiven to the inner world of 'my' with-world. 4 The inner world of the with-world and of the past and future world (as a perspective of expectations) is pregiven to 'my' own inner world as a sphere, i.e. all self-observation is—as Thomas Hobbes clearly recognized—only an 'attitude' towards myself 'as if' I were 'someone else'. Self-observation is not a condition but a consequent and a copy of the observation of others. 5 My own, and every other, lived body is *pregiven* as a *field of expression* (not as an object-body) to any division between corporeal body and body soul (i.e. the 'inner world').

From this it follows that the assumption of the reality and a specific form of *society* and *history,* in which man is placed, is not at all based on the assumption of the reality and a specific form of the so-called 'corporeal world' or of the contents of inner self-perception, as so many still believe. With good reason there are many philosophers who contested that there is a real, extended, inanimate world (Plato and Aristotle, Berkeley and Fichte, Leibniz and Kant, etc.). But there are only very few that denied the real existence of an animal or even a plant. Even the radically 'idealistic' Berkeley already maintained doubts whether his *'esse = percipe'* could be applied to plants. Never and nowhere has there existed a 'solipsist'! Apart from all the proofs for our laws that can be provided from all areas of developmental psychology—but which we cannot mention here—we can see clearly how much more deeply the conviction of the *reality of society* is rooted in us than is the reality of all other objects belonging to all other spheres of being and knowledge. We can 'doubt' all other realities or leave them as they are. But we can *no* longer doubt this reality.

But what follows from these laws for the sociology of knowledge? It follows that, first, the *sociological nature of all knowledge* and of all forms of thinking, intuition, and cognition is indubitable. But it is not the contents of all knowledge and, even less, the validation of such contents that are indubitable; rather, it is the *selection* of the objects of knowledge on the basis of the *prevailing social perspectives of interests.* It also follows from these laws that the *'forms'* of mental acts, through which knowledge is gained, are always, *by necessity, co*-conditioned *sociologically,* i.e.

by the structure of society.[8] And because explanation is always something relatively novel reduced to something known, and because society is (by way of the above-mentioned principle) always 'more known' than anything else, we can expect to be true what a large number of sociological investigations have already shown: the subjective forms of thinking and intuition, as well as the classification of the world into categories, i.e. the classification of knowable things in general, are co-conditioned by the division and classification of the *groups* (for example, clans) of which a society consists.[9]

It is not only the peculiar facts of the primitive collective world-view, which Lévy-Bruhl, Graebner, Thurnwald, and many other ethnologists discovered, that now become fully understandable, but also those penetrating *structural analogies* between knowledge of nature as well as knowledge of the soul,[10] moreover metaphysical and religious 'knowledge', *and* the structure and organization of *society* and the order of predomination of its social parts during a political age. It is a special object of investigation for the sociology of knowledge to trace the structural correlations between views of the world, of the soul, and of God and levels of social organization, which hold with regard to all basic forms of knowledge (religious, metaphysical, and positive) and with regard to all developmental levels of society. A systematic investigation of these structural correlates is still lacking,[11] and so is an attempt to reduce such discovered correlates to *simple laws*. All these attempts find their ultimate justification in our formal principles pertaining to the laws governing the givenness of the spheres. These laws also provide full clarification of the fact that in all developments of knowledge a 'biomorphic' view of the world always *precedes* genetically any view that recognizes the peculiarity and inner lawfulness of inanimate nature or wishes to reduce the living to the dead (as modern mechanistic biology does). Furthermore, these laws clarify the basis of the erroneous theory of projective empathy,[12] found in the sociology of primitives and child psychology.

The first types of knowledge

The 'formal' problems of the sociology of knowledge are also the problem of *classifying the primary types* of knowledge, which are investigated sociologically, the problem of their *social origins,* as well as the problem of their *'forms of movement'*.

Cognitional theorists refer to the foundation of all artificial and higher positive-historical knowledge—be it knowledge of salvation, cultivation, or positive [-scientific] accomplishments, be it religious and metaphysical knowledge, be it theoretical knowledge or knowledge of 'values'—as the *natural view of the world'*. They obviously mean by this term a way in which the world is seen as a minimum of constant factors to be found whenever and wherever 'human beings' live. Cognitional theorists use this natural view of the world as their 'point of departure', and they refer to it also as 'naturally grown', 'practical', etc. But this concept of a natural view of the world contains the very same traps as does the famous concept of a 'natural state', found in the old ecclesiastical and anti-ecclesiastical natural law. Ecclesiastical natural law identifies 'paradise' with this conception, and the *'status naturae'* was more or less similar to the state of sin, depending upon the dogmatic significance of the 'Fall'. Hobbes identified the natural view of the world with his *'bellum omnium contra omnes'* and consciously juxtaposed it to the teachings of the Church; Rousseau identified it with the idyll of the absence of private property; the Marxists, with the 'free and equal' who 'originally' lived together with common property and promiscuity. But in fact we know nothing of a 'natural state', and, in reality, the content consigned to it in each case is only a political foil and background for the future *interests* that all of these typical 'ideologies' seek to justify. Is the 'natural view of the world', as conceived by cognitional theorists, any better? I do not think so. Berkeley, for instance, holds that natural man is an idealist, in his sense of the term, and proclaims that 'matter' is only an 'invention' of eccentric 'scholars'. Others again conceive the natural view of the world realistically, and they assign to it a specific categorial structure, such as a plurality of inanimate things in space and time, uniformity of events, reciprocity, etc. Kant, Avenarius, Bergson, and, recently, N. Hartmann, describe the natural view of the world in very different ways—unfortunately in such ways as it would have to be in order to be a 'point of departure' for the preconceived theories of knowledge that each of them intends to prove.

The sociology of knowledge has to reject flatly this traditional concept of an *absolutely constant* natural view of the world. But it must introduce, instead, the concept of the *relative* natural view of the world.[13] We define this concept as follows: to the relative natural world-view of a group subject (primarily a genealogical unit) belongs whatever is generally 'given' to this group *without question* and every object and content of meaning within the structural forms 'given' without specific spontaneous acts, a givenness which is universally held and felt to be *unneedy and incapable of justification*. But precisely such objects and contents can be *entirely different* for different groups and for the same groups during various developmental stages.[14] One of the most reliable insights with which the sociology of knowledge provides us with respect to so-called primitives, the biomorphic world-view of the child, and the whole of Western civilization until the beginning of modern times, and which also is provided by comparing the relative (according to the above criterion) natural views of the world in the largest cultural units, is the following: there is *no one constant* natural view of the world belonging to 'the' human being *at all*; rather, the various images of the world reach down into the categorial *structures of the given itself.* Spirits and demons are given to the primitives in their acts of perception as 'naturally' and indubitably as they are *not* given to us here and now. *One* absolutely natural view of the world is, therefore, only a *limit-concept* to assess the developmental stages of the relative natural view of the world.

The absolute, constant natural view of the world, the idol of traditional cognitional theory, has to be replaced by an attempt to discover laws of transformation governing the structures of the relative natural world-views.[15] O. Spengler correctly writes in the first volume of his *The Decline of the West* what I wrote in 1914:[16] 'Kant's table of categories is only one of European thinking'. But an attempt at a theory of transformation, holding together the separate relative world-views, can only be successful if the sociology of knowledge is aware of the intimate relationship it has with *developmental psychology* and if it uses for its own purposes the *parallel coordinations* of developmental stages already found there. There exist such parallel coordinations among the various series of psychic development.[17] Any of these parallel coordinations, found in a large amount of literature, could be of great importance for a sociology of knowledge dealing with the relative natural views of the world and their transformation into one another. In many respects they already are, as is shown by the works of Edinger, McDougall, Thorndicke, Köhler, Koffka, Bühler, Stern, and Jaensch, the psychiatrists and neurologists, Schilder, Birnbaum, Storch, and Freud, and the ethnologists and so-ciologists, Preuss, Graebner, Lévy-Bruhl, Durkheim, Niceforo, etc. The sociology of knowledge has as its subject matter the sociology of truth and also the sociology of social phantasms and superstition and sociology conditioned errors and forms of deception.

'Relative natural views of the world' are organic growths which *advance only during lengthy periods of time.* Instruction does not affect them; they can undergo basic changes probably only by racial integration and possibly linguistic and cultural mixings. They belong at the bottom of the automatically functioning 'group-soul'—and certainly not to the group-'mind'.

It is on the basis of the massiveness of the relative natural views of the world that the types of knowledge belonging to *relatively artificial,* or *'learned', world-view forms* build up. Let us enumerate them, starting with those that have a minimum amount of artificiality: 1 *myth and legend,* as undifferentiated, preliminary forms of religious, metaphysical, natural, and historical knowledge; 2 the knowledge implicit in everyday *natural language* (in contrast to learned, poetic, or technical language), which already Wilhelm v. Humboldt has traced in his investigations of 'inner' forms of language and world-view[18] (recently also Finck and Vossler); 3 the *religious knowledge* in its various levels of fixation, ranging from pious, emotive, and vague intuition up to the fixated dogmas of a priestly church; 4 the basic forms of *mystical knowledge*; 5 *philosophic-metaphysical knowledge*; 6 the *positive knowledge* of mathematics and of the natural sciences and the humanities; and 7 *technological knowledge.*

Whereas the form of *movement* belonging to the relative natural world-views is the *slowest and most cumbersome,* the movement of knowledge seems to *increase* with increased *artificiality.* It is obvious, for example, that positive religions move essentially much more slowly than metaphysical systems, which break down into various groups within the scope of the great world religions. The main types of metaphysical systems are relatively few in number within *one* cultural unit, and their recognition and validity persists throughout longer periods of time in contrast to the positive sciences, whose results change from hour to hour.

Every type of knowledge develops its own special *language* and *style* through which it is formulated, whereby religion and philosophy are necessarily more attached to natural folk-language than are the sciences, which—especially mathematics and the natural sciences—develop purely artificial terminologies.[19] As every publisher knows, mathematics and natural sciences are much more internationalized than the humanities; apart from the nature of their subjects, this is also due to their artificial language. Only the *mystical* type of cognition is, as it were, the innate *adversary* of language and formalized expression. Mystical cognition has, for this reason, a highly individualized and isolated, solitary tendency, coupled, however, with cosmopolitan tendencies. Mystical knowledge is supposed, in principle, to be 'ineffable'. This holds true for both the 'bright' *spiritual mysticism of ideas* and for the 'dark' *vitalistic mysticism* by which one identifies himself with the *Urgrund* of self-creating nature (*natura naturans*). The difference between these two kinds of mysticism we can find in all cultures. It probably has its origin in the difference and tension between matriarchal and patriarchal cultures. Mysticism—religious as well as metaphysical—from Plotinus to Bergson regards language not only as an inadequate means for representing thought and what is experienced and envisioned in the mystical '*unio*' and '*ecstasis*'. But, moreover, representatives of mysticism even tend to see in language and in '*discourse*' an insurmountable *source of deception and error* that keeps them from the 'knowledge' they, as mystics, desire. All mystics agree with Friedrich Schiller's words: 'If the soul begins to speak, it does not speak anymore'. This also explains a basic concept of the sociology of knowledge: we find in all mystical orders, communities, and sects of every kind and in all cultures the '*sanctum silentium*' with regard to both the 'dark' mysticism of vital frenzy, which seeks to circumvent 'spirit', and the bright spiritual mysticism, which seeks to circumvent drives and sense perception. This is all quite independent of the positive *contents* of any religion or metaphysics (without which mysticism cannot appear). To keep silence over 'secrets' is not only here a dictum and norm to be observed with respect to outsiders, as is the case with official, professional, and other secrets; rather, it is a part of the *method* to find knowledge itself. Among the Quakers, for example, all solidarity of opinions and wills is supposed to come about through silent prayer among the members of their community. Through such prayer one member, seized by the 'Holy Spirit' Himself, finds the necessary word of the hour and thereby expresses the true volitional purpose of the community and of God.[20]

The *origin* of the more or less artificial types of knowledge is a *problem* of the first order for the sociology of knowledge. Here only the *principal types of knowledge* will be examined in regards to their origin.

The struggle for knowledge, in all these types, grows out of an innate drive impulse, which man has in common with the higher vertebrates, especially with the anthropoid apes. Already such apes reveal a tremendous *curiosity* when they investigate and examine objects and states of affairs that appear to have neither biological use nor harm for them individually or for the species. Everything unfamiliar, everything that disrupts the context of immediate, interconnected anticipations, releases this drive impulse, which no doubt belongs to the large group of *power* drives and is closely related to the drive to construct and to play. But from this drive affect (stupor and curiosity) emanate various other emotive factors. A form somewhat higher than curiosity is the *thirst to know* [*Wissbegier*], which can also direct itself to what is already known. From the latter arise affections and drives that are connected with the higher types of knowledge and that represent themselves already as *mental forms of manipulation* of these drives.

77

First, it is the incessant vital urge primarily of the *whole group,* and only secondarily of the individual person, that 'safeguards' and 'saves' its existence, fate, and salvation and brings about its knowing relationship with an 'overpowering and sacred' reality, valued as the highest good and ground of existence for 'everything'. This is the lasting emotive root of all *desires for religious knowledge.*

Second, it is the much more spiritual feeling of *astonishment* ($\theta\alpha\nu\mu\dot{\alpha}\zeta\iota\nu$) that functions as the foundation for a new type of knowledge. As an *intentional* feeling it must be distinguished sharply from all stupor affects, such as fright, bewilderment, amazement, astonishment, etc., as well as from all impulses for safeguarding, securing, and saving. Any object, including a most known and familiar one, can evoke this astonishment—but only under *one* condition: such an object must be grasped as an *exemplification* and representative of an ideal type, of an *essence.* In other words, such an object is then not related to its spatio-temporal, immediate and mediate environment, to what philosophy refers as 'secondary causes', but is present to the questioning mind: Why, how, and for what is 'something like this' *there 'at all',* and *not not there*? If this question is directed to the existence and essential structure of a world as a whole, 'metaphysical' astonishment has been reached. This act of astonishment and its accompanying feelings are the lasting source of all seeking for *metaphysical knowledge,* as Aristotle clearly recognized. It is due to the very nature of this cognitive attitude that the object placed 'in an idea' is investigated without regard to its fortuitous existence and essence or to the grounds for such existence and essence— without regard to its being there now and not somewhere else and its being now and not at another time, i.e. *without regard to its positional value in a spatio-temporal order,* an order which, according to the recent works of Lévy-Bruhl,[21] the primitives cannot yet separate clearly from material things. Rather, the object of concern, as representative of *its* ideal type of essence, is related *directly and immediately to a causa prima.*[22]

The third emotion, which generates a new kind of thirst for knowledge, grew out of the search (which only secondarily became volitional) for such experiences that *first* happened *fortuitously* through *action* and *work* in the world: it is the *striving for power and domination* over the course of nature, over men and social processes, and over psychic and organic processes. This striving even pertains to techniques of magic that try to guide and *bring under control* supernatural 'powers', or those that seem to be supernatural to us, and to *'foresee'* phenomena for the sake of such control.

This drive has its deeper basis in purposeless drives to construct, play, craft, and experiment. They are *simultaneously* the drive sources for all positive sciences and technology, which, with regard to their *drive* conditions, are closely related. Directly correlated to this drive to control and the spiritualized power drive is the ability, undoubtedly already present in the highest vertebrates, to adapt without behavioral experimentation to *new and atypical* situations, beyond instinctive training by 'trial and error', so that life-enhancing behavior is preferred to other kinds of behavior, viz. *'practical-technical intelligence'* (whose psychic definition[23] we are not yet able to give very adequately). It is essential for the origin of 'practical intelligence' that, considering the conditioning of even the simplest sensation and perception by drive and vital effectiveness (which today is scientifically established), our *natural* world of perception itself be of such a type that what is relatively constant and temporally regular in factual processes of nature has a far *greater prospect* and chance to be indexed by sensations and perceptions than what is relatively irregular or unique in time. Therefore, the thresholds of noticeability, always belonging to the so-called thresholds of stimulation, favor the *constant and the uniform* and all that offers a *gestalt of unified meaning* in time and space, for example, every symmetrical order. Furthermore, E. Jaensch has suggested that probably this tendency to select the constant and regular does not transfer itself from images of perception to images of representation, but grows equally into both series of images because both develop from a primal form, 'the images of intuition', which are far less proportionate to stimulation than to the perceptions of adults.[24] Therefore, the ultimate basis of the conviction guiding all positive research that there is a spatio-temporal lawfulness governing things in nature is neither so-called pure reason (rationalism, Kant) nor (as the empiricists thought) sensory experience—which is formed much more *after* and *according to* this tendency to select from possible attentions; rather it is the thoroughly *biological*—and not in the least the rational or 'mental'—*drive for domination and power* that determines *uniformly and co-originally* the intellectual attitude towards the world of perception, representation, and thinking, *as well as* the practical behavior in acting upon the world and changing things in the environment. The *unity* of both theoretical and practical comportments toward the world and *common* structural forms in both are guaranteed by this.

The growing need to find 'secondary' and lawful efficient causes is separated from the religious need for salvation, saving, and protection by the same chasm as it is from the metaphysical need to find causes, which drives close to the origin of the existence of a representative of an 'idea' in 'the' or a *causa prima*. In sharpest contrast to the metaphysical need for knowledge, the object of positive-scientific questions is not the ultimate ground of an object that is raised into an 'idea' and whose existence and essence solicits 'astonishment' (why death? why pain? why love? why man? etc.); rather, science seeks to predict only the *positional value* [*Stellenwert*] of an object in a *spatio-temporal context* for the sake of *controlling nature*. (*Voir pour prévoir*; knowledge is power; etc.) 'Why is something now here and not over there?'—that is *the* question of all *positive science*. And this is also the preliminary question of every *technology*, for technology wishes to dissect things, recombine them into a more desired spatio-temporal connection, and thereby predict what will happen after such interventions in the course of nature.

Because Comte's and Spencer's Positivism—which is no philosophy but only a typical Western European ideology of recent Western industrialism—recognized only the *third* root of human thirst for knowledge while not seeing its clearly biological origins, it was bound wholly to misapprehend the essence of religion and metaphysics as well as their history. It was bound to make the *three* entirely *constant* and *non-interchangeable* forms of human knowledge into historical *prefigurations* and *temporal 'stages'* in the development of knowledge. But only the emotions and the spiritual methods of knowledge in religion and metaphysics are *specific monopolies of the 'homo sapiens'*, by contrast to which the *single* root of technology and positive science (despite their obvious co-conditioning by the mind) is only a *gradual extension* of the capacity for 'practical-technical intelligence', which animals already possess. Thus, the later positivists, also were bound to *deny* the *essential* psychic-spiritual *difference between man and animal*.[25]

He who sees the three different roots of the three types of knowledge can also perceive clearly the following six states of affairs: 1 the different ideal types of *leaders* in these three types of knowledge (*homo religiosus,* sage, researcher and technologist); 2 the different *sources* and *methods of their acquisition of knowledge* (the charismatic leader's contact with God—idea-thinking—inductive and deductive inferences); 3 the different *forms of movement belonging to their development*; 4 the different *fundamental social forms* in which acquisition and preservation of knowledge are represented; 5 their different *functions* in human society; and 6 their different *sociological origins* in classes, occupations, and estates.[26]

Let us select from this wide area of investigation only what is most important for a sociology of knowledge.

3 Material problems

Concerning the sociology of religion

1 In the sphere of *religion* those religions based on the person of a
'founder' are always *preceded* by a religious and anonymous
group-consciousness that binds souls together, i.e. a genealogical-
tribal-*folk-religion*.[1] Religious unity and the unity of cults and rites
appear to be attached everywhere to *genealogical bonds and bonds
of blood,* rather than to economic, political, commercial, or learned
communities. Only when, in a *political era,* there appears an
exceptionally 'charismatic' *'homo religiosus'*—i.e. someone in
whom there is unconditional but non-rational faith in regards to
his personal and extraordinary links with the deity—be he a
prophet, or a war hero who has founded his authority on religious
grounds, or a magician, or a conscious 'founder', can religion
detach itself from its original blood ties. A sorcerer or a shaman[2] is
not at all yet a *'homo religiosus'*. He is a technician endowed with
supernatural 'powers'. And a 'priest', i.e. an official cult-technician,
always is dependent upon a *'homo religiosus'* above him.

The transition toward *religions of founders* is indirectly enhanced
by the already completed transition of the predominant forms of
genealogical units into the large *political* and mostly monarchic
ruling units. The latter grow in strict opposition to the genealogical
and family units with their patriarchal leaderships, and they grow
from the *perennially* emerging groups of war lords; they break up
the *religious* authorities of the patriarchal-genealogical units and
tend to dissolve larger genealogical family-groups into smaller
families. It is for this reason that religions based upon founders
and all religious movements and groups tied together by a *person*
never appear *prior to* this stage of societal development, which W.
Wundt termed 'the political society'. The political society is the

beginning of the formation of classes and the beginning of large-scale suppression of animistic, matriarchal cults and womanhood.[3] Religions of founders are of express *male* and *mental* origins.

The *sources* of religious knowledge are to be seen neither in animism nor ancestry cults—as has long been suggested—nor in metaphysical judgments of reason. Rather, they are to be seen in a *believed experiential contact,* accepted by the group, that eminent persons have with a supra-powerful, holy person himself. And such experiential contact is attested through certain rites and actions and proves itself to be true through belief in 'miracles'. The first bearers of these 'charismatic' qualities, prior to the appearance of a founder-religion, are the patriarchal leaders of a blood-community. The first bearers of the higher religions of founders comprise a lasting priesthood 'inaugurated' [*eingesetzt*] by the founder, and its membership is drawn without regard to lineage.

The source of ideas of the divine appear in various combinations. 1 They are to be seen in the flexible *traditions* of the prominent genealogical groups of families and clans (folk-religion). 2 They are seen in the *living visions of the divine* gained by charismatic *'homines religiosi'* with the rich ramifications of their 'holy words', deeds, teachings, and advice that have come down only by oral tradition or by so-called 'holy scriptures' (book-religion). 3 These sources are to be seen, furthermore, in new experiences gained *during the performances of cults and rites* pertaining to the divine and its functioning. This experiential source represents a one-sided technicality in the history of religion: it often tended to make itself the only source for religious knowledge. But it always has been only one factor that modifies this knowledge and not a source for the genuine formation of religious knowledge. 4 The sources of the ideas of the divine pertain, finally, to those ideas of salvation and God that come from metaphysics (for example, Plato's and Aristotle's philosophies as origins of Christian theology). When those metaphysical origins lose their service or modifying functions to become primary functions with respect to religious knowledge, they tend to destroy positive folk-religion and the authority of the *'homines religiosi'* proper (as is the case in all forms of 'gnosticism' from Plato to Ekkehart and Hegel). It is only when we have large institutions of salvation which claim to be of universal validity that a *formula* of faith in the name of the founder can be found. This is the so-called *'dogma'*. A dogma develops by means of *'via negationis'* against 'heresies' which seek to destroy the unity of a church.[4] But it is only when there are such dogmas that something like *'theology'* can exist. Theology is the most derivative and most rational form of religious knowledge. However, the proper *sociological condition* for religious knowledge by no means comes uniformly from these four sources, but first of all from family-, clan-, town-, and folk-*traditions* and occupational-technical *cults*. The latter sources are in sharp contrast to the four former sources. And it is through these latter two sources that the *division of classes, occupations, estates, and castes,* with their divisions of labor, are mirrored most sharply in the pantheon and pandemonium of the world of religious objects (functional gods)—not through the ideas of the divine belonging to *'homines religiosi'* or concepts of the divine in metaphysics. For the latter are much *less* conditioned sociologically.[5]

Revealed religion in Jewish and, even more so, in *Western Christian religions,* as societal and historical factors, has a tremendous predominance over the pure or semi-religious *metaphysics of self-knowledge* and of spontaneous self-revelation—a predominance which stands in contrast to almost all of *Asian* and the *ancient* world's religions, which were without churches and dogmas. This predominance is very likely to be based upon *sociological* conditions and upon the character of the peoples concerned. It is the desire of those peoples to transform the surface of the earth and to expand power politically, technologically, and economically, a process which entails consolidations of their masses by actively questioning the ultimate grounds of existence, and which entails the systematic pacification of those masses and providing them with final securities by answering such questions. Such can happen only in the highly personalistic-theistic religions of revelation and, in the political age, through 'ecclesiastical' organizations, which are always copied from the *state.* Peoples who think about the metaphysical sense of life on their own and who seek to find it *actively by themselves* cannot devote their thinking and will as exclusively to earthly affairs and things as can peoples whose revelation, authorities, dogmas, and universal institutions of mass-salvation provide them already with *final* and *absolute* solutions to such questions.

Ever since the Roman Church succeeded in doing away with neo-Platonism and gnostic sects[6] this predominance of revealed religion over the self-active metaphysical mind has become extremely powerful in the *West*. And it is no surprise how little social and historical effect spontaneous metaphysical thought has had in the West! Only Cartesian metaphysics, German classical philosophy up to and especially in the case of Hegel, and later Marxism has had temporary mass-effects.[7] In my judgment it was Descartes, alone among the great philosophers, who was able to change the categorial structure of thinking among learned people—his doctrines were, in general, *'la nouvelle philosophie'* during the

83

seventeenth and eighteenth centuries.[8] But this, too, had only small effects on ecclesiastical institutions! In addition to this, the Western development of sects and churches after the Reformation followed a general law of direction whereby revelation and grace became *increasingly* significant for religious knowledge, and man's free activity became *more restricted* in regards to the Divine and rational cognition (and with this the metaphysical spirit in general) the more *earthly* activities *increased* through work, technology, occupation, economy, and power politics. In also considering this fact one sees even more sharply, since the origin of Christianity, the very same law of direction underlying the development of the relationship between religion and metaphysics in the West: present-day numbness of religious consciousness among believers, the utter helplessness and anarchy among non-believers, the increasing sociological power of the most *consolidated* churches during the rise of democracy, and the increasing determination of social aims which those churches enjoy during the economic age, all have their primary reason in the *suffocation of metaphysical knowledge* and *free religious speculation,* which resulted from the growing seclusion of revealed religion and positive science. This makes understandable why people like Wilhelm Dilthey, Max Weber, and Karl Jaspers agree with the older positivists that objective metaphysics in general has been overcome and is nothing 'but a historical category' of human thought—a category that would have to be elicited psychologically and historically, only in its various forms and ideal typifications. Yet, these same researchers hold, in contrast to the old positivists, that religion is an *essential category* of the human mind.[9] But *we* are convinced—for I speak not only as a philosopher but also as a sociologist—that all who think in such a way are victims of a great deception which the not-so-distant future will correct.

But the most consequential process in the history of founder religions, a process which is thoroughly and only *sociologically conditioned*—the process which alone makes possible the formation of a true church with its claims of absolute authority in matters of salvation[10]—appear to me to be *the same* wherever such structures have appeared: it is the *objective,* more or less penetrating *deification of the founder,* as expressed in various formulations. More precisely: his change in status from a *'subject'* of religion— with whom one spiritually *'identifies',* whom one practically and theoretically *follows by cooperating* with his personal acts, whose advice and divine teachings one follows and believes, and who, as essentially a *'model person',* is a model of man's inner and practical ways to God—into an *object* of worship, an object of religion, is assigned a special ontological origin from the Godhead. The *cult of the elevated Christ,* which first came into full force and expanded with Paul, is the root for the Christian Church in the same way that the subsequent deification of Buddha transformed what was originally Buddhism's metaphysical theory of salvation and ethics into a 'religion'.[11] This process of deification, wherever it has taken place, has always been demonically ambiguous. On the one hand it elevates a founder *essentially* above all other men and obtains, in this manner, a special relationship to the Godhead; the founder's authority becomes *'absolute'* and can only become absolute in this way. On the other hand this process *eases* and *relieves* a community, especially the *masses*, from the harsh pressures of the founder's demands and advice precisely because a common person can no longer compare himself with a person whose origin is ontologically in God or who is, at least, of other distinctly divine origins. The deification of a founder is, therefore, always *distantiation* and inner alienation. It is *great relief* from the *responsibility* which so easily flatters human nature and which, *prior* to the process of deification, the founder, as *subject* of religion and *model person* of his community, bestowed upon his followers.[12] The process of deification is tantamount to the victory of the *pressures of the masses* and their leaders over the higher and purer forms of spiritual religiosity. All other objectifications and materializations in any specific 'ecclesiastical' development are only consequences of this *one* basic process. Such consequences we find, for example, in the development of personal faith into the *'fides quae creditur',* in the development from the founder's deeds and actions which commanded following to an *'opus operantum'* (i.e. to a 'merited' capital of objective salvation and grace which the church gives to believers according to rule), and the development of the charismatic priesthood of the person into an objective, sacramental, and legal dignity or office.[13]

2 I have excluded from this essay a treatment of the sociology of the inner structure of religious knowledge. Instead, I wish to mention some typical influences of religion and churches that either *further or curb* the development of *science and philosophy.* I consider this subject to be indispensible for an objective and penetrating treatment of our subject here.

Friends and foes of religion and churches have thus far only one-sidedly described, by enumerating historical *facts,* the furthering and curbing elements existing between religions and churches, on the one hand, and the development of other forms of knowledge, on the other. A systematic investigation of the *laws of typical relations* between religion and other forms of knowledge has only rarely been made in terms of a comparative sociological methodology. The relations concerned do not all come to the fore when one merely looks at such historical facts alone, for instance, the fact that the Christian churches and monasteries in the West preserved the treasure of ancient writings, the fact that scholastic theology and philosophy created an excellent exercise in and culture of thinking and making distinctions, which secondarily became fruitful for positive science and whose loss such an excellent scholar as R. Virchow deplored, and the fact that there had been men of faith in all forms of knowledge. The laws of said relations cannot come to the fore either when one looks at the church as a place of superstition and witches or as the source of terrible prohibitions of doubt concerning questions in philosophy and natural and human sciences which touch upon questions of dogma, or when one enumerates all those 'cases' where ecclesiastical authorities fell into the hands of philosophy and science (Galileo, Giordano Bruno, Vanini, Serveto; gospel criticism; comparative religion). By such a method one can never get beyond *partisan* standpoints and there will always be a point and counterpoint. It is only by comparing the larger totalities of cultures that we can trace *unities of style* between religious systems and systems of knowledge. These interconnections are far above such historical 'cases' and partisan world-views. What is needed here is a macroscopic, not microscopic, art of consideration. Furthermore, the *types* of knowledge must be distinguished precisely from one another.

First of all, one must abandon the commonly held and erroneous idea that *positive science* and its progress—as long as it stays within its proper domains—can affect religion in any way. Whether such a position is held by believers or non-believers, it is equally false. On the contrary, whenever an objective area, in the sociological sense of a general phenomenon, is to become 'free' for metaphysical and scientific study, religion is subject to a spontaneous change within its *own* domain. This is because, first, religion is not a preliminary form of metaphysics and science, nor does it come after them; rather it possesses its own *autonomous* evolution.[14] And, second, in every instance positive religion has already filled out the group-soul and group-mind of men when a metaphysics or science comes on the scene. What alone can shake a religion is not a science but the *dying* of its faith and living ethos, i.e. when a 'dead' faith and 'dead' ethos replace a 'living' faith and ethos, and, above all, when a *new* religious consciousness, and perhaps also a new metaphysics that wins over the masses, begins to replace the old religion. Taboos, which religions have imposed upon human cognition in all areas by declaring certain things as 'holy' or as a 'matter of faith', must lose their character as taboos, always on the basis of their *own* religious or metaphysical motives, should they become objects of science. Only when a 'sacred' scripture has lost its quality of salvation, on the basis of religious or metaphysical motives, can it be 'scientifically' investigated like any other historical source. Or, as long as nature is filled out by personal, volitional, and godlike, or demonic, powers for a group, it remains 'taboo' for scientific exploration. Only when a religious step is made into a more spiritual, less biomorphic, and, by necessity, more or less monotheistic idea of God—as it appears in the vast *political monarchies of the East,* along with their monarchical societies—can religion raise itself above blood ties and genealogical communities and can the idea of God become more spiritualized and less vitalized. Religion can then make the parts of nature growingly deprived of religion's activities and make the objective, 'inanimate' nature *free for scientific investigation.* He who holds the stars for invisible gods is not yet mature enough to have a scientific astronomy.[15]

The Judeo-Christian monotheism of a Creator and its victory over the religions and metaphysics of the ancient world has undoubtedly been the *basic* factor that made possible the West's systematic exploration of nature. This monotheism freed nature for science to such a degree that it perhaps surpasses everything that has happened in the West up to this time. Its spiritual God of *Will, Work,* and *Creation,* unknown to the Greeks and Romans, Plato and Aristotle—no matter whether His assumption is true or false— has been the greatest *sanctification of work and domination* over subhuman nature. And simultaneously it effected the *greatest de-animation,* deadening, distancing, and rationalization of *nature* that has ever happened in comparison to Asian cultures and the ancient world. Work and Science, however, belong *intimately* to one another, as we shall see.

The main phases of accepted and believed *relationships between 'faith and knowledge'* in the *Christian West* are of less significance. The direction of this development is completely clear: it begins with a vague admixture of faith and knowledge (from the Church fathers to Augustine there were hardly any distinctions between truth of faith and truth of reason, religion and metaphysics) and moves toward a sharp division between them while, however, retaining their harmony ('*gratia perficit, non negat rationem*', says Thomas Aquinas); from this the development moves toward a growing *dualism,* which necessarily is one of Will and Reason in God and man, progressing into nominalism (Scottish and Franciscan natural philosophy), and then moving towards the *co-original* opposition between the abrupt Reformationist *teachings of grace,* which reject all rational metaphysics, and *rational deism,* for which God is nothing but the almighty engineer of the world-machine (Herbert of Cherbury, who is also the point of departure

87

for the freemasons). This development then continues on through the moderate English and German Enlightenment to the radical romantic Enlightenment which comes to an end with positivism as its highest product (d'Alembert, Condorcet, A. Comte, etc.). Following Max Weber's and Ernst Troeltsch's methodology, P. Honigsheim showed[16] that this development *reflected the struggles among estates and classes* and that it reflected the abolition of feudal and contemplative (close-knit) upper estates by political, sovereign powers, united with cities, burghers, and religious separatism against the Emperor and the Pope. Honigsheim also showed how the various rejections of *'causae secundae'* (Cartesianism, Malebranche, Jansenism, Gallicanism, Calvinism, and the theory of sovereignty of Bodin, Machiavelli, and Thomas Hobbes) reflect *absolutism and individualism* in the growing *democracy* and *'nation'*. And he showed how the connection between religious ways of thinking and social structure had been disintegrated by the mutual victory of independent, liberal, middle-class democracy and the industrialization of economy, technology, and science over the 'absolute' states. The elimination of *mediating* causes and powers (i.e. the *causae secundae* in the metaphysical world-view and the independent [*eigenmachtigen*] estates within the state) until Bossuet's *'un dieu, un maitre'* and the abolition of absolute central power (materialism—French Revolution) are processes of the same *logical sense and belong together*.

Concerning the complex questions pertaining to the relationship between religion and science [*Wissenschaft*], both the positivist sociology of knowledge and Marxist sociology have thus far held only *partisan* opinions on the subject. It would not be surprising if they were faced with a series of new romantic movements which they considered to be 'reactionary' and which would prove *their* opinions of development to be wrong. For the wholly Roman Catholic Comte, for instance, religion coincides with the Catholic Church as it does for the French *traditionalists*; i.e. he conceives the Catholic Church wholly as a *medieval institution*. And, furthermore, 'metaphysics', in general, coincides, for Comte, with the Aristotelian theory of forms held throughout Scholasticism. Comte saw no value in modern metaphysics regarding its sociological function. But if these *Western* relationships between religion, metaphysics, and science are seen from the vantage point of an Asian culture, even from a Russian vantage point, one immediately notices a *unity of style* that encompasses all these conflicts. Already the Slavophiles, for example, who initially were more religious, tended to see in medieval high Scholasticism and its 'syllogistic' rationalism the *beginning* of the 'Western European' counter-religious *Enlightenment*. Kirijewski sees the development from Thomas Aquinas to Voltaire as *one and the same* line of Western 'disintegration of belief'![17] Dostoyevsky's 'Legend of the Grand Inquisitor' has the same meaning. And I would like to add that in Germany E. v. Hartmann foresaw, in what he called the immanent union of a 'socially eudemonistic Jesuit Church' and a socially eudemonistic social-democracy, many things that for us today appear to be almost reality.

A second fundamental point concerning the relationship between religion and other types of knowledge that has often been ignored in discussions of particular items within the subject is the fact that points of either agreement or disagreement over this relationship emerge only when religion, understood as an object and major premise for the 'science of faith', or 'theology', is nothing but formalized *dogma,* when knowledge *is genuinely metaphysical,* or when scientific knowledge unjustifiably transgresses the limits of its province by raising its own results to *metaphysical levels.* In the case of the Church's condemnation of Galileo, for example, the point at issue was not the scientific content of Copernicanism and Galileo's dynamics. The Church directed its thrust against the 'metaphysician of Copernicanism', against Giordano Bruno, and against *metaphysical vestiges* in Galileo's theories, as P. Duhem and H. Poincaré clearly showed to be the case in the correspondence between Galileo and the Cardinal who presided over the suit (vestiges which have no foundation for present-day physicists and which have been wiped out by the theory of relativity). In the preface to his work on the motion of stars, dedicated to Pope Paul III, Copernicus refers to the *'lex parsimoniae'* in support of his theory, and he made a distinction between his principle and 'philosophical truth' about absolutes. And in a letter to Galileo the Cardinal advised him to do exactly the same. The fact that Galileo did *not* do so and put forward *metaphysical* assumptions in a wrong place was the factor that decided that case against him. But a large number of other obstructions that the Church incurred upon scientific progress had hardly any influence upon the positive effect that it *indirectly* did have on the development of the *exact sciences*—even by its suppressions of philosophical and metaphysical thought and of free religious speculation. (This can be seen when one compares this state of affairs with Asian cultures where such suppressions did not occur and where *incomparably more energy* from human thought flowed into *metaphysical* thinking and spontaneous *self*-redemption.) Of direct benefit to the sciences also was the intense struggle between the Church and the growing rationalism of its clergy against myth, saga, legend, popular types of devotion, 'superstition', free mysticism, and belief in miracles. In these cases genuine metaphysics also benefitted because *all* higher types of knowledge form a *united* front against types of knowledge that are *organismic and psychic* in their nature. It is precisely because revealed religions increasingly delineate a 'supranatural' area of faith and assert it to be absolutely perfect and unchangeable that they have become indirect pioneers of scientific rationalism. In this way human energy to think is diverted in the direction of *exact* investigation; and this path is at the same time that of *technical-pragmatic* thinking. It is no wonder, therefore, that there exists a mutual understanding between positivists hostile to metaphysics and ecclesiastical philosophers in the politics of choosing a professor to occupy a philosophy chair, and when it is important to keep proper and serious philosophy away from the universities.[18]

Factors that are also beneficial to science are religious *ascetism,* which, as Nietzsche already saw clearly, helps to increase the *scientific knowledge of truth which itself is ascetic,* and censorship by ecclesiastic administrations, which helps bring about responsibility for possible assertions and leads to refinements of and precautions in style and choice of words, to the avoidance of rash generalizations, to increased carefulness in thinking, to criticism, and to an attitude above an odd and befuddled 'spirit of the time', hypnotized by a few ideas. It is not the Church, therefore, that obstructs science, but the presumptuous pathos of 'a scientific church' (E. Mach), which soon will also reject science itself. The history of Darwinism, which collapsed with the rise of the hereditary theories of exact science, is a clear illustration of this proposition. It may be true that the area of conflict between religion and the *human* sciences is much wider, but here also in conflict with dogmatic religion is the historically and culturally *philosophical* understanding of historical facts and not so much the critical investigations into sources (which goes back even to Benedictine monks who were followers of St Maurus).

Yet, the conflicts proper between religion and knowledge of the world are to be found whenever we are concerned with *metaphysical knowledge.* It is here, no doubt, that ecclesiastical dogma and the church are the *most powerful and inborn enemies of any independent development.* And this is all the more so when the church, either in full awareness or unconsciously, has aligned itself with a metaphysical system of the past by way of its own theology or even through dogmas. If, for example, the dogmas *themselves* contain metaphysical principles from a past philosophical system, as is undoubtedly the case in Roman Catholicism—for example, in the dogma of the transubstantiation, which contains the material principle of Aristotle (*materia prima*), in the Thomistic theory of the soul, dogmatized with tooth and nail at the Council of Vienne, and in the 'proofs for the existence of God'[19] and the theory of free will as freedom of choice—metaphysics is utterly and completely fixed.

Perhaps the most important *peculiarity* in the formation of Western knowledge is the fact that the powers of revealed religion, of exact science, and of technology have almost always won their common struggle against a *spontaneous metaphysical spirit*. Their common victory is rooted in the practical, Roman *spirit of domination*. It is a victory over the more contemplative and purely theoretical attitude of the mind which has its own ways of 'investigating'. By contrast, in all Asian cultures it was *the 'sage'* and a *metaphysical* mind that won over religion as well as science. This, it appears to me, is the *most significant difference between Western and Eastern cultures*. In the East metaphysics is *self-*cognition and *self-*redemption, and in this sense it is not primarily Buddhism but the 'religion' of the Brahmans that was a first metaphysics. For this reason also we find in the beliefs of the peoples of China, India, and even Japan, the predominance of the *ideal of the sage*[20] in contrast to the Western *ideals of heroes and saints* and their model persons—which, from the time of Benedictus until Ignatius's overcoming of the proper monkhood, became more and more practical, eudemonistic, and social. This also explains the typical Asian 'tolerance' concerning membership in a religion or more than one religion; and it explains, too, the absence in Asia of both rational science and specialization, industrial technology of production, and hierarchical, ecclesiastical institutions with stringent dogmatics of an imperial form. The Asian metaphysical idea of self-redemption also explains the widespread conviction, which to us Westerners looks so curious, that the emperor, sovereigns, and supreme leaders are responsible for everything that happens in the world, including natural events such as floods, destruction of harvests, etc. The exclusion of any traces of magic techniques by the Reformation equally eliminated from Protestant culture all tensions between techniques of *magic* and *positive* technology. But also for Catholicism, which preserved a few traces of magic techniques—for example, meteorological techniques ('weather'-pilgrimages), medical techniques (exorcism; final unction), etc.—such magic techniques had little importance for the progress of positive technology.

The most *devastating weapon* against metaphysics in the hands of the dogmatic churches, however, is the *prohibition of any doubt* in tenets and things relevant to faith. This principle holds that all but merely 'methodological doubt' is 'sinful'—in conjunction with the identification of the Platonic-Aristotelian systems, i.e. systems

91

of specific historical metaphysics belonging only to Greek culture, with a so-called *'philosophia perennis'*, or 'the' doctrine of 'sound mind' and 'universal' human reason. Not only does it suppress all development of metaphysical knowledge and misunderstands its historical and factual development, which reveals elements that are worlds apart (for example, the connection between Aristotle's God as the first mover or 'the thinking of thinking', νόησις, νοήσεως, and the Judeo-Christian idea of God), but this principle also *dogmatizes* and *petrifies* a *specific* metaphysics. Aristotle's theory of God as first mover cannot be disconnected from his logic, from his astronomy, and from the basic spirit of Greek religion, which is wholly different from the Judaic idea of God as God of Will and Creation. Also, Aristotle's logic[21] is not separable, except in some formalist games, from his metaphysics of 'form' and 'matter' and their applications in nature. The whole system cannot be disconnected from the intercontainedness of positive science and metaphysics, which, as a *form* of knowledge, has been completely lost in modern times; it cannot be disconnected either from Greek slavery, which allowed a small contemplative elite to venerate and admire the world as a realm of meaningful, teleological 'forms' of regulation rather than to attack and work with the forms in practice; nor can it be disconnected from the *biomorphic* type of thinking in that community, which had not yet discovered the peculiar nature and laws prevailing in *inanimate* nature and had no knowledge of mathematical applications in nature and technology, and which, as a whole, was characterized by workmen and the use of tools. When such a *historical system* becomes inflated into a so-called *'philosophia perennis'* it must empty out its living, clear, and concrete contents. A so-called *'scholastic'*[22] method must arise whose nature it is to be a philosophico-historical interpretation of a philosphical authority and, *at the same time,* a systematic comprehension of things and states of affairs—i.e. to be a *twofold source of deception* for all historical interpretation *and* the understanding of states of affairs. But historical interpretation and understanding of states of affairs [*Sacherfassung*] have to be *distinguished* from one another. What happens here is the following: a specific and strictly historical stage of metaphysical thought, out of the anxiety of a new metaphysics which could be perilous to theology, is artificially conserved in an age whose lines of thinking are completely different and can—if properly understood—only exist as an anachronism. Positivism, especially through the authority of Comte, openly or tacitly accepted this idea of scholastic philosophy that the metaphysics of timeless forms and essences, such as the Platonic-Aristotelian system, would coincide with metaphysics *as a whole.* And it was in this fashion that metaphysics *became nothing but* an atavistic phenomenon because, as Comte clearly saw, the Platonic-Aristotelian systems are tied, indeed, to the present-day thinking of a modern society to which they are wholly alien.

One cannot be too surprised today about the growing popularity of the churches, especially the Roman Catholic Church and all parts of its philosophy (natural right, social philosophy), when one examines the exact powers that are sworn against any independent metaphysical activities and free, speculative activity in religion, powers which in hiding or openly work together.

As A. von Harnack often emphasized, it is the ideological indifference of the *masses* that is the strongest basis for the oldest and most inflexible conservative powers; they are the strongest preservers of things past. Blind churchgoers belong to this, and this 'rotten wood on Christ's vine' is not likely to be rejected by the churches while the churches direct more of their attention to *mass-guidance* in regard to social welfare problems, and the more—as they have learned to do since the French Revolution—they bring themselves in contact with democracy and the right wing of socialism. Positive *science*, as we saw, cannot do anything about this because it cannot enter into competition with the churches, which seek to solve the eternal needs of knowledge. But scientistic and positivistic currents, as well as all metaphysical 'agnosticism'—all of which, it is true, are anti-ecclesiastical—*do help* the churches in this (although hiddenly) because they also tend to suppress metaphysics on the grounds of their own epistemological and sociological errors. The motto here is: 'Foes of my greatest enemy are my friends'. Messianic *Marxism's* substitution for religion, the 'future state', pays, however, for its role in this. Where Marxism holds sway, as in Russian Bolshevism, there is a pure reversal of the cultural politics of the Roman Church, as shown by the Bolshevik censorship of books, the new *'index librorum pro-hibitorum'* (including the Bible, the Koran, the Talmud, and all Western philosophers from Aristotle to Fichte). Also the *mysticism* of modern circles, sects, and other groups is sworn against genuine metaphysics. Expanded *democracy,* however—which once had been an ally of free research and philosophy in a struggle against ecclesiastic supremacy—slowly turns out to be one of the greatest dangers to spiritual freedom.[23] There is *another* type of democracy—not the type that goes hand-in-hand with free research as was the case at the times of our youth—*the* type of democracy, which, in Athens, Socrates and Anaxagoras rejected and which in modern Japan opposed all acceptance of Western methods in technology and science, begins to win ground again in the West and perhaps also in North America. Only the struggling and predominantly *liberal* democracy of a relatively 'small elite', as the facts already show us today, is an ally of science and philosophy. The prevailing democracy, expanded to include women and half-grown children, is no friend but rather an enemy of reason and science [*Wissenschaft*]. In Germany this process has begun with professorships for those holding ecclesiastic world-views, with 'punitive professorships' for social democrats, and with pressures being placed on lesser State authorities by Parliament in all questions pertaining to filling vacancies of academic chairs. But this process will continue! The new *relativist theory of 'Weltanschauung'*—as it has been introduced by W. Dilthey, M. Weber, K. Jaspers, and G. Radbruch even in the philosophy of law—is a theoretical reflection of this democratic parliamentarism that reaches into *Weltanschauung*. In this parliamentarism one discusses all possible opinions without making assertions and negotiates without coming to decisions; and one abandons mutual convictions based upon knowledge in the manner which parliamentarism, at its peak, always presupposed.[24]

Concerning the sociology of metaphysics

Let us now look at *metaphysics* itself. Its sociology of knowledge has been given the least consideration.[25]

From a sociological viewpoint metaphysics is, among other types of knowledge, one of an *intellectual elite*. Free from religious or any other tradition of their life-communities and free from economic ties and work, this elite has the time to look at the ideal [*ideelen*], *essential structures* of the world from a purely theoretical attitude and, in conjunction with the state of *scientific* knowledge at a particular time, it establishes *probable hypotheses about the ultimate ground of things*. But because the totality of the *world* is only a totality that is theoretically accessible to a *person,* metaphysics is by necessity tied to a *person* or borne by so-called 'schools' of metaphysical wisdom which group themselves around a person. Furthermore, metaphysics belongs essentially to a cultural field and even is tied often to the *spirit of a nation* and is incomparably more specific than are the international disciplines of science with their divisions.[26]

Since metaphysics always represents an interconnection between *a priori* synthetic knowledge of essences and the inductive and deductive results of positive science, the possible types of metaphysics, to a certain degree, are *a priori* construable within a cultural field by way of a pure theory of *Weltanshauung*.[27] In their historical manifestations the *most general types* of metaphysics in a cultural field are *side by side* with one another during the process of cultural development. During such a process each type *'grows'* along with and seeks to absorb the experience of inductive, positive science, but by no means do they have their bases in such experience. Viewed from a second aspect of growth, different from the one above, metaphysics itself grows throughout history in fullness and comprehension of world contents in so far as any new metaphysics tries to incorporate at least elements of truths contained in all other metaphysical systems. But it relativizes them under the guise of a higher, more comprehensive, creative, and basic thought. The 'conflict' among various metaphysics can never be settled in the same sense and by the same methods as are conflicts among the sciences. This follows by necessity from the *first* object of metaphysics, which is to deal with undefinable, basic concepts to which one can only point [*aufweisbar*] and with unprovable principles that govern the *essential* interconnections of the *world* and which necessarily underlie all possible proofs. And this follows also from the fact that metaphysics in full consciousness abandons the principle of positive science, viz. that every question that cannot be settled by observation, measurement, and mathematical calculation is to be *excluded* as senseless, and that it thereby wishes to furnish a hypothetical *total view* of how all things, ordered according to ultimate essences, are *rooted in 'absolute reality'*. Its aim is therefore a systematic representation of the systematic interconnections of things in their being.

It is because of its very object that metaphysics cannot be organized into the same sort of divisions as the disciplines of positive science can: a totally comprehensive view of the world can be given *only* to *one concrete person*. It is also for this reason—and not because of historical chance—that metaphysics' sociological form of existence is by necessity a *'school'* with a *'sage'* as its center. The ultimate value of metaphysical cognition is not to be assessed according to the positive sciences' measure of provability—at least not in so far as its primary function is to provide a detailed, *a priori* theory of essence. Rather, it is to be assessed in terms of the *richness* and *fullness* through which the *metaphysician as a person is in unity with the world,* mediated by his inner solidarity and participation in the totality of historical world experience. The concept of man as *microcosm,* incorporating all essential domains of the world and its ground and laws (*'homo est quodammodo omnia*[28]), repeats itself here, albeit in a *relative historical* sense, in so far as he who possesses the *totality* of *hitherto* world experiences, as well as its thought in its most concentrated and rational form, is also he who possesses the possibility of the deepest metaphysical cognition. By contrast, positive science pays

95

for its universality and universal provability because its special object—which can only be separated by abstraction from the total reality of the world—is *relative to man* in so far as the term, 'man', is understood in the *essential* sense of a vital, rational being—not in the empirical sense of earthly man with his fortuitous characteristics. For science also seeks to raise itself above this 'man' and indeed makes him an object of its investigations in all directions. Metaphysics, however, is the *venture of reason to penetrate into absolute reality,* for which man, with all his essential, personal powers, is always *personally* responsible. Its results are *continuously hypothetical,* in contrast to the hypotheses of positive science,[29] and they remain only *probable* because of its second, positive-scientific cognitive function. Metaphysics' results are 'valid' only for those who feel its nature to be in spiritual unity with the nature of a metaphysician who corresponds to their own ideal person-type.

Whereas science has to avoid all value decisions the more perfect it becomes, metaphysics is both *cognition of reality* and *theory of absolute values.* Metaphysics shares with religion participation in 'absolute being'—but not through faith and free obedience to a person who is believed to have experiential contact with the Deity: revelation, grace, illumination, or a special ontic relationship to the Deity. Rather, the metaphysical participation in absolute being is through *spontaneous,* evidential *cognition* of matters in themselves which can be re-thought by anyone. This proposition is valid only when metaphysics is not regarded as the 'handmaid of theology' or as in the service of religion. And in this regard metaphysics is not only the path of salvation but a *spontaneous* one. It shares with religion a basic orientation towards being-in-itself (*Ens a se*), but only to the extent that this appears in the world of experience (essential experience and insight, such as the fortuitous experience of spatio-temporal facts and their laws) and with express *renunciation* of all so-called 'supranatural' sources of cognition. On the other hand metaphysics shares with science stringent, rational method and a basic orientation towards the world. At all peaks of its historical existence metaphysics is in closest and creative contact with positive science, much as science, on the other hand, at all of its peaks, bends back into its philosophical foundations. It is only on the relatively lower plains of their mutual movements that metaphysics and science fall apart and lose their interconnections.

Since *cultivation* [*Bildung*] and growth, in respect to the re-awakening of human forms of cognition, come about only when knowledge of the *essence* of the whole world's structure *becomes functionalized* with random areas of the world from which this knowledge has been gained, and since a *complete* view of the world is never accomplished by inductive or deductive means, meta-physics is also the main lever for all intellectual and *spiritual cultivation of the person* because its forms of looking at the world are applied ever anew to any and all fortuitous facts. This is in contrast to the changing results of other areas of knowledge whose primary concern is not *'cultivation'* (in the true and good sense of the word [*Bildung*]), but solely *'accomplishment'* by which they are at the service of the basically infinite process of scientific progress. Beyond this function the other areas of knowledge are valuable in regard to 'cultivation' of the person only to the extent that their problems touch on philosophy itself.[30]

The presupposition for the re-awakening of an independent metaphysics that goes beyond a 'lonely thinker' (as Eduard Zeller pointedly stressed with regard to Greek philosophy) is always the absence of a *'church'*, as an institution for mass-salvation, hierarchy and dogma, and the beginnings of its dying (Buddhism). The greatest sociological power over the history of human groups has been exercised, up till now, by the following meta-physicians, in order of decreasing greatness: Buddha—in-comparably the greatest effect in history, far greater than Christ—Laotse, Plato, Aristotle, Descartes, Kant, Hegel, and K. Marx. Beyond their schools they have co-determined, in basically different ways, the *types of thinking* of whole ages and masses. And they did this to the extent that the cultural *elite,* which metaphysics can affect directly, did not know anymore how much it was influenced by those thinkers—only indirectly can metaphysics affect the *masses* by influencing ecclesiastic dogmatics, 'public opinion',[31] or class-ideologies, as is the case with K. Marx. Prevailing metaphysical systems are never crushed by positive science, which itself is determined by metaphysics—more than it suspects. Rather, metaphysics is crushed only by *new* metaphysical systems or by a religion. The more a metaphysics remains unformulated, and the more its followers are *not conscious* of its origins, the stronger its power is on the human mind. The sociology of knowledge has to trace such hidden metaphysics, as has been done in a magnificent manner by E. Troeltsch in his *Historismus* of many German historians, and by Radbruch in his legal philosophy of political parties, which also are strongly co-determined by metaphysics, or by thought very similar to meta-physics.

The *estates* and *classes* to which metaphysicians belong are of greatest significance for the structure of a metaphysics. In contrast to the *homines religiosi,* who on the average come more widely from the lower classes, the metaphysicians come mostly from estates and classes of *cultivation and possession*. The difference between the founders of Christian religion, which, as Max Weber stated, was a religion of 'migrant, young craftsmen', and Greek philosophers shows this clearly enough. It is true that some of the philosophers belonged to the class of slaves (where, in the sense of public law [*staatsrechtlich*], cultivation and possession must have had little meaning), as, for example, Epictetus. But such exceptions appear, in general, to be confined to the individualistic and cosmopolitan, ethical-practical schools of the *cynics* and to post-Aristotelian philosophers, especially the later *Stoics*. In its ethics and social philosophy Stoicism became more and more an *ideology of a suppressed class*—which Spengler with some justification compared to modern proletarian socialism.[32] In contrast to pre-Socratic, colonial philosophy of nature and to Anaxagoras, and Socrates, who 'could not learn anything from the trees', the *difference between country and city* clearly appears with the earliest theories of mind and of '*nous*'. *Asian Indian* metaphysics is one of 'forests' (as Tagore pointedly says in his book, *Sadhana*), one of immediate contact with *nature,* of identification with and immersion of the soul in life, and it also presupposes an almost metaphysical-democratic conscious unity of man with all sub-human life[33] (even already in pre-Buddhist developments). By contrast almost the entire metaphysics of the *West* is a product of *city* thinking. This explains the fact that Western metaphysics rests on an entirely different consciousness of self[34] and an entirely different interpretation of man himself, viz. as a *sovereign* being *above* all of *nature.* Until now the history of philosophy has paid too little attention to this state of affairs,[35] although many phenomena of this kind can be made understandable only by sociology. *French* philosophy has been a philosophy of the *enlightened nobility* since the overcoming of the medieval Scholasticism of priests and especially monks until Rousseau—the father of revolutionary, emotional radicalism and romanticism. It is borne, no less, by the spirit of this estate: it is world-open, non-academic, and non-pedantic; it has the character of men of the world; and it is given in a form that directs itself to the entire learned world.[36] This is similar to *Italy* where the patrician city-nobility has accomplished much more for the cultivation of the mind than in *Germany*, where the difference between castles of nobility and burghers of the town was fundamental to the history of German nobility. *Modern German philosophy* has been the achievement of the learned *Protestant middleclass,* especially those of the parsonage. This explains its forms and styles, its often horrible terminology, cut off from the world, its strong tendencies towards schools where ideas have become increasingly fixed; this also explains many of the traits of its contents, for example, its

98

relatively small connection with mathematics and natural science, its non-political[37] and contemplative spirit, its meagre radicalism (which stands out when compared to other Western philosophies of the Enlightenment), and its almost complete inner lack of 'spirit' with regard to industrialism and technology, which is so conspicuous with the *British philosophers of the larger bourgeoisie,* who are both statesmen and economists. These factors account for the very different frontiers of German philosophic thought as compared to Romance countries, for in the latter the opposition between ecclesiastic philosophy and the non-religious, anti-metaphysical currents has always been much sharper than in Germany. These factors also created in Germany the *opposition between theory and power* which permeates all of German life. A conscious class-philosophy, a proletarian science—a non-thing in itself—has been attempted in Germany only by Karl Marx.

Also of considerable importance for the sociology of knowledge is the *relationship between systems of metaphysics and nations.* Nations express their nature also in the methodologies of exact sciences, but they more explicitly and more immediately reveal their nature in metaphysics.[38] It would be a fruitful undertaking for the sociology of knowledge to establish a theory relating the phases in the history of philosophic theories to the *types of groups* from which they came. The following points would have to be considered in such an undertaking: 1 the traditional scholastic-Latin, *supranational, ecclesiastical philosophy,* derived in its essence from the estates of priests and monks, and against which especially mysticism and humanism as well as modern philosophies rose (Telesio, Campanelle, Bruno, Descartes, Bacon); 2 the philosophies of the young *European nations,* which are characterized by national-mythic contents and the usage of national languages, not intended to be national *as such* but which presented themselves as *'cosmopolitan'*—whereby they easily overlook that their cosmopolitanism, however, is only hidden *Europeanism*—and which, as a phase, includes the traits of all so-called 'modern' philosophy, from Nicolaus Cusanus and Descartes to Kant; 3 the expressly *nationally oriented* philosophy of the nineteenth century, which, since Fichte, has been a strong ferment in the rise of national, cultural consciousness in Germany (Fichte and Hegel in Germany; Gioberti and Rosmini in Italy); 4 the slowly emerging and truly *cosmopolitan world philosophy,* engendering vivid discussions among leaders and representatives of larger cultural units as a method of its investigations—a phenomenon whose earliest well-spring in our own country began with Schelling, Schopenhauer,[39] Paul Deussen, and Eduard v. Hartmann's incorporation of Asian Indian wisdom into the philosophical discussion, and which, following the World War, has gained substantial ground as 'mankind's first global experience of itself'.

Concerning the sociology of positive science: science and technology, economy

In contrast to metaphysics, which, as we saw, stems from the work of learned people of the upper classes who have the leisure to contemplate essences and to devote themselves to their own 'cultivation', *positive science* is of another *origin*: there are two social levels which first were separated from one another but which increasingly must permeate each other if a systematic and methodologically sensible and cooperative, *disciplined* research is to come about. This proposition, I claim, contains an element of inner lawfulness: that is to say, there is, on the one hand, a class of people who have accumulated experience in work and crafts. The latter's inner drive towards increased social freedom and liberation prompts an intensive *interest* in those images of and thoughts about nature that make possible the *prediction* of natural processes and *control* over them. I do not believe that *one* of these groups alone can account for the existence of positive science, because only under the influence of free contemplation could science extend its purely *theoretical mode of cognition* and its logical and mathematical methods to the whole of the world. But without the influence of the other group, science never would have found its essential and close connection with *technology*, measurement, and, later on, free *experiment*, not restricted merely to technical and occasional functions. Above all, science could not have learned to restrict its interests in any area of nature to the *measurable and quantifiable* aspects of the world, or to laws governing the *spatio-temporal interconnections* of phenomena as they are or could be under various conditions: it could not have rerestricted its interests, then, to what can be conceived as dependent upon possible *motions*. No matter how the formal-mechanical principle of natural explanation appears in this or that form, it stems no doubt from men who move material things from place to place, and whose continual success in this work brings about ever new experiences of the nature of bodies and energies. The basic sociological origins of positive science are always *economic communities of work and commerce* to be found in patriarchal, expanding cultures—not in blood or cultural communities, where the religious, holy person and the metaphysical sage can be found.[40] I assert, therefore, that it is wrong both to see the origins of science only from a technological, pragmatic (here one speaks with reservation), Marxist conception of the relation between work and science (L. Boltzmann, E. Mach, W. James, F. C. Schiller, A. Labriola, etc.), or to see its origins only from a purely intellectual view, which has value and meaning only for the development of philosophy. Positive science, wherever it arose, in Europe, Arabia, China, etc., has been the *child of the marriage between philosophy and work-experience*. It always presupposes *both*—and not only one of them. Because the *mixing of classes* was, in comparison to Asian theocracies and castes, strongest in the West (starting with Hellas)—a condition that became obvious after the abolition of the 'chthonic' gods and remnants of maternal laws—the division of scientific disciplines *in the West* grew from a unique historical condition, that is, from the talents of the masculine and logical people of Greece, and to a wider, global, and *systematic* extent only among *Western city people*.

This very origin of science would lead us to an assumption which the history of science has already confirmed: the forms of *production techniques* and human *work* (in the technical sense) are *parallel* to forms of positive-*scientific thought*. Neither of these two forms can be assumed to be the origin of the other or to be a variable independent of the other. The independent variable that determines *both* these forms is rather the prevailing *drive-structure of the leaders* of a society (many different drives can be predominant here; to detect them is a problem of psycho-energetics in conjunction with the psychological theory of racial heredity)—in close interrelationship with what I have called an *'ethos'*, i.e. the prevailing and valid rules for spiritual acts of value-preferences. In simpler terms we can say: the independent variable is the unity of the drive-structure with the guiding values and ideas toward which those leaders and, through them, their groups are directed. The mental, *economic attitude* is only *one* among many bases for an ethos, and, by its very nature, it must be explicated only through a *history of the mind,* much as the drive-structure must be explicated through racial integration and hereditary laws of *vital-psychic* characteristics. I consider the following to be *one of the important propositions of the sociology of knowledge*: technology is not a subsequent 'application' of a theoretical, contemplative science characterized by the idea of truth, observation, conservation, pure logic, and mathematics; rather, the more or less prevailing *will to control* and direct this or that realm of existence (gods, souls, society, organic and inorganic nature) co-determines the methods of thought and intuition, as well as the goals of scientific thought, and, indeed, it co-determines as though behind the back of the consciousness of individuals, whose changing motivations for investigation do not matter in this process. This proposition is just as firmly proved by the *history of cognitional*

101

theory and developmental psychology as by the factual *history* of science and technology.

I cannot go into the details of the difficult reasons, based upon both the theory of cognition and developmental psychology, why all perceptions and thoughts, with regard to the laws governing the *selection* of their *possible* objects, and, not any less fundamental, all our actions, are rooted in the *conditions of valuation and drive-life*.[41] I only wish to emphasize, though, that these investigations into valuation result in a very relative justification for the theory commonly referred to as 'Pragmatism' and 'economism' (in Mach's sense). This justification is relative because it pertains not to the *idea* of knowledge, truth, and *pure* logic, as in the case of pure 'Pragmatism', but to the *selection* of the sides of the world that are 'interesting' to *positive science* and that science develops as *true, i.e.* develops correct and adequate propositions and theories. The condition for knowledge and the forms of its acquisition by the technical development of worldly goals for our possible actions, however, does not pertain to metaphysics. Yet, it is precisely the *essential* difference between philosophy and positive science that the former is *not* determined by possible *technical goals,* but it makes into an *object* of 'genuine' knowledge and establishes for its own foundation precisely those 'forms' of thought and intuition and their corresponding forms of being within which science thinks and finds its objects already standing.

Let us at this juncture say something about the *historico-sociological* aspect of the *relationship between technology and science.*

The first who clearly recognized the sociological and historical interconnection between technology and science—apart from Bacon's generalizations and one-sided treatments of the subject—was the Count Saint-Simon[42] in his later life. In his first period of thought, which A. Comte followed, Saint-Simon was, like Comte himself, an intellectualist; he believed that the development of science was also a leading factor in economic and political progress. However, Saint-Simon was also the one who, with other French historians and socialists, strongly influenced Karl Marx's so-called 'economic interpretation of history'. What was said above implies that I, too, see the justification—although very small—for such an economic interpretation of history, which has stimulated sociological thought considerably in regards to the *technological* interpretations of the very ambiguous term 'relations of production' [*Produktionsverhältnisse*] as they were given later by A. Labriola. But the limitations of the economic interpretation are so numerous that I have almost nothing more in common with Karl Marx than the rejection of intellectualism, which holds technology to be only a 'subsequently applied' and thoroughly 'pure' science. Marx holds that not only positive science but *all* mental accomplishments are dependent upon the economic relations of production. *I* hold that *only* positive science has this dependency, and only in terms of a *parallelism* that has a *third common, primary cause*: *the hereditary drive-structure of leaders*, their biological [*blütmassige*] descendence, and their relation to a modern ethos. Marx wants to conceptualize the prevailing religion and metaphysics, moreover the ethos itself, in terms of the economic relations of production. It is my stand that these three factors *co-determine* to high degrees any *possible* formation of positive science *and* technology—hence, they represent a *second* independent variable which can be conceived *only* through the *human sciences*.

Let us give some examples: *Buddhist* metaphysics and its ethos, as well as pre-Buddhist religions, also developed a will to control, which was no less than in the West. But this will to control was not directed towards outer material production, and it entailed neither an increase in population and material needs nor a perpetuation of them. It was *inwardly* directed towards mastering the automatic flow of psychic processes and all processes of the lived body—directed towards mastery for the sake of mortifying inner desire. This explains, to use an example contrary to the way it is with us, the adaptation of the child population to *static* relations of production, say, by killing young girls, etc., an extraordinary psychic and vital technique but not a significant technology of production or war. Also, Greek religion and metaphysics, likewise but to a lesser degree, excluded strong *will* and any positive *valuation* of production techniques that made use of machines, even after the development of the very rich pure mathematics and investigations into nature. There arose much less *actual* technology than could have developed within the technological possibilities that Greek science, mathematics, statistics, and the beginnings of dynamics provided; the technological capacity of Greek science by no means had been exhausted. True, Greek metaphysics and religion, in principle, *affirms* the world, its nature and existence, but neither as an object of human *work,* human building, ordering, or prediction, nor as the object of a divine creative and architectural deed which man has to continue. Rather, their world is the realm of living and noble *energetic forms to be seen and contemplated and to be loved.* It is also here, then, that the prevailing religion and metaphysics exclude any inner connection between mathematics and studies of nature, between studies of nature and technology, between technology and industry; a connection which is the unique and powerful stamp of modern civilization, but which, however, presupposes the beginnings of free

103

labor and increasing political emancipation of the great masses in contrast to the manifold forms of unfree labor (slavery, bondage, etc.). The beginnings of positive science (astronomy, mathematics, medical arts, etc.) in *Egypt* and in *China* were closely connected with the vast technological tasks posed by the geographic and geopolitical conditions of these powerful monarchies, especially the tasks of regulating the Nile River and the two great river systems in China, navigation, coach-building, and architecture—all of which had been at the service of *political power* interests. If among these people there did not develop a methodological and cooperatively organized, positive disciplinary science[43] which encompasses the whole universe and its divisions, it is here obvious that the *lack of free philosophic speculation* explains this failure. In China all powers of the ruling classes were directed towards the *'cultivation'* of human existence, mores, and inner dispositions. This occurred during the reign of Confucianism, with its humanistic classicism, with its official ethics, spanning throughout the magical solidarity of nature with the emperor and up into the order of the 'heavens', and, not the least significant, with its hieroglyphics, conductive to rigidity and inflexibility in thought and linked to the books of the great classical writers. Very little mental energy was left here for extensive war production, technology, and systematic science—despite strong economic incentives, population increases, and eagerness for possessions. The ruling classes of *Babylon* and *Rome,* which set the patterns for *legal systems* in subsequent ages, reveal that in the area of private law the *technical impetus* behind the origin of human sciences out of myth, saga, and tradition, i.e. from the *souls* of the peoples, manifests itself, as does the origin of the natural sciences. Also, philosophy, pure logic, and a drive to play and experiment in legal thinking—similar to Greek 'pure' mathematics, which for centuries remained without physical and technical applications—is what brings about unity, logic, and system in the science of law and gives it the character of embracing all social concerns. But the *content* of the law and the stratification of given legal goods within the prevailing ethos is determined by the direction and the content of the social will to *control* found in *political* ruling groups and classes, i.e. is not determined primarily by economic motives or intellectual insights. R. Jhering[44] recognized the creative power of legal judgment. But legal judgment was not, as Jhering meant in his one-sided technicism, the sole source for the development of Roman private law. Rather, the power of legal judgment is side by side with legislation, the 'purpose' of the legislator, and the *logical* motivation of legal thought. Yet, the considerable *Roman* technology displayed in communication, fortifications, war, and architecture did not lead to large-scale productions of machines as is characteristic of modern European nations. And this was so because, first, the extent of the will to control nature remained within the confines set by the *political* will to control, and the political techniques for ruling in the form of a political, ruling capitalism—thus there did not arise a pure will to control nature for the sake of such control and for the sake of purely economic purposes and economizing work—and, second, the psychic hereditary dispositions of the leading Roman classes lacked the sense of *philosophical* contemplation that was proper to the Greeks.

If we want to understand *the origin and developmental stages of modern science*—one of the most attractive tasks in the sociological dynamics of positive science—and if we want to understand these not only historically but sociologically as well, viz. as a total outcome of the criss-crossing laws of *ideal and real historical* processes, then we can do so only by linking the types of knowledge from various sources and areas of specialization with one another. It informs us very little when W. Windelband[45] says, in consideration of all Copernicuses and Keplers, that the Platonic-Pythagorean mathematical science of nature, with which the qualitatively oriented, anti-mathematical Aristotelianism of Scholasticism had done away, has been revived in modern times (for example, Aristarch of Samos, the predecessor of Copernicus) and that this acceptance of Platonic-Pythagorean science has formed the creative origin of modern mathematical science. The Hellenistic neo-Platonists took primarily gnostic-mystic contents from the *same* systems of thought, and the Florentine Academy took something else again! Much as the ancient trains of thought had in fact been assumed and were sources of stimulation, one must ask the question: *Why now*—and not, say, in the eleventh century? The beam of interest, which, like the beam of a lighthouse, illuminates only a part of the past, is also the work of the historical *present,* coming first from *futural tasks* hovering above the spirit and will and later from a will for a new 'cultural synthesis', as E. Troeltsch pointedly says. One of the most important problems within the complex question concerning the origin of modern science is, above all, to understand the conspicuously dense *accumulation* of inventions and discoveries of experimental and mathematically useful knowledge of nature in the period including Galileo, Leonardo, and Newton. We are faced here with a *sudden* process which occurred by fits and starts and immense leaps and not a continuous and roughly uniform process, developing step by step, as an intellectualist hypothesis necessarily would want us to expect. This is so despite all preliminary work done on the subject and despite all presentiments—which especially Pierre Duhem in his intense studies discovered for the history of physics since the eleventh century. It is this sudden process that led from the medieval world-view to modern scientific methods. I do not believe that the above-mentioned revivals (Democritus and Epicurus, ancient atomists who were forerunners of Boyle, Gassendi, and Lavoisier; Aristarch, Proclos, and Plato, logicians who were the forerunners of Copernicus and Kepler) have ever meant much for the origin of modern science: science would have begun also *without* this.

Let us distinguish *negative* and *positive conditions* for the rise of modern science, and let us also try to trace the importance of some factors and laws that determine the effects of those of the conditions. 1 A negative and only moderately effective cause for the rise of science is the elimination of certain checks on thinking due to the *disintegration of the ecclesiastical hierarchy* and power through *religious reformations*—which from a purely scientific viewpoint appear to have been highly reactionary. The prevailing ecclesiastical powers had been more enlightened and more friendly towards science, more circumspect, and, above all, more rational than the great reformers, who were characterized by a gloomy fanaticism, irrationalism, and, in general, indifference to culture. This is proved by the very ambiguous relationship the humanities had to both religious parties; it is also proved by the destinies of Serveto and Kepler, who had to witness his mother being burned as a witch. Yet, it would be incorrect to assign to this negative causal factor no importance at all, for it must be assigned at least an *indirect* significance for the rise of modern science—although, as we saw, the ecclesiastical mind favored to high degrees exact, positive thought.[46] The partial collapse of ecclesiastical power had significance also because of unified factors that were only indirectly connected with the changing dogmatism. One of these factors is to be seen in the *disintegration of the ancient biomorphic metaphysics* with its conceptual realism and ontological orientation. This disintegration went *hand in hand* with the disintegration of large parts of the old dogmatics, especially those related to Church and sacraments. Biomorphic metaphysics was *much more* of an obstruction to the rise of science than dogmatism, the Pope, the hierarchy, monkhood, etc. Of course, the inner development of the European peoples themselves toward a new social aggregation also had its share in the disintegration of this kind of metaphysics, which rested in the relative natural world-view of the time. But no doubt it was the reformers who played a great part in the abolition of the ancient scientific formulations of biomorphic metaphysics. Nevertheless, the main reformers, whose character and lines of thinking are far away from those of the founders of modern science, such as Galileo, Ubaldi, Descartes, Kepler, Newton, etc., share a number of albeit *formal* but important traits: 1 They are *nominalist in their thinking*, something which is always connected with a revolution against an old and petrified age. 2 They hold that man's *will*—and not only a contemplative mind—dominates his nature. 3 Both founders of science and reformers stress *problems of consciousness and certitude*: certitude of cognition precedes 'truth' with Descartes, and the question of the certitude of one's salvation precedes objective theological problems. 4 Both put *freedom* of investigation and judgment in matters of faith at the basis of an ontically conceived capital of truth and capital of grace, which one must possess in order to be free ('truth will make you free', it was said, but now both scientists and reformers say 'freedom will lead you toward truth'); *independent thinking,* in contrast to dependence upon traditional doctrines, is demanded by science as well as reformers for reading the 'Bible'; faith is a *personal* voluntary act—not an 'order of the will over reason' to accept certain doctrines from outside or from the *Church.* 5 Both the scientific and religious movements have in common a new *dualism* between mind and flesh, soul and body, God and world. This is clearly articulated in Luther's *Freedom of a Christian* and in Descartes's *Meditations* and *Principia philosophiae.* This dualism abolishes the *specifically* 'medieval' *interwovenness* of the material-sensible and the spiritual, which belongs to the biomorphic world-view of all 'life-communities'. Theories of sacraments, magic techniques in saying mass, the obscure interwovenness of public law, local law, and family law, the theory of the substantial unity of the soul and the *'forma corporeitatis'* (later dogmatized at the Council of Vienne)—a Thomist theory which Descartes, Luther, and Calvin abolished simultaneously—and a partial identification of the ('struggling') kingdom of God with the *visible* institution of the Church: all this, and much more, are inner effects and consequences of *biomorphism.*

The following question is of eminent interest here: What precisely is the *sociological* meaning of these peculiar, *common* factors to be found in such very different movements of reformers, on the one hand, and fathers of modern science, on the other? The answer is this: the unifying factor of these mental attitudes is to be seen no doubt in new forms of thinking, valuation, and willing belonging to *one class*, the rising class of *bourgeois entrepreneurship*, standing in contrast to a contemplative class of monks and priests, on the one hand, which dominates by political means reminiscent of ancient Roman patterns and methods, and to the forces of the feudal world, on the other hand, which was characterized by the bonds of estates and which was politically and economically based in the 'power of wealth'. The common agent behind *both* movements is a new will to *work* and the so-called *individualism* of the bourgeoisie (dissolution of guilds, etc.). And it is this factor that renders to the *law of aging* pertaining to cultures (from biomorphic to additive, 'mechanical' world-views) its distinctly *historical* mark.[47] A nominalist way of thinking, for instance, is essentially *interconnected* with a decline in contemplative, religious classes [*Schichten*], such as the old orders of monks patterned after Benedictine models, giving way to juridical, regimental *ecclesiastical branches of power* (resulting in Occamist voluntarism and the later Scholasticism whose authoritarian petrification helped bring about Reformationist agitation). Furthermore, a nominalist way of thinking is interconnected with the fall of a biomorphic world-view in favor of a *mechanical* one because any 'general' conceptual object that is pertinent to the vital sphere—especially the (organic) idea of 'species'—and is not found in the sphere of the inorganic, possesses, indeed, a reality and unity independent from the criteria for individuating the spacio-temporal manifold. Finally, it is also interconnected with the rise of *'society'* as a group-form based upon contract and which slowly begins to take the place of the 'life-community' based upon blood, tradition, and preponderance of an ideal, psychic total-experience [*Gesamtkapital*]. *The categorically biomorphic world-view itself is connected essentially with a social, life-communal form of existence with its own tool-techniques and a predominance of organic (in contrast to inorganic) ones.*

2 There is another sociological and psychological interconnection between the rise of science and the Reformation. It consists of the *channelling of all psychic energy quanta into work within the world and into one's calling* [*Beruf*], energy which in the priestly Church had been directed into inner and outer 'works' for the deity and things divine, along with magical technique and *relative* self-redemption. The exclusive activity of the deity towards man in regards to religious justifications and sanctifications—virtually the only common criterion for the dogmatics of *all* new Protestantisms—i.e. their exclusive religiosity of 'grace' (along with the polemics of Protestant theologians saying that the old Church represented Pelagianism or semi-Pelagianism), is the simple result of this *redirection* of vital-psychic energy. Later, as these religious bonds *dissolve* altogether, as soon happened at the beginning of the Age of *Enlightenment* among the powerful cultural elite, a *purely* world-immanent rationalism and a complete *autonomy* of mundane cultural areas from all religious ties is what remains as 'residue'.[48] It took a century for what originally were only 'artificial' ideas of the Enlightenment, of an elite gathered around absolute sovereigns, to develop first into 'public opinion' and then slowly into a 'relative natural' way of thinking among the masses. The cultural

108

elite was frightened by and perturbed about this process's *social consequences* and attempted a weak, pliant, and faceless revival of older genuine religiosity within the historical and excessively numerous forms of the so-called new *'Romanticisms'* (O. Spengler's 'second religiosity'). This was the same religiosity that their spiritual predecessors themselves had dissolved and destroyed and whose influence they were not quite able to camouflage with their new protective colouring for their souls.[49]

3 With the growing separation of Church and State in the later Middle Ages, which replaced their so-called 'organic' relationship during the high Middle Ages—as A. Comte pointedly observed— there also grew a stronger guarantee for the *freedom of science* because this enabled the scholars to play off the various authorities against one another. But also the authoritative ties to the sciences had to diminish when churches and sects *increased in numbers* and held each other *mutually in check* and balance. Thus it could happen that the new universities and research institutes (the 'academies'), created by the absolute state in opposition to ecclesiastical organizations of knowledge (including the Paris, Petersburg, and Berlin academies), brought with their new tenured chairs for the specialized sciences also an entirely *changed atmosphere* to the life of the sciences—an atmosphere which, in regard to the *human* sciences (mercantilism, chamber politics [*Kameralismus*], court historiography, theology of state churches and of court preachers [*Hofprediger*], judicial theories justifying the absolute state) brought wholly new bonds with scientific freedom, lacking during the Middle Ages. But the *natural* sciences greatly benefitted through the technological and economic impetus (war technology, communication technology, and nationalized technology of production). The medieval science of priests and monks—a *science belonging to an estate*—dissolved except for scarce traces. Only during the nineteenth century, when the political age was replaced by the age of predominantly *economic* causal explanations, as described by the sociology of real factors— in terms of the limitations of such explanations in the history of mind, as we conceded in the first part of this treatise—did the *form* of dependencies upon and ties with the sciences, and first of all with the human sciences, change, i.e. with the origin of strong *economic* concerns of all kinds, including those of employers and employees, for the development of the state itself.[50] The danger of tutelage, of which *only* philosophy as *pure* theory, and *never* positive specialized science because of its technical co-conditioning according to essential laws, can rid itself (although in only a few cases), does not anymore come from Church and state but rather comes from new economic forces, which increasingly align

themselves with scientific staffs (industrial test centers, 'secretaries' of concerns, professorships of national economy, the so-called punitive professorships of the left and right, etc.). Academic representatives of *the latter's* ideologies of interests seek to enhance, directly or indirectly, these new powers with their wealth or by whatever means, including pressures on the state: through their presses and publishing houses—they laud them, reject them, or silence them, just as they please.

True and absolute *scientific freedom* grew in history, never out of the autonomous power of the scientific spirit itself, but only through the *mutual competition* of those *real-sociological* factors— in conjunction with an independent *philosophy*. What is called 'freedom of science' is only a *relative* freedom, i.e. a change in its bondage to risks. This competition between the real-sociological factors and institutions for the bonds, degradation, and leadership of science—and precisely with this its semi-automatic liberation—is a *sociological process* that pertains not only to science but also to *all* basic tendencies and areas of culture. According to the principle '*divide et impera*' this competition affects all secularization and autonomization, even of language (origins of national learned languages), art of all sorts, religion and mysticism, and, at the climax of the political age, also economies. All of these things were ecclesiastically inspired during the Middle Ages, being subordinated to the Church, first organically and in a hardly noticeable manner, and then, at the end of the Middle Ages, more artificially and mechanically—only secondarily were they subordinated to the state with which they were organically connected. They were embedded in the Church's supranational world of ideas and faith and always guided and controlled by its authorities. From our viewpoint today all of these things were *supranationally* unified and borne by certain *estates* which cut *across* the unified souls of peoples and clans and which were sustained economically by sovereigns, the upper classes of the town population, and the Church alike. There was the unity of the learned Latin language; there was a medieval world economy through which the large commercial cities of the various countries traded with one another directly. Learned classes and all artists united by estate stood above their peoples in a conscious, effective relationship. Basically, the *secularization* and discarding of ecclesiastical inspiration *and*, following the increased *differentiation* of cultural areas, the *new* unification and integration of their separated and autonomized parts into a new and growing group-type are *one and the same sociological process*: a process leading to the *unity of growing nations* and their growing national 'minds'. *Autonomization* and *nationalization of cultural areas* are thus only two sides of *one* process. National learned languages, national economies, nationally tinged philosophies and mysticisms, nationally tinged methods of the sciences (like those of the bourgeoisie, as opposed to the nobility and the priesthood as estate-based cultural forces), and continual reshuffling together form those new cultural force centers to which we refer as national 'minds'—in sharp contrast to the 'souls' of peoples and clans, towns and provinces, bound together organically and by their soil. These centers gradually absorbed the older, horizontal, universal culture of estates, and, aided by the new unity of growing nations, the distinct national activities again entered into communication with one another. The order in which this happened is not of any sociological interest, but rather is a concern of history.

4 Another sociological law of knowledge expressed in the development of modern science is what I elsewhere have referred to as the priority of 'those with a sense of appreciation over those with mere expertise', the priority of dilettantism over the scientific expert, or the priority of 'love over knowledge'. Throughout its history, any new area that science has subjugated for itself must have been grasped first through an emphasis upon *love*—only then can an age of more sober and more intellectually objective investigation emerge. Hence a new natural *science* presupposes also a new natural *feeling*: a new valuation of nature.[51] This emotional breakthrough ensued in the European Renaissance, beginning with the still intact Christian-linked Renaissance of the Franciscan movement and its various forms in Europe, which became, however, more and more mundane (Telesio, Campanella, Leonardo, Petrarca, Giordana Bruno, Spinoza, Shaftesbury, Fénélon, up to Rousseau). This breakthrough pertained first to the skies, and then it also spread to parts of organic nature. Heinrich von Stein correctly remarks: 'People of the seventeenth and eighteenth centuries think first of the skies when they use the term "nature"; those of the nineteenth century think of a landscape'. Emperor Friedrich II, with his partly occidental, partly oriental-Arabic circles—he was the founder of the University of Naples—is a most powerful source of this emotional trend. There is a secretive, frenzy-like attitude of men towards nature from *within* (to which Goethe's words refer: 'Is not nature in man's heart?'), which no faculty of rational understanding can replace. The connections with such novel natural *frenzy* are new emotional relationships to animals and plants, i.e. to everything that is most near to man as a living being. But the extent and type of this *sympathetic process of empathy and identification* with nature are very different throughout periods of history. During the high Middle Ages they are minimal in their extent and intensity. During the Renaissance this

111

spiritual power of man breaks through with vehemence, no doubt beginning with a new emotional relationship between man and woman.[52] The orphic-Dionysian wave of 'dark' mysticism always returns. In the Western history of science emotional breakthroughs of such a type result in constantly new impulses. The diverse provinces of being, nature, and history can be affected by them: in the Humanist movement with regard to the Middle Ages; in the seventeenth and eighteenth centuries with regard to the world structure and all artificial 'machineries'; in the nineteenth century especially with regard to organic nature and the landscape (geography); in Hölderlin, Winckelmann, and the new German humanism again with regard to antiquity;[53] in W. v. Humbolt, Schelling, Schopenhauer, E. v. Hartmann, and P. Deussen with regard to Indian philosophy and religion; in K. Marx with regard to the history of economy and the struggle of the masses for their existence; and presently in the Russian and Slavic world with regard to cultures of the far East.

There are a number of definite *criteria and laws* that underlie these historical rhythms of feeling and valuation and that, to be sure, are to be found in all types of knowledge (including religious knowledge as the Reformationist and Baptist [*täuferische*] 'longing' for primordial Christianity shows).

These rhythms first appear with a philosophic nominalism[54] and are joined with attempts to rescue oneself from a petrified, stable, intuitionless, and merely abstract culture. They are the strongest adversaries of 'Scholasticism' throughout Western Christianity, throughout the Arabic world (Sufism), throughout the Jewish world (Jewish mysticism, Spinoza), and throughout China (Laotze versus Confucius). Secondly, they always require 'autopsy', 'self-experience', 'immediate knowledge', and 'intuition' and always greatly underrate the necessary *rational* forms of all knowledge. The officialdom of an overcome level of knowledge (be this an ecclesiastic or national level) can be dissolved only by such emotively exaggerated intuitions. Galileo asks the bookish scholastic astronomers: 'Are you going to pull down the stars from the skies with your syllogisms?' Furthermore, such rhythms follow laws of *generation,* that is, principally a *biological* rhythm, not one belonging to the history of mind or to institutions. They are always connected with '*youth movements*'. This was referred to in the Renaissance as the opposition between '*moderni*' and '*antiqui*'. Ernst Troeltsch[55] showed very clearly this state of affairs in the relationship of Romanticism to the present German youth-movement among scientists, but he did not see the *general* sociological nature of this in so far as it co-determines all history of science. Such movements are also 'dilettante'—not only in the good, etymological sense of the word, but also in the negative sense of being unmethodical and turbulent and often overestimating and giving excessive *ontological value* to a novel area of interest. This last point is the most important. As a rule, the contents of a newly grasped area of being are first misplaced into the '*absolute*' sphere of existence, whatness, and value, viz. knowledge of it always aspires toward 'metaphysical' validity and its object tends to be a variable *independent* of all change. According to the law of analogous transferrence, whereby already proven laws and schemata[56] are transferred to other areas of being, the whole world, or the better part of it, is now thought in analogy with the new, preferred area of knowledge. This is shown by the following examples: For Descartes the analytic geometry that he discovered is 'the' natural science 'in general', and even a natural metaphysics. The so-called conservation principles of the new dynamics are successively transferred (a) into all qualitative natural phenomenon (sound, light, color, etc.), (b) into chemistry (atomic and molecular mechanics) and into the world-structure; (c) into psychic facts (associative psychology) and physiology (Dutch and French medicine); and (d) into social sciences, political sciences, ethics, and jurisprudence (Hobbes, Spinoza, etc.). For Marx whatever is called culture or religion becomes a function and an epiphenomenon ('super-structure') of economics and the dynamics of class struggle—for the modern dilettante biology of 'Life-Philosophy' they become, strictly speaking, 'life' (Bergson, Simmel).

The hypnotic concepts of the great fool or the overgrown child, which one calls '*Zeitgeist*', originate in these emotional movements and frenzy-like *generational* affects. According to the laws of *drive energetics* the direction of drives, which for a long time had been bound and repressed (by any dominant *ascetic* system that restricts certain drives and hence stresses others), free themselves in such frenzy-like affects—begin, as it were, to revolt. The *new drive-structure*—and also its accompanying new form of drive-restricting *ethos*, which is always relatively ascetic and relative to changing drive directions—originates through blood and blood mixtures of an elite as well as through their psychic expression. And along with this there is also born a new *mode for selecting* the possible world impressions and a new direction for man's *will* against the world. The *theoretical world-view* and the actual, practical (political, economic, and social) *world-reality* coincide not because one of these causes the other, but rather because they are *co-original* in the new structural unity of *ethos* and *drives*. Any such emphatic and enthusiastic-ecstatic epoch is followed always by an epoch of sobering, during which there is novel objection of disciplines and a new beginning permeated by inductive and deductive,

113

rational elements belonging to a new positive-*scientific* discipline. The formation of such a discipline is characterized by its objects, by the accompanying social need for technicians and engineers of the state and the economy, and by the need for physicians, etc. in the society. Excessive emotions—and the directions they take—affect mostly religion, art, and philosophy equally—and then they affect also the *sciences by means of a new philosophy*. Natural *philosophy* precedes science as does 'the mother-lye the crystal' (Comte), and, moreover, wherever there was a great philosophy it was not a mere 'Minervan owl' of positive science but rather the *pioneer* of science. Often philosophic hypotheses first become subject to scientific provability only quite late. This is shown by Bruno's theory of the chemical homogeneity of the world—rejected by Comte as 'metaphysical'—which was subjected to Bunsen's and Kirchhoff's spectral analyses; by the pure mathematics of the Greeks, resembling philosophy and being an extension of logic (for example, Proclos's theory of conic sections), which Galileo, Huygens, Kepler, and Newton subjected to proofs; by Riemannian geometry, which Einstein subjected to proofs; and by the ancient philosophic theory of the dynamic constitution of matter (Leibnitz and Kant), which H. Weyl subjected to proofs.[57]

Now analogical relationships of style and structure among art (and among the branches of art), philosophy, and science in the greater historical epochs need *in no way* rest upon *conscious* transference as in the cases of Dante with Thomas Aquinas, Racine and Molière with Descartes, Goethe with Spinoza, Fr. v. Schiller with Kant, Wagner with Schopenhauer, and Hebbel with Hegel. Rather, these relationships display their proper meaning whenever changes in the depth of a *new generation's* soul, changes which absorb the older differentiations of handed-down, established cultural values and renew them, follow upon one another *independently* of personal and conscious factors. This has been the case, for instance, with the analogies between French classical tragedy and French mathematical physics of the seventeenth and eighteenth centuries (which Pierre Duhem described), between Shakespeare and Milton and English physics; furthermore, it has been the case in the analogous styles of Gothic architecture and the architecture of high Scholasticism, Leibniz and Baroque art,[58] Mach-Avenarius and graphic Impressionism, Expressionism and modern, so-called life-philosophy, etc. Changes in the forms and directions of these individually *structured* emotional impulses are entirely beyond conscious 'purposes and interests', but *they* co-determine all subsequent purposes: they are *prior to knowledge and will*. They are biologically conditioned—not necessarily in a natural scientific sense as results of new objective blood mixtures through racial conflicts and interaction, but to the extent that either other *tribes* of people provide the spiritual elite[59] or other present *blood-classes* [*Blutschichten*] gain power either through the extinction of such a prevailing blood-class (such as the Franconian and Norman nobility in France and England) or through revolutionary means (for example, the Jews' loss of power in Russia due to the Bolshevik revolution). Such biologically conditioned changes are proved already by the very generationally recurrent rhythm of these movements.

Disappointment among the upper classes *coincides* with the *generationally* determined changes in the souls of the same groups, brought about by a new elite (as in the case of German romanticism's disappointment over the consequences of Enlightenment ideas and its experience with later phases of the French Revolution), and thus this disappointment determines even more strongly the direction of the *spiritual revival of a bygone age*, for example, of the Middle Ages and its spiritual world. As W. Dilthey, E. Troeltsch, E. Rothacker, and others have very pointedly shown, the 'historical sense' of the German human sciences of the nineteenth century—which L. v. Ranke termed as 'sympathy with everything human'—and that which grew out of it, the various so-called 'historical schools' of religion, theology, law, economics, philosophy, art, etc., were born out of such a dually motivated *romantic movement*. For it is a peculiarity of all human history that, indeed, the visible processes, accomplishments, and states of affairs do not repeat themselves, but the dormant powers of the soul that once filled a whole epoch are able to be re-lived in so-called 'reformations', 'renaissances', and 'receptions' *again and again* and can *be actively awakened*. This happens when congenial pioneers and elitist groups—that had long been forgotten—wake them up and call them forth, and when these powers, breaking out into new future plans and actions, at the same time begin to cast, like a powerful cone of light, new *retro*spectives on the otherwise silent and dead world of the past. For this reason the *re-living* of spiritual and psychic *functions* that created works of the past culture must always *precede* the *objective study* of those *works themselves* and their 'forms', i.e. the philology of historical sciences. But what results from these new epochal powers is not a 'copy' of the old cultural accomplishments, even when these have served as 'models'. The artistic activity of Humanism is as remote from 'actual' antiquity as reformed Christianity is from early Christianity. The monks copied truthfully and exactly the work of the ancient author—he who stood *most remotely* from the former's own mind. A man highly preoccupied with antiquity, or a Humanist, not infrequently misrepresents such a past work by

115

subjective assumptions and interpretations, and he creates some-thing which, most of the time, is not classical. But the scientific philologist, who presupposes the Humanist, *unites* the 'spirit' of a past culture with sincerity and philological strictness.

In all of these typical and frequent phenomena in the history of all types of knowledge, there appear, expressing themselves on general and collective scales, laws such as those that we find on a smaller scale among individuals. One of the first of these laws is the following: any *intellectual* comprehension of *what* something is *presupposes* an *emotive value* experience of the object. This proposition equally holds for the simplest perceptions, re-membrances, and expectations, as it does for all types of thinking; it equally holds for the intuition of first phenomena (i.e. the primordial forms of things as detached from sensation and their *hic-nunc* existence) and for the immediate thinking of ideas, both of which lead to *a priori* knowledge. And it holds no less for the cognition of all fortuitous matters of fact based on observation, induction, and mediate reasoning. *Value*-ception always precedes *per*ception. Desire and expression of feelings are already contained in the first words that a child utters. Psychic expressions are what he first perceives.[60] The child first grasps the 'agreeableness' of sugar before he grasps the sense quality, 'sweet'. The functions of animal senses develop only to the extent that they can function as signs for what is harmful or good to them (and only secondarily are their own central and peripheral organs structured accord-ingly). All creative inventors and researchers have attested to the fact that what they found was given to them first in the form of a 'premonition' [*Ahnung*] more felt than thought. All beginnings of novel scientific epochs are replete with such 'premonitions'. Whereas in a scholastic age knowledge of the world is considered to be more or less complete and ordered, in periods when a new world-view emerges men view nature or any area of this new knowledge as an unpredictable learning *process.* Even the most familiar data become questionable during renaissance periods. Every problem, i.e. every problem that is independent from the subjective questioning of individuals, and every dubitable state of affairs leads incessantly to new questions so that nature assumes the character of enigmatic depths. There is a general comportment among men that resembles early periods of child development when children incessantly ask, 'Why?' As psychic and mental *processes of rejuvenation,* such renaissance movements also show an apparent return to more *primitive* conceptions of the world. The mind rejuvenates and integrates itself in order to differentiate itself anew. The period of transition from high Scholasticism to the modern views of nature was filled with witchcraft, superstition,

116

mysticism, belief in ghosts and demons, and similar things, which were *not* known in the high Middle Ages. Nature suddenly became a huge field of *expression* for vital and unordered forces, which astrologers, alchemists, and physicians like Paracelsus thought they could control. All kinds of tendencies toward primitive magic techniques again appeared. There was—as W. Dilthey pointedly put it—a 'dynamic natural pantheism' that mediated between the Scholastic world-view and modern rational science. Also erotic tendencies at the time, seen as a whole, were 'mostly pubescent'.[61] It would be a mistake to see only rational thought in the powers that overcame the *anthropomorphism* of the medieval world-view, or to hold that rational thinking occurred here first in time. For the Scholastics were much better in the subtleties of thinking, its art and methods, than were men belonging to the more modern generations of researchers. What led beyond book knowledge and narrow anthropomorphism was, rather, an orgiastic and ecstatic *emotional devotion to nature* and a new attitude that opened up the world; in it was sensed, through one's own drive-life, a continuation of the vital powers and currents bearing all nature. This devotion to nature was followed by a new hunger for 'autopsy' (a favourite term of the Renaissance) and it led beyond book knowledge and narrow anthropomorphism. It was a wave similar to the one that ran from the orphic movements of the Middle East, across Thrace, and into Greece, and which produced not only an ancient tragedy, but also Plato's and Aristotle's classical philosophy through a marriage with 'Apollonianism', as Nietzsche saw. It is for this reason also that Plato's theory of *eros*—as a theory that originated in the orphic movements and the accompanying mystery cults—was a favorite subject of both philosophers and poets during the Renaissance.

In light of the above and many other analogous factors, the history of human knowledge poses for itself a question deserving the greatest attention, but which I do not venture to answer here. We know that to what ethnologists refer as 'advanced cultures' have always been in their beginnings mixtures of predominantly *matriarchal and patriarchal cultures*—mixtures that include mentalities and world-view forms that, in both types of cultures, first were distinct from one another and later developed in their own ways. It looks as if the principle of procreation by the females and males, which governs the breaking waves of organic life among individuals and their bodies, is *once again* active and effective among *collective* groups as well as in the psychic and spiritual processes and activities from which culture grows. And we can consider it to be more or less established that *ecstatic* comportments in perception, feeling, and drive-impulses *precede* ego-related

117

and 'conscious' comportments in all psychic developments. We may also consider it to be very likely that the two basic manifestations of ecstasy, which recur throughout all history, especially that of mysticism— the (dark) identification with the dynamics of *natura naturans* in which spirit is set aside and the (lit up) ecstasy of ἰδεῖν τῶν ἰδεῶν, blocking off drive-life and, therefore, resistance, in which the reality (*hic et nunc*) of things is primarily given to us—have their *first sociological roots* in matriarchal and patriarchal cultures. But is it not then probable that the 'conception' of a *genius* in all areas has its basis in the *amount of tension* between the two opposed ecstatic types of comportment and in the concentration [*Innigkeit*] and depth of this tension's loosening? Would not the same hold true for the conception and creation of *new cultures* by whole groups of peoples? The deep mystery of all cultural sociology, why specific and often very short-lived epochs stand out so much over other epochs as the genius stands out over the human average, may well be illuminated on this basis. And it could perhaps also explain why the analogous factors in the oppositions between Scholasticism and mysticism, classicism and romanticism, rational philosophy of ideas and intuitionist life-philosophy which seeks identification with nature, reveal *periodic changes* and *rhythms* that we find in the history of all cultures, even though in various historic and individual forms—changes in which the second term of the opposites usually *precedes* the first.

5 If *love* and *control*, as I have maintained for many years,[62] *are the foundation* for two attitudes of cognition—complementing one another necessarily and essentially in the human mind—modern science, in its development from puberty to maturity, also must be based in a new direction of the *will to control*. And this is precisely so. For the *second* source of modern positive science is the unrestricted tendency of the city-bourgeoisie toward a *systematic*, and not only occasional, *control over nature* and an endless accumulation and capitalization of knowledge for controlling nature and the soul. This tendency is not checked by any needs but is supported by the ethos and the will of the people concerned. Although aimed at the control of nature and the soul alike, this tendency is not exactly commensurate in nature to the knowledge of control itself—which was Bacon's narrow, all-too-English, practical restriction and which led him to speak so foolishly about the astronomy of the fixed-star heaven as a 'vain' science, a train of thought which Comte[63] unfortunately continued. Nature and soul nevertheless are *conceived* as being controllable and manipulable [*lenkbar*]. The 'soul', for example, can be controlled and manipulated through politics, education, instruction, and organizations (of

the masses first).[64] It takes subtle reasoning in this area, if anywhere, to fall neither into the folly of traditional intellectualism and pragmatism, including the economic theory of history, nor into the errors of psychologism, sociologism, and historicism, which tend to devalue modern science by clarifying its sociological 'origins'. Our own method already prevents us from making this mistake, for it never explains the *meaning* of spiritual culture and its value but rather the *selection* of this or that meaning from equally possible spiritual meaning-contents *as described by a sociology of real factors* [*realsoziologisch*].

One must not confuse all this with *motivations* or subjective intentions of learned *individuals* who do research; such motivations can be infinitely many: technical tasks, vanity, ambition, greed, love of truth, etc. What we declare is the *sociologically conditioned origin of the categorial apparatus of thinking* and of the objective goals of investigation with its impartial [*versachlichten*] methods, which in the 'new science' (*'nuova scienza'*) are effective beyond the will, wishes, and subjective intentions of individuals. Why, for example, does the category of 'quantity' gain primacy over that of 'quality', the category of 'relation' gain primacy over the category of 'substance' and its accidents,[65] or the category of 'laws of nature' gain primacy over that of 'form', 'gestalt', or, furthermore, 'type' or 'force'? Why does the continuous production of motion through spatial gestalts, according to an analytic formula, gain primacy over the category of qualitative spatial gestalts (Descarte's analytic geometry)? Why does the logic of relationalist thinkers gain primacy over that contained in the syllogism? Why does the prospective and forward-looking *'ars inveniendi'* gain primacy over the *'ars demonstrandi'* of a stable, thoughtful, theological or philosophical truth, based on the ecclesiastic Christ and on the 'prince among those who know' (Dante), i.e. Aristotle, as highest authority? Why has the modern experimenting and mathematically deducing *'researcher'* leadership, and no longer the medieval *'scholar'* who had many books and always looked backwards? Why does one proceed from phenomena of *consciousness*—and not from beings themselves? Why does there arise criticism of origins as the principle for all historical investigation and a new hermeneutic, which explains the meaning of handed-down writings out of their author's environment and which *sharply distinguishes* between the past and present, which during the Middle Ages were so curiously intercontained, killing thereby, as it were, the living present and present impressions and distorting the image of the past by unconsciously interpreting it through present interests? In the latter case one even seriously argued, for example, that Aristotle's *'nous'* was roughly identical with the God of Moses and the Gospel. Why is it that critical historical science—which as a whole is a self-analysis, self-liberation, and self-salvation of society—pushes back so much of what is still 'present' and 'lived' into the past—from whence it came—by virtue of the deceptions of unconscious life-communal traditions, continued through generational contagions, but at the same time sharply distinguishing their *peculiar* historic nature? Spengler judges modern science here correctly, if also somewhat one-sidedly and distortedly:[66]

> Within Baroque philosophy Western natural science stands entirely by itself. Something like this happened in no other culture. For sure, natural science was from its beginnings onward not the hand maid of theology, rather it was the *servant of the technical will-to-power and only, therefore,* was it mathematically and experimentally directed and from its youth controlled by *practical* mechanics. And because natural science is first technique before it is theory, it must be as old as Faustian man.[67] Technical works from an astounding energy of combination appeared already around 1000. Already in the thirteenth century Robert Grosseteste treated space as a function of light, Petrus Peregrinus (1289) wrote the best experimentally based treatise on magnetism before Gilbert (1600). And the disciple of both, Roger Bacon, developed a scientific theory of cognition as a basis for his technical experiments. But the audaciousness in the discoveries of dynamic interconnections goes further. The Copernican system is already more or less sketched in a manuscript of the year 1322 and had been mathematically developed a few years later in Paris by Occam's students, Buridan, Albert of Saxony, and Nicolaus of Oresme, in connection with the anticipated mechanics of Galileo. One must not be deceived in evaluating the ultimate tendencies underlying those discoveries: pure vision had no need for experimentation, but not so the Faustian symbol of the machine, which already during the twelfth century led to mechanical constructions and turned the idea of a *perpetuum mobile* into the Promethean image of the Western mind. *The working hypothesis is always first.* It is precisely what has no meaning in any other culture. One must accustom himself to the astonishing fact that it is not natural for man to turn any knowledge of natural phenomena into immediate practice, except for the Faustian man and those who, like the Japanese, the Jews, and the Russians, are living under the spiritual spell of its civilization. The very concept of the working hypothesis already contains the dynamics of our own world-view.

The force of the *technical impetus* for the application of

mechanical schema to facts has been revealed by E. Dühring, P. Duhem, E. Mach, and L. Boltzmann for mechanics and physics, by Kopp for chemistry, by G. Cantor for the history of mathematics, and recently from a sociological perspective by C. Bouglé,[68] by E. Ràdl for biology,[69] and by Bergson, Scheler, and Grünbaum for psychology. They have shown how the *theoretical representation* of facts has somehow always been *transformed formally and mechanically*—within pure mathematics by the natural-scientific task of physical application; within the exact sciences generally by technological problems; within technology by technical and practical problems of industry and by techniques of defense, war, and communication and, moreover, those of scientific experimentation and measurements; even within biology by animal breeders and plant growers and the diagnostics and therapy of diseases; and within psychology by the techniques of psychic control and guidance in education and politics (beginning with Ignatius's exercises based in associative psychology and continuing with Spinoza's theory of affectation and English associative psychology up to recent applied psychology and medical 'psychoanalysis').

Pragmatisms and fictionalisms of every sort, like all formal technicalities in mathematics, and even the Marxist technicality of the primacy of economic production technique for science,[70] have drawn their weapons and apparent justifications for their theories from this historical knowledge. The outstanding physicist, Boltzmann, wrote that the ultimate proof for theoretical natural science is that 'machines do run' built upon its principles, and that one knows through his theories how to tackle nature so as to bring about whatever one desires![71] Even thinking itself, according to him, is only 'an experiment with images and signs' of things rather than with the things themselves, and 'laws of thinking' are only rules that finally proved and fixated themselves after many well-done, i.e. *successful,* interferences in nature through controlled thought experiments with such signs. If 'work' were the source of culture and science (Marx in the *Communist Manifesto*), then, indeed, at least *one* considerable part of the Marxist theory would be proved.[72] But then man is *not an 'animal rationale'* but rather a *'homo faber'*—he does not have hands and a grasping thumb because he is rational, rather he has become rational because he has hands and because he learned how to extend these organs as tools and finally to do without them as much as possible in production. And, furthermore, he understood how to economize his sensible intuitions and representational images in favor of *signs* and their relations and to economize human volitional and vital kinetic energy in favor of *machines*—the latter being initially at the expense of organic energies belonging to subhuman nature (agriculture, breeding of animals, burning of wood) but mostly, however, at the expense of inorganic energies (water, sun, electricity, etc.). Historically, one strong current of thought in epistemological theory and the social sciences, which circulates throughout the cultural world, has seen the matter in this way. It thereby does not miss the suggestively amusing fact that the mutual adversaries of older, scientific rationalism and intellectualism, the sociological Marxists and positivists, on the one side, and modern romanticists of all sorts, on the other, *both* avail themselves of arrangements of data of this sort: the one, in order to show that only convenience can be assigned to science, but no 'truth' because truth would belong to 'higher' sources of knowledge (intuition, dialectics);[73] the other, in order to show, as Th. Hobbes has already asserted, that truth does not *consist* in anything else but 'univocal [*eindeutig*] and convenient designations of facts'.[74] I do not believe that either one of these sociological [*wissenssoziologischen*] interpretations of the above historical data—which effectively have been proved—hold any degree of significance. But the older scientific rationalism is equally wrong in holding science to be the pioneer of the modern world itself, and in tending for a long time to consider the scientific world-view not only as something true but also as an *absolute* representation of *absolute* things.

6 Hand in hand with changes in the logical systems of categories, whose main traits we discussed, there exists another process that we can refer to as the *increasing division and separation of the intellectual and emotional-volitional functions* of the human mind in the *new leading classes,* extending from the Middle Ages to modern times. This process led consequently also to a more articulate *separation of all problems concerning value and oughtness* from problems of existence and essence.

We would also consider it to be a grave error to assume that in this area there are *only* new theories about the same states of affairs. On the contrary, since Duns Scotus the theories regarding the primacy of Will in God and man and the dualism between Will and Reason, representing themselves in a variety of forms,[75] are themselves only rational attempts based in *new sociologically conditioned attitudes* of Western man. They arose from genuine and effective processes of *differentiation* within the human mind *itself.* Increasing dualism is more developmental-psychologically conditioned, but primacy of Will over Reason is more sociologically conditioned. *Medieval thinking,* as a social form of thinking, found itself structurally within that real developmental stage of all thinking which developmental psychologists call 'emotional thinking' [*Gefühlsdenken*],[76] viz. a thinking in which *valuating 'prefeelings'* largely determine the unitary formation of meanings, the

122

contents of and connections among judgments, and the objectives of syllogisms as mental activities, and, moreover, a thinking in which the practical, dynamic schemata of the whole organism's *comportment* predominantly determine the comprehension and structure of the world-content. And precisely *because* medieval thinking found itself within this developmental stage—precisely because *there was* such subjective, anthropological thinking—it could not gain cognition of itself as such. Such a type of thinking had to conceive itself as *purely* theoretical thinking. But man *knows* only what he is no more—never what he is.[77] If beings and essences—with the aid of pre-feelings and schemata of this sort of unconscious guiding thought—are perceived according to *systems of preferences* corresponding to the laws of preferences and selections within such feelings, then the result must necessarily have been a basic idea that was *fundamental* for all medieval-scholastic thought and also for ancient thought, at least ancient classical thought, and which undoubtedly was dominant. This basic idea can be formulated in two propositions: 'Every thing is good to the extent that it *is*, and bad to the extent that it is *not*', and 'Every thing within the order of good *and* bad is either a higher good or a lesser evil the more *independent* its type of existence'. These propositions, which naturally the whole scholastic philosophy took to be ontologically valid, designate, in fact, an apperceptive functional law of the human mind, in so far as the mind is linked to a *life-community*. The whole world, including matter and God, is, by its very existence and forms of existence, a hierarchy of goods whose peak is the *summum bonum,* i.e. God Himself: God functions here as the first independent being (*ens a se et per se*) and He is the infinite being in terms of *'existence'*—a verb which for the medieval mind implied increasing *activity*.

Sociologically this type of thinking, which analytically deduces value-being from being itself, is seen as a specifically *life-communal* type of thinking, bound necessarily and according to laws of meaning to a biomorphic world-view, and a type of thinking *related to estates* [*ständische*]. Church, state, estates, and principle occupations are necessary parts and consequences of an ontic world-order, as are all ethical and aesthetical values: a rigorous, stable, and objectively teleological 'world-order'—not unlike the societal and estate order reduced by Plato and Aristotle to a world-order in itself ('born' slaves and masters). The Pope was the sun; the Emperor, the 'moon'. But in reality the opposite is the case: the order of life-communal estates is unconsciously projected into the world-order—according to the law whereby social structure is primary to all other structures of being, i.e. the primacy of the 'thou' before the 'it'. For thinking connected with estates the

123

following holds true: he who belongs to a lower estate is not only regarded by someone belonging to a higher estate as a *different* being (one is a particular being and not merely someone else only *within one and the same estate*), but he also is relative *non*-being, or one whose *type* of existence is *more dependent*. Nietzsche already pointed to the possible etymological root of the term '$\dot{\epsilon}\sigma\theta\lambda\dot{o}s$': it designates someone who *is*—the common man, however, is someone who is *not*.[78] Analogously the concepts of 'action' and 'passion'—an anthithesis that the modern concept of causality views only as subjective and relative because passion brings about counter-action and both are reciprocal actions—are ontic concepts for Aristotelean-medieval thought. The relatively independent form of being is activity, while the more dependent form of being suffers activity's effects. Primary matter, the '$\dot{\epsilon}\nu\delta\epsilon\chi\dot{o}\mu\epsilon\nu o\nu$', is 'the' passiveness absolutely and the lowest substrate of all forms, and for Plato even a $\mu\dot{\eta}\ \ddot{o}\nu$. The man of the lower estate *is* simply not in the same way as the man of the higher estate; whether he is a good man or a bad man is a wholly different, moral problem and a wholly different antithesis from the one with which we are concerned. He 'stands' less on his own and *is* more dependent, just as man, as the unity (*'unum ens'*) of his spiritual-vital soul (*'substantia imperfecta'*), also *is* more dependent than the *'angelus'* (*'forma separata', 'substantia perfecta'*).[79] The concept of a hierarchical order comes to man first of all from the *social* world, and it is then easily carried over into organic nature, as a *stable,* ever-present order of perfection in regards to types and species that God 'created' within a world of realistic concepts. But such an order can be extended to *all* beings, even the inanimate and the suprahuman, invisible transcendent, *only* within a biomorphic, life-communal world-view, borne through timeless dynamics and not through temporal evolutionary processes. The formal structures of society, organic and inorganic nature, and the heavens were, in the world of the Middle Ages, always the same: the *stable hierarchy* of powers and *existences* was at the same time and purely analytically a *hierarchy of values.*

But this type of thinking and valuation also undergoes basic *changes* in the predominantly *societal* world. First, the human soul *differentiates itself.* Thinking, as a living function, increasingly *emancipates* itself from both emotional and organic-schematic guidances, and the spiritual soul emancipates itself from the vital soul. With impressive and exalted words Descartes brought the completed process of this emancipation to expression: *cogito ergo sum.* The new singularism, individualism, rationalism, and ideal-ism, the *new distance* between man and *sub*human nature and the new *direct relationship to God* (not mediated by the world and its

order), the incomparable soaring of the human, rational consciousness of self—all these new experiential qualities of a *new type of
man* this powerful thesis brought to expression in three words. Seen
from the standpoint of objective philosophy [*Sachphilosophie*] this
proposition is a web of errors,[80] but it is nevertheless the most
grandiose expression and drastic formulation of a *new sociological
type of man* ever to be found. With this differentiation, which
seems to hold analogously not only for the values of Truth and the
Good but also for the Good and Beauty and their subjective act-
correlates, even the order of things and goods, of natural objects
and values, of causes and purposes, which in the Middle Ages
remained identical (the Middle Ages as a life-communal epoch), in
principle fall *apart*. Thinking can become individually 'autonomous' only when it also becomes free from the emotional and
organic-somatic schemata that direct it—the experience that no
doubt laid the foundation for the new *division* between the vital
and spiritual soul, which the Council of Vienne condemned.

Another basic change in the societal world is the *elimination* of
the idea of a *hierarchic order* of formal activities—which previously
had given to all things the determination of their becoming,
existence, and nature. As powers, these were called entelechies,
and, to the extent that they struggled through the various levels of
matter, they made things *both* exist *and* 'good'. Along with the
hierarchical order there was eliminated a whole living world-view
containing a categorial system, which was reduced to a *theory* and
preserved like a fossil in the traditional schools of ecclesiastic
philosophy. But the elimination from modern sociological thought
of the idea of a *hierarchical* order among things and of the
objective, stable theology, so that only the antithesis of good-bad
remained, is undoubtedly conditioned *sociologically*. It is a
consequence of the increasing *disintegration of the order of estates*
that first took place through a prevailing arrangement of
occupations, and later, during the course of the nineteenth century,
through a prevailing arrangement of *classes* in Western society.
The 'forms'—which during the Middle Ages were ontic and God-
given and had fixed meanings—become, throughout societal
thinking, consequences of acts of human *subjects,* viz. they become
regarded primarily as human forms of thinking only (Descartes,
Kant). Objectively one regards them as consequences of dynamic
processes, and certainly as containing 'laws' that can be mathematically formulated, or at least of a *formal*-mechanical type.
That is to say, their stability vanishes and the status of the world,
previously conceived as basically spatial and in terms of timeless
dynamics, is now replaced by the schema of a *becoming stream in
time,* in which, as by necessary laws, always new 'forms' (of

125

society, of organic and inorganic nature) appear and disappear. This, primarily, made possible the modern historical thought that considers all factual forms and arrangements of human society as principally *transient* and relative, and which tries to explain them as consequences of demonstrable [*nachweisbarer*] *historical processes*—without influences from higher powers.[81] For the study of organic nature the idea of evolution and descendences among the species first arise; for the study of inorganic nature the idea of a uniform and formal-mechanical explanation of nature arises.[82] But while the idea of an objective hierarchy (as co-given already with the factual, real world-order) and of an objective teleology of the world, signifying simultaneously the unity of all human will, completely disappears in societal thought and valuation—because this idea was dependent upon theories of 'objective forms'—the other dimension of value differentiation, that of good-bad, became subjective and *relative* to man.[83] Values are now as subjective as sense qualities, and they are only shadows that our desires and antipathies, our feelings of pleasure and displeasure, cast upon things. Either there are *a priori* laws of the will and preference (peculiar in human reason) that condition concepts such as good and bad (for example, Kant, Herbart, Fr. Brentano) and historically changing goods, or there are only organically conditioned experiences of pleasure and displeasure, or, respectively, desires and antipathies, that possess a certain *social uniformity*. This value-theory of society—which is only a 'dogma of society' as is the theory of an exclusive subjectiveness of senses—successively affects all domains of values, for example, economic values. The theories of 'objective values' belonging to the Church fathers, scholastics, etc., and their resulting concept of the '*justum pretium*' were replaced by a theory of 'subjective needs'.[84]

Only with the collapse of the mechanical theories of nature in the *current* physical, biological, and psychological sciences do theories of the *subjectivity* of forms, qualities, and values and the theory of the absolute *dualism* between values and being also disappear. It becomes evident that laws of nature based upon formal-mechanical structure are nothing less than metaphysical laws and they are not laws that our understanding necessarily prescribes to manners of appearance so that they become objectivated through time in terms of a universally valid context of nature (Kant)—they are only *laws of large numbers*. It also becomes evident that the extensive magnitudes and other extensive spatial and temporal determinations of matter and natural events are no *more* absolute and invariant than qualitative determinations of senses—as related to nature's absolute reality. But it also becomes evident that—if these qualities are related to the world of

126

objective appearances and images, which, although independent of human consciousness, is a manifestation, a *'phenomenon bene fundatum'*, of this dynamic reality—colors, sounds, and other qualities are no *less* objective than extension and duration. It becomes increasingly evident that statistical and dynamic gestalt-laws and form-laws, which determine partial processes by whole processes, also extend into physical existence,[85] and in no way is such lawfulness physiologically and psychologically relative to the activity of a subject. It becomes evident, furthermore, that values are no less and no more subjective than qualities and that they possess ranks of their own—that only goods, which during the Middle Ages had been regarded as static and as functions of 'existence', are relative throughout history. The value-freedom of objective existence, which all *modern philosophy* (for example, all types of Kantianisms) accepts, and which was also for mechanistic theories of nature as apologetics, rested on a *phantasm* belonging to a specific attitude. Curiously, this phantasm itself was conditioned by values and practice: namely, by the life-value of a world containing nothing but elements of nature that are subject to *control,* while all other elements are reduced to *artificial abstractions*.[86] The one-sided categorial system of societal thought is thereby set aside—certainly not through a return to the life-communal thought of the Middle Ages, as some have foolishly suggested, but rather by a *new synthetic conception of World and Knowledge* that overcomes the opposition between mechanical and teleological dependencies through an encompassing principle of regularity that is *neither* mechanistic *nor* teleological, viz. through a concept that also *sociologically* finds its correlate in a new essential form of *intersubjectivity* in which life-community and society both begin to be overcome in the *formation of group solidarity among irreplaceable individuals*.[87] I wish to leave for another study an explication of the structure of the world-view belonging to this modern, slowly developing formation of human groups.

The voluntarist philosophies in the modern West, from Duns Scotus, Occam, Luther, Calvin, and Descartes to Kant and Fichte, are not merely new 'theories' of the same state of affairs. Rather, these trends reveal *new sociologically conditioned forms of experience belonging to new classes of leaders,* as W. Dilthey had already stated clearly.[88] They formulate the new idea of *control* and the new absolute value of control belonging to a new type of man, the Faustian man, who continually extends his power over nature *ad infinitum*—and also his power within the state, until he meets an opponent of equal power. Faustian man neither recognizes logical ideas and their interconnections nor an objective order of values and purposes that precede and limit his sovereign will. Replacing the central *locus* of the ego—the ego is neither a thing nor a specific activity but has only a positional value [*Stellenwert*] within the structures of acts—near which, during the Middle Ages, *theoretical and intuiting* acts stood, was the *sovereign act of the will* in the new societal types of leaders within the Church, the state, economy, technology, philosophy, and science. Naturally this happened equally in 'God' as well as in man—even historically and consciously first in God, then in man. The replacement of a contemplative and intellectual caste at the peak of society by an actively producing and regimenting caste in the actual course of history requires from itself a new image of God and soul. All this means, *sociologically,* the new 'Voluntarism'. It is this voluntarism that, as a vital function, transformed the intuiting 'intellect' of the Middle Ages, from the beginning, into the technically relevant 'understanding' of the new experimental and mathematical naturalism. It is very characteristic that the Franciscan school, in which Nominalism and Voluntarism began, was also the pioneer for the new experimental naturalism in which the natural philosophy of Aristotle was overcome (Roger Bacon, etc.).

In order to solve *sociologically* the extremely difficult *problem of the relationship between science and technology,* one must first determine the *series of meaning-correlations* [*Sinnentsprenchungen*] *between the structure of modern science and that of technology* as well as between *technology itself and economy*—and, in fact, without causal explanations. Only when such an independent study has been accomplished can and must a causal explanation be attempted—but within the above-mentioned limitations.

Let us enumerate some such series of meaning correlations among all three phenomena (while claiming no completeness), and let me restrict myself only to the period from the Middle Ages to modern times and to some of its larger phases. The following correlations have already been developed by me in a series of partly published, partly unpublished works and are presented here without further details.[89] I begin with the most formal and more methodological ones and proceed to those that refer more to the content of world-images.

1 To the same extent that, during the main phases of capitalist economies[90] (early capitalism, high capitalism, later capitalism), the city bourgeoisie worked their way up, an entrepreneurship ('publisher', manufacturer), on the one hand, and a lifelong and ultimately hereditary, traditional class of journeymen [*Gesellen-schaft*], on the other hand, emerged out of the disintegration of the guild (the beginning of a 'proletariat'), and to the same extent that, due to the need for taxes and money by the powerful feudals who had arisen to territorial sovereigns, the combined forms of work

belonging to the political and military sources of power stepped back in favor of 'free labor', a *new form* and *redirection of the power drive* emerges in such new 'upper classes'. The form and direction of the power drive belonging to the class of feudal lords was essentially gauged toward domination over *human beings*—it was, of course, also directed towards territories and things, but only to gain domination over men. The new form and direction of the power drive goes, on the contrary, for the productive transformation of *things,* or better: for the 'capacity' and the power to transform things into valuable goods. This process expressed itself *simultaneously* and *co-originally* in two events: (a) In the displacement of spiritual-contemplative and priestly groups, who formed a sociologically homogeneous whole within the society's highest leadership and who ruled by means of ecclesiastical, ordered, holy, and magical techniques for salvation, like the feudal classes (nobility and hierarchy), who ruled successively and through tradition by means of primitive martial powers. Only the highest leaders of the feudal class of landed proprietors [*Grossgrundherrn*] became territorial sovereigns with the help of the new bourgeoisie and entrepreneurs—supported by the reception of the individualistic Roman private law. They harnessed their own political will-to-control to the new economic, thing-directed power drive. And during the mercantile age they became the *second* great point of departure for capitalism, besides which we have added the 'publisher' [*Verleger*], viz. State-Capitalism (W. Sombart). (b) In a *new valuation* of possible controls over nature, which lets arise co-originally a new *technical will-to-control* over nature as well as a new *type of vision and thinking* (a new system of 'categories') in regards to nature. I place the greatest stress on the *simultaneity* of all these processes. Technical needs did not condition the new science (as Spengler one-sidely maintains), nor did the new science condition technical progress and capitalism (A. Comte). Rather, the basic transformation of the logical categorial systems belonging to the new science, as the new concomitant technical drive to control nature, have their foundation within the *new type of bourgeois humanity,* with its *new drive structure* and its *new ethos.* *Technology and science* thereby stand together in the fruitful, mutual effort in which we find them, and they 'fit' with one another because they are together parallel consequences of this *one* psycho-energetic process.

It is, in my judgment, a new *will to control* nature and soul—in sharp contrast to an attitude of love-filled devotion to them and to a merely conceptual order of their appearances—that now gains primacy in all cognitional comportments. The tendency towards knowledge of cultivation and salvation becomes subordinated to this will-to-control. But the will-to-control is in no way the same as the will to put things to use. Bacon not only misconstrued the nature of science, but he also misconstrued the nature of technology. Utilitarianism not only misconstrues the proper meaning and rank of 'spiritual goods' and values, but it also misconstrues the driving wheel that put modern technology into motion. The basic value that guides modern technology is not the invention of economical or 'useful' machines, whose uses one can already recognize and assess beforehand. It aims at something much higher! Its aim is—if I may say so—to construct *all possible* machines, first only in ideas and plans through which one could direct and control nature toward any useful or unuseful purpose whatsoever if one wished to do so. It is the idea and value of *human power and human freedom vis-à-vis* nature that ensouled the great centuries of 'inventions and discoveries'—by no means just an idea of utility. It concerns itself with the *power* drive, its growing *predominance* over nature *before* all other drives. It in no way concerns itself with a drive towards mere exploitation of present forces for specific purposes—an attitude that was prevalent during the Middle Ages along with philosophic-contemplative attitudes. And it concerns itself, furthermore, with the change in direction of this power drive away from God and men but toward *things* and their meaningful places in a spatio-temporal system. This explains, also, the many playful and impossible, technical experiments, designed to 'make' anything out of anything, which preceded the blossoming of the technological age (alchemy, automatons, etc.).

2 Compared to the intellectualistic comprehension of the history of science (Comte, Kant, etc.), we understand the *sudden* and *leap-like nature* of this process in which the 'Age of Inventions and Discoveries' was born and which replaced the 1,500-year domination of the theological and biomorphic world-view. We understand, furthermore, that the new mechanics became and remained, until recently, a model and schema for all world explanations, although the new theoretical physics, biology, and philosophy prepared the final downfall of such a world-view.[91] But we understand also that, in the course of modern historical processes, science has preceded and stimulated technology at least *as often* as technology, science—and technology absolutely did not only one-sidedly precede and stimulate science, as Pragmatism and Marxism lead us to believe. The same holds true for the relationship of 'pure' mathematics to physics and chemistry.[92] I cannot offer here a proof for my claims about this state of affairs, but I do offer them with strong emphasis. We understand, furthermore, that mechanistic conceptions of nature, the soul, and

130

society in no way arose only 'accidentally' because one *first* studied, only historically and in a secular manner, the motion of heavy masses and sought to 'explain' only the 'relatively unknown reduced to what is known' (E. Mach, H. Cornelius). Conversely, the formal-mechanical *scheme of ideas* as a whole had greatly *anticipated* everywhere their realization within the various branches of physics, chemistry, biology, and psychology and thoroughly *determined for their own time only* the *direction* of all experiments, all observations and inductions, and, furthermore, the *application* of pure mathematics to knowledge of nature, which the Greeks, especially the qualitative physics of Aristotle, almost missed entirely.[93] The new 'science' did not arise from occasional inductions whose results had been transferred by analogies to other areas of knowledge; nor did it arise from occasional technical problems—no matter how important such problems may have been, especially at the beginning of the modern world-image, perhaps with Galileo, Leonardo, and Ubaldis. With Lagrange and his analytical mechanics, for example, such tasks lost their importance entirely. The conception of the new formal-mechanical world-scheme aims, especially from the beginning, at something much more general, more encompassing, and thoroughly *whole* and *systematic*: toward an interconnection of stringent causes and effects of states of affairs and exact definitions of concepts. But this is so restricted in content that one can 'direct' through a *thinkable*—not 'real'—action any event of nature according to any wish, regardless of whether one 'willed' it on the grounds of utilitarian motives, and regardless of whether one 'could' actually do this.

Under the presupposition of 1 pure logic, 2 pure mathematics (neither of which are pragmatic disciplines), and 3 observation and measurement, the uniform and systematic *power* of thought and will belonging to a new type of leader projected and prescribed the scheme of this world-image—not in any way, therefore, the technological or even economic 'needs' of industry. That is an entirely different position! For entirely contrary to what is assumed by Pragmatism and especially by the economic theory of history, it is *science*—although in its limited sense of potential technical objectives—that developed ever new technological possibilities in its own *self-legitimizing* progress of a purely logical sort. These technological possibilities were then actually subjected to *two further selections*: first, to the option of the *technologist* to realize one or another of these possibilities through some machine that serves as a model, and, second, to the option of the *entrepreneur* to make such machines, which are only fashioned by the technologist, 'ready for industry', and to produce and use them for any sort of

131

production. The error of Pragmatism is revealed by the 10,000 examples that one can cite showing that, in entirely unexpected ways, technological and industrial utilization considered the discovery of a law often in terms of its highest, mediate consequences and primarily in wholly different connections.[94] But as scientific thinking stands minimally in the service of particular technical tasks and far more primarily *develops* and brings forth 'possible' tasks, so also the technologist stands minimally in the mere service of already described tasks that have grown out of industry, communications, war industry, agriculture, etc.[95] It is much more technology that actively develops industrial needs out of itself through new means and ways of production and arouses and calls forth such needs, as, for example, the whole growth of the modern electrical industry clearly reveals. Also, the special scientific techniques for experimentation and measurement did not fall from heaven to produce science—as Labriola means to suggest! The tools of science themselves are only *realized in matter—embodied theories, as it were.* And, at the same time, they are, as natural bodies, *applications* of the same theoretical systems they are supposed to support through extended and more refined observations, which in turn make such theories possible. Thus, the *theoretical meaning* of what they report with respect to the measurement and nature of things is always also an ingredient of the so-called 'facts' themselves that comprise this data. Duhem[96] elucidated this interrelationship excellently, and the history of relativity physics is one of the great examples proving Duhem's point. Thinking, therefore, is so little an 'experimenting with images and thoughts', that, on the contrary, real experiments are only the material garment and preservation of logical cause-effect relationships among the contents of thoughts.

And the formal-mechanical scheme itself is *not* a result of 'pure' theories, as the old logicism and intellectualism held.[97] It is the product of pure logic (and pure mathematics) *and* pure power-valuation in the selection of observable data in nature. And only within this second *power* factor lies the *sociological co-condition for this principle of selection of natural phenomena.* For this reason alone a question has no meaning for positive science when its affirmation or negation cannot be developed within logical consequences that yield various measurements [*Massausschiläge*], *observable* by the subject, within this scheme and its projected mathematical possibilities. For philosophy, however, such a 'question' may *very well* have 'meaning'. Indeed, philosophy, as cognition of reality, begins precisely where appearances are related to something *'absolute'*—quite different from positive science where they are related to their function of filling out this schematization.

132

If one wanted to refer here to an epistemological 'guilt' of modern society—which, indeed, is also primarily ethical—it would not include the application of this scheme itself, proven so fruitful for so many centuries. Rather, this guilt consists in the *philosophical ignorance* of the *limits of the formal-mathematical scheme's validity,* viz. its being regarded as an absolute scheme, or in the elevation of the formal-mechanical model of selection to the level of a metaphysical 'real' that is behind appearances. But with this there is also the diminution of all genuine metaphysics, whose objectives, methods, and epistemological principles are, as we saw, wholly different from and, in part, antithetical to those of positive science. (For philosophy, for the sake of *its own* objectives, rejects the principle of selecting from possible technical objectives, a principle born out of the absolute valuation of power.) It is in this way that philosophy temporarily turned from being a *'regina'* to an *'ancilla scientiarum'* and, along with this destitute *technicism,* became the master of mind, determining essences, goals, and values.

3 Also the other correlations between modern economy and modern science have as their highest principle the sociological processes mentioned. Capitalist *economy* is based in the *will to endless acquiring* (as an *act*), *not* in the will to *acquisition* (as a growing *possession* of things).[98] Modern *science,* too, neither administers a given, stable possession of truth nor investigates only for the sake of solutions to tasks and problems stemming from needs. Rather, it is *primarily* a *will to 'methods',* from which, it was once thought, ever new material knowledge comes forth—almost on its own—in an unlimited fashion, in endless processes, and as specialized [*arbeitsteilig*]. Hence, we find the enormous abundance of works on 'method'—which anyone can use like 'protractors and rulers'—from its beginning onward (Bacon, Descartes, Galileo's methodical explications, Spinoza, Leibniz, Kant's critique of pure reason as a 'Tractatus on Method', etc.). And just as the primary psychic tendency toward acquiring *separates* and spreads from the subjects of the leading classes through laws of imitation, and as it becomes a universal tendency of groups and, indeed, a supraindividual vehicle of the economy that turns goods, indeed, basically all possible things 'between heaven and earth', in so far as they can be regarded and valued only as being powerful and effective for any sort of acquiring (i.e. in relation to possession: powerful and effective for *profit*), into 'capital'—so also the acquiring will toward always new knowledge of the type described above, a will objectified in 'methods', lets all things and all processes appear as *quanta* of kinetic energy and kinetic subjects (= matter). This is a dynamic *correlation* [*Sinnzusammenhang*]—and in no way just an analogous relationship. Modern economy is, furthermore, a

133

mercantile and financial economy, so that every thing and every commodity [*Sach- und Nutzgut*] appears only as a possible quantity that may act as a medium of exchange, i.e. as 'merchandise money'. That is to say, everything appears first as 'merchandise'. As Karl Marx so clearly saw, the basic formula for economic motivation in a 'free market' (i.e. ideally free) is: Money → Merchandise → Money, and not, anymore: Merchandise → Money → Merchandise. Correspondingly, the category of *'relation'* precedes that of 'substance' in societal thinking. Likewise, the search for quantitatively determined, lawful relations among appearances then replaces the search for a conceptual order among the things in the world (Scholasticism) and a classificatory pyramid of concepts that alludes to a teleological 'realm of forms'; the idea of 'types' and qualitative 'forms' surrenders its authority to the idea of quantitatively determined 'laws of nature'. Everywhere production aims at *inexhaustible* stocks of merchandise or goods of knowledge. Everywhere a new *spirit of competition* emerges, surpassing every given phase (unlimited 'progress'). And every person partaking in production seeks to surpass every other person by a wholly new *ambitiousness* for inquiry and research, unknown to a medieval 'scholar', who—at least in his intention—preserved knowledge only as a good in itself. The medieval scholar tried to pass off 'new' ideas, even in the mundane sphere of knowledge, as old and traditional, because he assumed that 'truth had already been found' long ago—the modern researcher, conversely, tries to pass off as something new and original what has for a long time already been known. Thus arises a new ambitiousness for research and a new form of scientific cooperation, which is to be established as *'competition'*, wholly alien to the Middle Ages and its alliance with authority—as the scholastic mind characterizes it. The fundamentally *critical* attitude in reading an unfamiliar scientific work thereby follows. The legal concepts of 'mental property' and patent, and other analogous legal concepts, are as alien to the form of knowledge in the life-community—or any 'scholasticism'[99]—as is the issue of priority in scientific polemics and criticism. But these phenomena belong as much to modern science as does the objectification [*Versachlichung*] of knowledge through 'method', i.e. a kind of logical, supraindividual machinery.

4 Until the Age of Liberalism modern economy became more and more a *predominantly individual and societal economy* amid the dissolving remnants of semi-*communal* economy and *communal* law. *Subjectivation* of qualities, forms, and values belongs essentially to the science of a *'society'* because artificial, exact, mutual understanding among *individuals*—for each of whom the

world is given as primarily 'his' world—about the *identity* of things is possible *only* through the measurement of phenomena by standards mutually agreed upon and through the arrangement of all things into a universally accepted, spatio-temporal system of laws. Thus, there is not just a new 'theory' of the subjectivity of forms, qualities, and values in contemporary philosophy and science—no man has yet 'proved' this thesis in a purely theoreticaly manner. Rather, there is a totally *new attitude of man himself,* which philosophy and science have only *subsequently* defended with all thinkable and diverse 'reasons' (almost every philosopher with different ones). So, one can easily see that the position was believed subjectively *prior* to its supposed reasons and justifications: it is only a 'dogma of society', belonging to this present, predominantly *societal* group-form of men.[100] Also, the *principle of source criticism,* such as Descartes formally developed from his idealism of consciousness, is a result of this new scheme of thinking, which follows from the *'cogito ergo sum'* (which is itself only a totally unfounded expression of an *historical* attitude of mind that necessarily belongs to a society, and which is anything but 'evident'). In such an attitude the source renders to this consciousness only the 'representations' of its author anew—and not the historically real itself, so that one must construct these 'reals' primarily from many sources that have proven themselves to be without contradiction and with continual consideration for the presumed interests of individual authors to falsify matters. *Distrust,* as a primary attitude among members of 'society', whose expression is curbed by conventions of hospitality, successively pertains also to the claims of historic men of the past. One forgets that past generations did not have these personal 'interests' in falsifying at all—they had at best a corporate interest. And, moreover, from the same principle of modern society came forth contract theories of law, language, and the state, which modern, individualistic natural law and language, legal, and political philosophies of the Enlightenment further developed. This 'system of human sciences', stemming from the Enlightenment (Dilthey) in all its aspects, became part of the older history of the Western peoples and part of all cultural fields, became integrated, for example, with the idea of *'homo economicus'*—whom in no way the classical economist[101] regarded as just a conscious 'fiction', as C. Menger, for example, has recently and one-sidedly suggested to us—with the same naiveté as did the mechanical world-view and its basic conceptions ('absolute mass', 'absolute extended substance', 'absolute space', 'absolute time', 'absolute motion', 'absolute power'), with the exception of only a few skeptical outsiders whom no power won over to positive science and, even less, to its ways of

135

thinking (for example, Leibniz, who wanted to bridge the opposition to the Middle Ages). Indeed, the idea is recognized as *adequate*, not only as a true and correct, representation of reality. Thus society projects its own structural *form* as a 'thing in itself' behind nature (materialism). It is only Kant who, although insufficiently, shook this assumption; it is only the historicism of the nineteenth century that shook the dogmas of the human sciences stemming from the Enlightenment.

5 Finally, the *implementation* [*Versachlichung*] of *scientific means of production* itself, i.e. scientific technique and materials, is also exactly the same formal process that we find in war technology or the technology of material production and communication. It is the same process, also, by which nearly all ecclesiastic orders, and slowly the medieval Church itself, became what they were after the Council of Trent, following the model of the mechanistic and absolutist structure of the Jesuit order. It is the same process as the one we find in the replacement of private book-keeping by 'enterprises' and their book-keeping.[102] The same process pertains to the soldier of a modern army, now equipped by the state, in contrast to the medieval knight, who owned his own horse and sword; to machines, materials, buildings, etc., which are now 'furnished' to the worker for mutual cooperation—also to the laboratories, observatories, collections, institutes, test centers, and technical plants belonging to the *methodically* developed and implemented [*Versachlichung*] sciences, in contrast to the previously *isolated* researcher, who is now compelled to share these institutions with others. The medieval study parlour, with its diverse accessories and private property, has disappeared. But is this process economically conditioned? In no way! The implementation and systematization of technical means for all occupations represents a wholly *universal and formal direction of civilization* and is no more basic to economics than it is to science, church, or war, for example. The officialization (by the state), or semiofficialization, of researchers under the direction of a manager who organizes their work, an officialization joined with this implementation of scientific techniques and materials, also results only from the same sociological rule. According to this rule, for instance, out of the warlike followers of the medieval feudal lord [*Feudalherrn*], grew the 'officer' of a 'standing' army (after the French Revolution) *in the service of the state*—no longer primarily in the service of the sovereign as a *person*. Or, out of former honorary offices, based in political power-relations and acts of trust among sovereigns, and out of the feudal officials and lawyers, who were provided with continued enfeoffments and authoritative powers, grew the specialized officials and professional lawyers of the

modern state, employed on 'salaries'. Here there exists only a national difference. In German scientific institutions the state's officiation of researchers became and remains much stronger than in England and the Romance countries due to the principle in German universities of unity of research and doctrines [*Lehre*]. In England the medieval system (Oxford and Cambridge) lasted longer, and the independent amateur scientific researcher[103] is much more common than in Germany. In France research and doctrine are more *distributed* among particular state institutions—a system that even our modern German 'research institutes' are adopting in part.[104] And in North America the 'endowed university', established and nourished through the domestic economy, has gained a special place.

The differentiation of the special sciences, as they are developed by the immanent logic of the scientific processes (for example, psychophysics, physical chemistry, developmental mechanics, and exact hereditary science), partly by the economy of the researchers' mental powers and dispositions of talent, is, beside the above-mentioned two motives, only *secondarily* co-determined *sociologically* by the differentiated societal *needs* of an expert officialdom (preachers, teachers, school-masters, physicians, officials of the state, community, and economy, judges, engineers, etc.). Meanwhile, the motive for the differentiation and limitation of the sciences does much more harm than good to the inner logical connection among scientific theories—one of many reasons why I believe it necessary in Germany to *separate more sharply from one another* research institutions and learning institutions [*Lehreinrichtungen*], especially 'cultural institutions'.[105]

Another special task of sociology would be to trace also the *forms of science and economy that correspond to the individual phases* from primitive *magic technique*, which tends to differentiate itself later in religious rites and positive techniques (depending on the failure or success and the type of these successes and failures), to present technology.[106] It seems to me that the completion of such a task is not possible at the present because much too little has been done in this area from a *sociological* perspective. But we can say that it is *technology* that *primarily ties science and economy together* and that knowledge, and its movement, is more dependent upon technology the less developed are the total conditions of a society. It appears to me that the following are the most important transitions in this somewhat overlooked historical complex:

1 the transition from magic technique, which rests on the assumption that it is not ordered according to laws and secondary causes through pure will or words (verbal spells and verbal superstition) to control spatially and temporally distant powers,

to positive technology in general, especially the technologies of arms and tools, which are basically closely related;

2 the transition within the technology of agriculture from the hoeing of matriarchal culture to agriculture connected with cattle breeding (the plough) in the mixed cultures, which are the presupposition for all formations of states (formation of classes) and for the 'political era,[107] as well as the foundation for all 'higher' civilization;

3 the transition from predominantly manual and empirical-traditional tools (or tool-machines) to the era of scientific-rational technology of power-machines still using energy originating from organic nature (early capitalism); and

4 technology that begins with the use of coke and takes most of its energy from solar energy that is stored in coal (high capitalism). Whether or not electricity and an eventual technological use of immense energies from radioactive substances will one day bring about a technological era still more distinct from the age of coal than the latter era is from technology that uses predominantly organic technics of wood burning and water power, and whether or not a substitute will be found for the decreasing coal, remains uncertain at the present.[108]

There is no doubt that the above rough classifications, which have permeated all technologies of production, communication, and war and scientific technology itself, have been most closely connected with more important *changes, too, in scientific world-views*. The following quite clearly distinguish themselves from one another as parallel phenomena of science: 1 the magical view of nature belonging to the primitives; 2 the rational-biomorphic view of nature (the stage of tool-techniques); 3 the rational-mechanical view of nature; and 4 the electro-magnetic view of nature.

This technical development, as an entirely *autonomous* subject in its 'progress', must, from our perspective, become wholly distinguished from economic development. True, it is influential in the highest degree on economy, but it also is determined by its opposite, secondary influence—a reciprocal influence. And certainly the technical development interferes here, in the first place, in the development of *managerial forms*. But it effects no less the development of the state, in so far as the state has managerial form, and it likewise influences the political corporations of 'power' (big powers, world powers) and their imperialistic tendencies. The development of the state reveals the same tendency towards 'large management' as does economy itself. The historico-philosophical idea extending throughout all Marxist literature and resulting from economism, not technicism, that a universal control over nature by man[109] would make superfluous the domination of men over men and the 'state'—as a coercive unity by contrast to the state as a welfare organization—cannot withstand a sharp critique.[110]

Concerning a synthesis of Western and Asian technologies (cultures of knowledge) and a revival of metaphysics

The question remains entirely open whether in the future of European-American civilization there will develop *psychic techniques* or *inner vital techniques,* known thus far only to the great *Asian* cultures as technical correlates of their predominantly metaphysical, non-scientific cultures of knowledge. I hold the answer to this question to be a decisive one for the destiny of Western technicism. Because, under the brilliant victories of his admirable technological accomplishments, Western man during the last centuries, like no other creature in known human history, has almost completely neglected and forgotten how to control his own *self,* his *inner* life, and, moreover, his *self-reproduction* through systematic psychic and vital techniques, so that today Western peoples as a whole appear much less self-governable [*unregierbarer*] than in former times. The art of self-control, however, is the root of the art of control over individuals as well as groups. Western man knows this inner art only in its ethical form but not in the form of a *systematic,* self-developing *psychic technique.* It appears to me that the most noble and most promising fruit of the new 'cosmopolitanism of cultural fields', characterized earlier and based in the spiritual exchange between *European-American peoples* and Asian culture, would be if the inevitable Europeanization of these peoples, with regard to positive science and technological and industrial methods—a process that cannot be hindered even by reactionary movements like those of Mahatma Gandhi[111]—were *complemented* and compensated for through the systematic *takeover of their psychic techniques* by the European-American peoples. Until recently this was only a dream, in which the deep-thinking psychologist, William James, was already passionately immersed during his last years, and today still only sparse signs of its possible realization can be found. But surely these signs resemble a young dog's first attempts to walk and, with regard to their value and final success, have to be assessed, in my opinion, rather critically. As social 'movements', however, they are of great interest to the sociology of knowledge. Such attempts include, for instance, the anthroposophic movement, the Christian Science movement, and the psycho-analytic 'circles' of Freud and Adler. The fact that questions concerning the psychic techniques could already gain so much *popularity among the masses* is a sign of a

139

direction of social needs that deserves the greatest interest of the sociology of knowledge. The present-day efforts of individual and social *psycho-therapeutics* are only loosely connected with it (against whose exaggeration important physicians, such as the internist, Fr. Kraus,[112] have already warned). Such efforts, on the one hand, are reminiscent of older forms of pastoral medicine and, on the other, have brought once again the professions of physician and clergyman so unusually close together from both sides that one is reminded of social eras when the physician and the priest were not generally sociologically distinct.[113] But these psychic techniques, in which the goals of health, salvation, and philosophic cognition strangely intersect, must be strictly distinguished from the psycho-technical efforts that want to tackle practically problems concerning occupational fitness, advertising, and similar things on the basis of experimental individual and mass psychology and differential psychology. Such techniques place themselves consciously into the service of higher production and sales of the present economy.

The sociology of knowledge points out a tendency in positive, value-free science towards *'individual control'* (which characterizes all positivistic currents of thought) and also a tendency towards the *degradation of science* into *technicism.* This we already know from the very *origin* of positive science: only when science *does not lose sight of philosophy and metaphysics,* as *pure* theory, not limited by the principle of possible control, i.e. as the forms of 'pure' thought, is it able to save itself for long from the fall into technicism. But, on the other side, metaphysics is also closely connected with, and even essentially conjoined with, *psychic technique* in the above-mentioned sense—as the *joint* predominance of both metaphysics and psychic technique in Asian 'cultures of cultivation' [*Bildungskulturen*] reveals—in so far as psychic technique neither serves only ethical and practical objectives of exercise or training nor serves only ascetic, religious, or purely theatrical aims. Rather, it also serves *epistemological* goals.

The problem of the technical production of inner *dispositions* of mind and feelings, as it relates to the philosophical cognition of *essences,* has been known to all great metaphysicians from Buddha, Plato, and Augustine to Bergson's 'painful effort' to envision *'la durée'* and E. Husserl's 'phenomenological reduction'. The latter represents, generally, an epistemological-*technical,* hitherto inadequately solved problem regarding the specifically philosophical attitude toward knowledge and cognition, cloaked by Husserl only in an apparent logical methodology.[114] *Inner, philosophical and metaphysical cognitive technique* is a problem quite its own[115] and must not be confused with the cognitive techniques of positive-scientific and other psycho-technical procedures for other 'purposes'.[116] It always is a matter of one thing: to bring about *pure 'contemplatio'* of genuine ideas and primordial phenomena and to produce, in their congruence, 'essence' free of existence through an *act of blocking out* [*Ausschaltung*] those acts and drive-impulses that yield the objects' moments of reality (reality is always, also, the highest and ultimate 'principle of individuation'). But these acts and impulses are of a *drive-like,* dynamic nature, as Berkeley, Maine de Biran, Bouterwek, the later Schelling, Schopenhauer, Dilthey, Bergson, Frischeisen-Köhler, Jaensch, and I together learned. For reality, in all modes of perception and remembrance, is given only as 'resistance' against dynamic, drive-like attentiveness.[117] But these *blocked* acts—not a merely logical procedure of 'setting aside' from modes of existence or 'bracketing' from existence, as Husserl believes—are also the sources of the will-to-*control* and the valuing of control, which, as we saw, are the pre-logical sources of both positive science and its techniques of control. The philosophical *technique* of cognition—which is to be sharply distinguished from the problem of a 'logical and epistemological theory of philosophy', i.e. the theory of the cognition of an *a priori* object and the *forms* of intuition and thinking themselves, meritoriously rediscovered recently by E. Lask—is not only different from, but wholly *antithetical* to, the positive-scientific attitude of cognition, which demands the very *elimination* of all questions of *essence* in favor of the cognition of laws pertaining to apparent spatio-temporal coincidences (of the *'hic-nunc'* of what is) and which likewise requires a conscious *insertion* of technical goals.

If Western man, as well as the Asian, were able to perform, *both* easily and alternately, these acts of consciously inserting *and* blocking out, belonging to *each one's* opposing attitude of consciousness—so that both would learn and practice the other's new and 'alien' attitude—then *all cognitional possibilities,* slumbering in the human mind, would be exhausted: metaphysical *and* positive-scientific attitudes alike. And by strong analogy: if in the greatest common task of humanity, namely, the elimination of ills and suffering and the production of goods—a task connected with both forms of knowledge and their corresponding techniques—the external, evolving Western production of goods and active *struggle* against ills (i.e. by eliminating their *external* causes) becomes *unified* with the active, heroic art of sheer *'endurance',* based upon psychic technique, (i.e. the *inner* inhibition of 'suffering') and the spontaneous, active care for the soul, in contrast to all religiosity of grace, *complete* power over outer *and* inner nature—considering the reciprocal, essential relationship between suffering and ills—

would be gained.[118] With the execution of this same technique, which eliminates, along with automatic resistance, the moment of objective reality, *all possible suffering* of the world becomes co-eliminated, because 'suffering' never rests only on its external causes; rather, it rests, no less, on an automatic, *drive-like,* and motor process against such causes—a proposition that is already valid for the most simple sensations of pain. The Western technicism of outer nature and its correlate in the realm of knowledge, positive science, threatens man with enmeshment into the mechanism of things that it intends to control *to such an extent* that this process, without the counter-balance of the two completely *opposite* principles of knowledge *and* power, essentially belonging to one another, can end only in the certain fall of the Western world.[119] The sociology of knowledge teaches us that, in all areas where ills may be encountered and in all areas where goods of positive vital values are produced—whether it be for war and peace, disease and health, growth of population and its inhibition for the sake of higher quality, for economy and industry—we must learn systematically to posit *both basic principles of all 'possible' techniques* and their correlate forms of knowledge *simultaneously* and *alternately* in order to restore a meaningful balance of humanity.

This is not the place to present in detail the program, implied above, for a new distribution of the culture of knowledge and technical culture. But we wish to emphasize all the more the principal deviation of our sociological dynamics of knowledge from those of *positivism,* which teaches for all humanity a death for metaphysical knowledge and its correlate technique of 'endurance', i.e. the elimination of resistance against ills by psychic technique. And no less we wish to emphasize our disagreement with all metaphysical and romantic gnosticism, which, in principle, turns against positive science and its correlate technique—in a *reactionary* negation of values and in infantile *ressentiment* of a petty bourgeoisie—for whatever reasons. In contrast to positivist and Marxist doctrines of all sorts, and also in contrast to the enforced inhibitions upon the spontaneous, metaphysical mind, which seeks self-redemption through churches of revealed religion, we are of the conviction that in *Europe* and North America a *vigorous epoch of metaphysics and psychic techniques* is likely to follow the positive and technological epoch of so-called 'modern times', while in Asia an epoch of *positive science* and *technology* will replace the strongly one-sided metaphysical epochs of these cultures.

Effects of the second principle characterized above in the struggle against ills and suffering exist already in all present-day teachings of *negative politics of 'non-rule'* and *heroic non-resistance,* as represented in modern times by Tolstoy, Gandhi, R. Rolland, *et al.* For centuries the Quakers and the American Mennonites held these teachings. They rest ultimately on fundamental knowledge that psychology and physiology have thoroughly proven: that all willing, besides simple affirmation and negation of projects, is either only an *inhibition or a releasing of drive impulses* and correlative motor nerve processes that are apt to be realized in the process of the volitional project, depending upon one's choice either to inhibit or release such impulses and processes. This is to say, willing does *not* possess a *positive* power to produce anything. Each supposedly positive effect of mental willing is also, always and by necessity, not a *'pure'* willing but only one mixed with drive factors. True 'willing' as causation is always, therefore, only either a *'non fiat'* or a *'non non fiat'*; only by contrast to the project as *ideal value-complex* is it either an absolute (positive) *'fiat'* or *'non fiat'*. Hence, a *politics* that seeks realization of such an ideal value-complex by purely spiritual means—whether this is possible we leave here unanswered—can only be, in principle, one of *non-resistance*. This is so because any positive resistance is volitionally sustained by the same drives and desires that are effective also in an adversary. Therefore, the principle of non-resistance expressly states also that valuable non-resistance is present only when the *power* to resist is established explicitly as *present* and that endurance of insult [*Beleidigung*] an injury does not result from feebleness, cowardice, or anything similar.[120]

Closely connected with the principles of negative politics, which result from the metaphysical position of the active, heroic technique of enduring suffering and from the doctrine that restricts the function of the mental will to merely inhibiting and releasing drive impulses, is a system of *eugenics* and *qualitative population politics*. Such a system would rest on a principle absolutely contrary to the one that has predominated in the development of Western history and that demands special objective and subjective justification for *non*-participation in procreation for the sake of effectively decreasing the number of children, *ceteris paribus*—be it through asceticism or through various means of birth-control. The principles of vital technique, just as they are in accord with the art of endurance and the *primacy* of man's self-control *prior to* his control over nature, must necessitate the opposite principle: that all *participation* in the procreation of the human species is to be tied to the special right and even *privilege of a minority* of people who promise 'good' hereditary qualities and who are certainly or with only average probability exempt from negative hereditary qualities. The simple aim of material production technique and positive science is based, first, upon the conviction that someday good hereditary values will be a function of the *quality* of fertilized eggs (a prejudice of the Darwinian chance theory, which has destroyed modern heredity research). And it is based, second, upon the conviction that the potential progress of technology and science, moreover, the progress of positive science, will make it possible for every new person to produce eventually *more* economic goods than he will use himself. For science [*Wissenschaft*] both convictions prove to be more and more *untenable*.[121] Their practical realization has not only been responsible for the ugly condition belonging to the *enmassment* [*Vermassung*] *of life,* a condition which is the first independent variable for all wars and revolutions in a Europe much overpopulated in relation to its future food production and its future growth. But it is also the ultimate cause for the qualitative law governing Western (and American) populations, a law which is becoming increasingly interwoven with the development of capitalism, namely, that the increase in the European population is *at the expense* of more relatively *good* hereditary values than bad.

It appears to me that a principal question (whose scientific answer faces insurmountable difficulties today) is whether or not world population as a whole has acquired, on the basis of hitherto existing principles, a reproductive tendency that is *incommensurate* with the expanded utilization of land for food production, made possible by technological, scientific, and economic progress—a tendency which *must* lead, in its development, to terrible and relentless class-struggles and eventually to the destruction of all spiritual culture. And because every species, including the human species as a whole, is subject, according to the insights of modern biology, to birth, aging, and death (natural death of a species), it is becoming impossible to ignore the fact that mankind, within its natural life-span, has reached an age where only a *fundamental overturning of its ethos* promises prosperous development and potential progress—as measured by the eternal hierarchy of values. Such an overturning changes the ethos, consisting of maxims (which direct and guide the drive potencies of procreation) pertaining to the duty of *not* practicing birth-control (i.e. of procreating descendants), into the common duty of *avoiding* offspring and *demonstrating justification for procreation.* I am far from the opinion that this question can today be answered by purely scientific means—although I do not see why it cannot be answered sometime in the future. I only say: it may well be. It could, therefore, just as well be that mankind, in a great phase of its natural life-span, has had to choose that principle as a principle of progress, a principle which previously was considered to be the metaphysical, wholly one-sided (not false) principle of *young* people, viz. that existence is better than non-existence, and which places *non*-participation in procreation (in any case) under the burden of proving special *justification*. And it could also just as well be that there is a *turning point* in mankind's total life and aging in which—it is concluded—only the *reversal* of the burden of proof, i.e. the ethos of a special *justification for procreation* (and the institutions and sanctions corresponding to this ethos) would be able to guarantee any further possible progress—as measured by the eternal hierarchy of values. In this case the very *contrary* of hitherto existing sanctions would become valid. It is only a wholly unproven prejudice to assume immediately, along with the hitherto existing maxims and principles, for example, of the Christian Church, that one and the same principle must always and everywhere be beneficial for humanity. To investigate the technical and institutional, or non-institutional, realization and realizability of eugenic thinking, which in America promises to become almost a new religion, is out of place here. The exclamation of a great poet on present-day Europe sharply expresses a feeling of life and being that sees perhaps much deeper into the ultimate roots of all social questions than many scientific investigations do in treating their causes: 'Already your numbers are an outrage'.

It is not without interest to the reader to become acquainted with some *objections* made to our thesis concerning the future *completion* [*Ergänzung*] of Western and Eastern culture and their two kinds of techniques. They were advanced by partisans of Marxist sociology as we presented the above thesis to the sociological conference in Heidelberg in September 1924. There were *two objections* in particular, one by my respected friend, Rudolf Goldscheid, to whom I am deeply indebted for furthering my presentation of sociological problems, and the other by Max Adler, the moderator for my paper.

Goldscheid's elaborations were meant as a partial defense of my theses against Max Adler's attacks. But they also contained a factually and logically more cogent criticism than Adler's. He argued that the technique of overcoming suffering through active endurance and its basic metaphysics belong absolutely to a higher and more positive value, even in relation to Western science and its material production technology. But this value, he also argued, is only *relative* to an economy and technology of production that is still too little developed. Naturally this statement—were it correct—thoroughly destroys all that we might show. But he turns what is originally a not-*willing* into a not-*able*. He does not regard metaphysics, religion, and the ethos of cultures as *co*-determining *sources*, at least in the sense of guiding and controlling, of economy, the kind of technology, and technology's direction. But rather, he regards them as *indices*—in the sense of an economic-technical theory of history—of the levels of economic and technological conditions of production. These indices, of course, are assessed by measures of value belonging to European, rational metaphysics and Marxist theories of progress. Also, the very prejudice that I and, in great detail, Sombart have attacked has here been presupposed: that there are laws of economy—be they stable and assumed to be universally valid, like those of classical national economics, or be they laws of development—that are *independent* of *primordial* ideas and valuations.[122] But this is a primary 'European' prejudice, which Marx certainly shares with Hegel, Comte, and the greater majority of Western theories of history: that their theory of history, its laws and direction of development, for example, the development of economy towards a capitalist phase, with its accompanying science and technology, should apply to the *entire* development of humanity. They assume, moreover, that the respective economic, technological, and scientific levels would have been present at one time even in India, China, Russia, and Japan—even if these economic conditions had *not* been imposed by force upon these cultures during a certain historical period. Goldscheid's objection fails to see that this presupposition is not even true for Russia, let alone for the other great Asian cultures, and that, moreover, economism and the theory of class-struggle is valid only *for a very limited and late phase of Western history.* And with this he also ignores the *co-originality* of the *different,* indeed, even *opposite,* fundamental directions that human knowledge in the West and in the great Asian cultures (despite their wide inner differences) has taken, and he thereby overlooks the *magnitude* of the *adjustment* that would someday allow the convergence of originally separate cultural units towards a slowly integrating 'humanity'.

Max Adler's objection placed my thesis among a whole group of theories, investigations, theses, and 'moods' to which he referred as 'modern predilections' for the 'metaphysical pessimism' of Asia and India, the 'mood of decadence', and unjustified scepticism of technical and economic progress, and as examples of which he mentioned Spengler, Sombart, and me. This group of opinions and judgments he explained as ideologies of fear and anxiety, 'sociologically' represented by a declining class. As a later section of this treatise of mine will show, the tendencies and perspective interests of classes and their intellectual representatives in the world and in history, in so far as they pertain to present logic and the formal *'type* of thinking', are not unknown to me. The (logical, ethical, aesthetic, and religious) *theory of idols* pertaining to all human groups, especially *classes,* has always been a special subject of my research. In addition, I consciously wish to overcome it for the sake of my own position—within the limits, though, of a *perspectivism* governed by essential laws, a perspectivism which is inherent in all historic knowledge because of history's incomplete nature. Max Adler agreed with me that class prejudices can be overcome, thereby showing that he is no genuine Marxist, for whom material existence precedes human consciousness. He is rather a Kantian who has always supposed that there exist *constant* laws of consciousness and reason. A genuine Marxist, or a representative of the 'absolute' class struggle, could *not* maintain this. I am, in this regard, even more 'Marxist' than Adler in so far as I, too, have reduced all consciousness to *being* and all supreme laws and forms of reason to the processes of functionalization within the formal comprehension of being—but certainly not as Marx did. Rather, I have reduced them not only to material being but to the *whole* being of man. In contrast to Adler, I do *not* suppose—as this discussion shows—uniform, immanent, and constant functional laws in human reason, viz. the constancy of categorial apparatus. In this regard—and only in this regard—my theories are more similar to the teachings of Positivism and Marxism than Max Adler's. It is precisely the theory regarding the relativity of thought forms that Adler, with Kant as an authority, attacks. But what should one say when Max Adler, under this presupposition and in view of the enormous chasm he opens between bourgeois and proletarian science—whereby he places all non-Marxists on the same side with Sombart, Spengler, and myself, as well as Schelling, Schopenhauer, and v. Hartmann, who, as I have criticized, had a much stronger predilection for India *prior* to the decline of the 'bourgeoisie' than I, and who, contrary to my own theory, had made pessimism a part of their own particular metaphysics—finally comes to the more than strange conclusion that there is *no* difference between the categorial system of primitives and that of men living today in Europe (be they proletarians or bourgeoisie), but there *nevertheless* is an irreconcilable difference between present-day proletarian and bourgeois types of thinking! I cannot possibly imagine how a 'rising proletariat' can feel different from a 'declining bourgeoisie' in an age when the former class lives miserably enough and capitalism is stronger than it ever has been. A view and doctrine leading to such an absurd conclusion certainly must be wrong.

We view this progress of ours not as 'wishful thinking', but rather as a probable result of the whole development of all human knowledge as a *new synthesis* of scientific and technological cultures of history until now, a synthesis which has already prepared itself extensively: the peculiar positivist idea of judging the development of *all* human knowledge on the basis of a small curve segment that shows only the development of the *modern West,* must finally be halted. One must come to the insight—through the *sociology of knowledge*—that, in view of different racial dispositions, different relative natural world-views, and probably different mixtures of matriarchal and patriarchal cultures, *Europe* and *Asia* have approached possible problems of knowledge from fundamentally different directions: Europe's predominant direction has been *from matter to the soul;* Asia's has been *from the soul to matter.* One also comes to the conclusion that the stages of this development must be basically different up to the point where they begin to meet in cultural synthesis. It is only in this latter stage that a possible *Everyman* can be born.

We see a *new 'metaphysical epoch' in the West* being introduced today not only by the (hitherto weak) start of a new metaphysics within philosophy proper—which sociologically means very little—but also, no less, *by the start of a psychic technique correlated with metaphysics.*

But we see above all an important *negative* condition for the newly arising metaphysical age in the fact that the objective idealism of the corporeal world and 'extended substance', like that of the dynamic theory of matter, has developed, through relativity physics, from a philosophical stage (Leibniz and Kant to E. v. Hartmann) into a positive-scientific one—now called a stage of serious discussion.[123] For if 'extended substance', in all its final determinations, proves to be only an objective appearance and manifestation of forces, the distinction between primary and secondary qualities completely falls apart. The philosophical theory whereby reality is nothing but resistance against acts of vital movement and given *prior to* all other qualities of 'corporeal' things (duration, gestalt, color, etc.), coincides very closely with the results of *theoretical physics* concerning the ultimate subjects of physical statements. Whether one explains the changeability, from the standpoint of the observer, within the extensive magnitudes of bodies and atoms and within the relation of these magnitudes (for example, before-after) by claiming that even magnitudes have a subjective meaning so long attributed to secondary qualities—*or,* conversely, whether secondary qualities are *just as* independent of human organization as the so-called primary qualities and are only *objective appearances* of changing relations among *force centers* and force fields—is a question whose answer depends on whether or not one assumes, from the viewpoint of philosophical biology, a *uniform and supraindividual life.* If one assumes such a position then inorganic nature, as the image [*Bild*] of extended, temporally determined bodies and all their qualitative determinations, is

148

completely *in*dependent of *man* and his organization. But, in contrast to the forces underlying this image, ideal being and 'objective appearance' alone cut out only various perspectives of this 'image' for the *subject of this supraindividual, universal life* and the various subdivisions that exist as partial specifications of this life. We believe that this assumption, which restitutes, by a curious detour, the natural view of the world, is essential, but we cannot discuss this metaphysical question here in detail. The newly emerging mathematical discipline of topology—a deep foundation for what Leibniz already had intended with his *analysis situs*—can provide sufficient means for determining the order of the force centers themselves, as distinct from all their secondary determinations, such as those of extended magnitudes and gestalts.

The *changes in the idea of causality,* requiring a more stringent investigation into quantum theory, are no less significant for philosophical metaphysics and the theory of cognition. In an article entitled 'Die Grundlagen der Quantentheorie und des Bohrschen Atommodells', A. Sommerfeld recently wrote:[124]

> Very noteworthy in these rules of intensity is the interchangeability of initial and final states. It looks as if what happens is not given by what is probable for the initial state of the atom and what is probable for its passing into a final state. Rather, it looks as if both initial and final states are equally determined by their respective quantum weights. This would, indeed, contradict our traditional notion of causality to a certain extent, a notion by which we readily think that a process is determined by its initial state. It seems possible to me that quantum theory can change our notions in this respect. It has often been said that Bohr's stipulations about radiation imply that the atom must already know the state into which it finally will go before it can radiate. We take also a teleological standpoint, and not a causal one, when dealing with the principle of the smallest effects. Such a teleological reformulation of causality seems to me, indeed, less contradictory to quantum theory than to classical theory. In any case, we must require, so long as there should be a natural science, the univocal determination of observable events and the mathematical certainty of natural laws. But we cannot *a priori* know whether this univocity is given by initial states alone or by both initial and final states. Rather, we must learn this from nature.

If this idea of causality prevails, it would probably reduce to nothing the difference between causal-mechanical and teleological relations in nature—as well as the main difference hitherto believed

149

to exist between inorganic nature and organic life. It becomes evident that the preference for mechanical causality, according to which consequential states were clearly determined by immediately prior states, has come about only through *practical* motives, because it is easily seen that nature could be univocably *predicted* and *directed* by us as long as it followed the causal model of thrust [*Stoss*] and the *vis a tergo*. Teleological and mechanical causalities would both be anthropomorphic perspectives of one and the same causality that is *neither* mechanical *nor* teleological, each suggesting itself to be the stronger and predominant by reference to different groups of phenomenon (mainly inorganic-organic). It is thereby self-evident that the *forces* one has to suppose on the basis of a dynamic theory of matter and on the basis of this causal form of phenomenon, have been permitted neither in punctual space nor in fixed moments of objective time. Their origins must be both supraspatial and supratemporal because they must first make clear and understandable *how* that, in the sphere of objective appearance, is due to spatial and temporal determinations of matter and of events and their relationships to this. Leibniz's idea that space is a product of forces and a *'phaenomenon bene fundatum'* would find, therefore, a wholly new application to time and even to the gestalts of a four-dimensional spatial system.

Theistic metaphysics as metaphysics—questions of faith do not interest us here—is untenable, as E. v. Hartmann saw with complete clarity, when things develop in this fashion. For a theistic metaphysics *presupposes* the absolute, real existence of a *matter* independent of all forces—including not only that which is extended, but also the 'principle of extension', which constitutes Aristotle's 'primary matter'. But if bodies are only manifestations of forces, such *forces* lack, above all, a subject. However, a force without a subject is an impossibility. What else could this subject be then but the *unreal itself*? This efficacy of God alone is excluded by metaphysical theism, which stands and falls with the *secundae causae* and *independent material substance* that it penetrates—as well as with the assumption of substantial, created souls. Although we are aware today that we are only at the beginning of a basically new concept of nature regarding the above matters and that there are deep contradictions within theoretical physics that still need to be solved, we wish to show with the above examples—without providing metaphysical conceptions—how positive science today is crowding, out of necessity, into unquestionably metaphysical problems.

Another negative condition for the rise of metaphysics shown above is the relativization of the second adversary of metaphysics, the *relativization of 'historicism'* through the denial of a historic 'thing-in-itself', through the assertion of an ontically valid and *necessary perspectivism* for all 'possible' historical images and cognitions throughout the content of individual moments, and through the unique place of the observer in a time necessarily regarded as absolute for organic processes and psychic run-offs. In the doctrine of the essential relativity of all historic 'being' *itself*— and not *only* its cognition—historicism as *Weltanschauung* has been overcome (*by* overcoming *itself*) just as in the theory of the relativity of physical, extended *being itself*—not only the relativity of our human *cognition* of it—the 'absolute' mechanism of an 'absolute' corporeal world has forever been overcome in favor of purely lawful and absolute constants and force-centers. Also in this respect physical science, because it has excluded from its realm of investigation all factors, viz. all *pseudo*-metaphysical elements, that contradict the principle of observation and mathematical de-duction, has *opened* the path to a 'metaphysics of nature' and completed the process of differentiation, which, contrary to the positivist and historicist doctrines on the dying out of metaphysics, has been actively present from the beginning of modern history. Analogously, 'historicism' has shaken, with full justification, all 'absolute' historic authorities, especially all those of a 'church' founded in an *absolute,* positive, concrete world of goods and salvation—a church which has been the great adversary of independent metaphysics, so as to become, in its turn, put out of action by a doctrine based upon one absolute system of *value-ranks* and the simultaneous theory based upon the historical per-spectivism of essences belonging to historical being itself. The path toward metaphysics has been opened up also by this extremely interesting process of knowledge unfolding.

One kind of principle of relativity pertaining not only to historical cognition and valuation but also to *historical facts,* to the determination of values connected to them, and to the essential incompleteness and variable meaning of historical fact. I first put forward in an essay on 'Repentance and Re-Birth'.[125] Here, after having discussed the nature of psychic causation and lived time, which continuously fragments itself into the three dimensions of 'present' (sphere of perception), 'past' (sphere of immediate remembrance), and 'future' (sphere of immediate anticipation)— dimensions unknown in objective, physical time—I stated:

Historical facts are incomplete and, as it were, redeemable. True, every event in nature that, for instance, belongs to Caesar's death, is as complete and invariable as the eclipse of the sun predicted by Thales. But everything that is historical fact, as well as that which is a unity of sense and effect within the fabric of human history, is *incomplete* and becomes complete only at the end of world history.

The thought that the nature, meaning, and value of historical fact and historical being *itself*—not only its historical cognition and cognizability—is *relative* to the vantage point, changeable in lived history, of the historical observer, was first taken up and appreciated by Ernst Troeltsch in his *Historismus*. But he did not yet see it in its full importance. I am all the more happy to see, however, that all of a sudden—I know not whether dependent upon or independent of my own writings—this idea has been articulated sharply and precisely, not always from the same starting point, by many other scholars: by Eduard Spranger,[126] more acutely by Theodor Litt,[127] in great detail by Karl Mannheim,[128] most clearly by William Stern,[129] and also by Nicolai Hartmann.[130] Mannheim states:

> The historical object (the historical content of an epoch) is identical to its being-in-itself. But the nature of its experienceability implies that it is grasped only in its aspects because of the various historical vantage points of the mind.

W. Stern remarks more extensively:

> Napoleon's deeds not only represent themselves differently in the eyes of German and French historians, but they also arrange themselves in the historicality of the French people according to quite different objective structures and accentuations than they do in the historicality of the German people.

The so-called question of 'what actually happened' is for Stern only a limit concept: it is only the raw material for a certain threshold and model, which can not be applied yet to such an example, in order to distinguish what is historically valuable from what is not and then to structure it. The 'Reformation', above all, has for Stern its own contemporary value-structure, but, in addition, it necessarily has *one* particular objective structure of value and meaning belonging to possible views from later phases because the Reformation means something new and different (in an ontic sense) for such phases.

> There is the obvious paradox that not only the future but also the past is plastic (i.e. subject to changing influences). The petrification of the past pertains only to scientific abstraction, not to history. Even now figures like Plato, Aristotle, Jesus, and Goethe continually *change* as true historical potencies, displaying meanings and significations that were foreign in their own time.

Stern's position is, therefore, that the 'changing' meanings and values of psycho-physical states of affairs, which we call and permit to be called historical facts, are not various adequations of historical *cognition* nor various comprehensions that the historian construes from 'universal values'—and thus there does not pre-exist already a univocal fact from which it is 'selected' (as is the case with H. Rickert). Not only our cognition (which has its *own* levels of relativity) of 'historical fact' but *'historical fact' itself* is *relative to the being and essence*—not just the mere 'consciousness'—*of the observer*. There is only a metaphysical, never a historical, 'thing-in-itself'.

A historical fact *constitutes itself* in rays of remembrance that hit it and in intentional coincidences whereby 'sources' and mediated 'monuments' represent only objectified symbols of possible remembrance. Since mediate remembrance is essentially dependent upon *dynamic directions of interests* contained in *im*mediate remembrance and upon the attention implied in immediate remembrance, and since these themselves are dependent upon effective, living *systems of value-preference,* which determine the observer's vantage point in real, living history, the very nature, value, and meaning of the historical fact is *itself essentially relative*—and not just its reflexive historical cognition, whose object is the historical fact. Furthermore, because the living systems of value-preference, as factors that pre-select their *possible* empirical contents, directly determine the mediate and immediate sphere of anticipation, as they do the mediate and immediate spheres of remembrance, so, too, the historical *perspective* and correlate 'aspect' of historical reality, its 'modelling' (as Stern says), its place and location within changing phases of living, real history, must *simultaneously change with futural anticipations* and their ideal constructions for a new 'cultural synthesis' (E. Troeltsch). It is always within an indivisible process and act that historical reality and cultural synthesis change. The objectivity of historical science and the univocity of historical facts, as seen from one vantage point, has absolutely nothing to do with this. They remain, of course, as requirements, along with the entire historical metho-dology. But, indeed, so-called *historicism,* as a world-view and as a bad cryptic metaphysics, pervading all true metaphysical problems, has been uprooted along with this view. We will return to this point later. The historicism that relativized all cognition, first in metaphysics (Dilthey), then also in natural science and mathe-matics, and finally even in its own cognition (Spengler), is *itself* relativized by the above insight. Historicism has made history into a 'thing-in-itself'. And what else does this mean but that it attributes to historical reality and to its cognition a *metaphysical* meaning and sense? If, as we stated earlier, all positive historical worlds of *goods* become relative, viz. relative to the absolute system of non-formal [*materialen*] *values,* historical whatness and value-being is *itself relative.*

A similar development shows the relationship between positive science and the *metaphysics of values.* The dream of the Enlightenment and Positivism has been to ground an ethics, an order of values, and an order of norms in positive science, sociology, and evolutionary theory. This dream is finished. Positive science, the more positive and strict it becomes and the more it excludes disguised value-judgments, speaks only to the *techniques* of life, *not* to the *ethics* of life.[131] Here also the process of differentiating philosophy from science gradually has been completed. Positive science has sharply rejected the cryptic metaphysics of value contained in the evolutionary philosophies of Comte, Spencer, and Marx just as it rejected the absolute systems of rational norms belonging to the enlightenment and the authoritarian norms belonging to the older churches of revealed religion, in so far as they claimed absoluteness. Such a metaphysics of value has tended to justify the very fortuitous European, and even national, prejudices and myths—not only class prejudices or chiliastic utopias (Marx)—and to predict its claims as an 'unconditionally necessary, consequential phase of development' by means of 'scientific' insight ('scientific socialism'). But also, on the other side, historicism, which in general dissolves all 'absolutes' into the problem of value and absolutizes only the value of *'historia'* and common success, has been *uplifted* [*aufgehoben*]—and with it *historical relativism of value in general*—by historical *perspectivism* and the principle of the primacy of *value*-comprehension *prior to* comprehension of the *whatness* of things, even things of 'the past'. Only the worlds of *goods* and *norms,* accessible solely to history (as positive science), are relative, even entirely relative—by contrast to the order of *'values' themselves,* which are independent of goods. Goods, purposes, and norms *presuppose* the comprehension and validity of such values. The theory regarding the 'dimensions of the relativity of value-complexes'[132] makes it possible not only to anchor all historical morals and ethoses in a system of relations—but only one pertaining to an order of *value* modalities and qualities, not one of goods and norms—rather it also provides the latitude—only *negatively,* to be sure—within which each positive historical age and every individual group must find *its own relative* system of goods and norms. The *historical* form of the *penetrations* into the metaphysical and absolute world of values by ethoses of various ages and groups lies within the *essence* of this world of values (of which the order of values represents only the most formal and general *a priori* constitution) and its own timeless becoming. Thus only the universal and solidary *cooperation of all ages and peoples*—including those of future history—can exhaust such a world of values and be *co*-realized *in* 'primordial being', in so far as this realization has been assigned to man in general. The value-metaphysics of any age formulates *its* own historical and individual conscience and 'public opinion' and manifests itself in *those* persons who have solidly united themselves with the fullness of human life surrounding them; it is simultaneously an *absolute* and *yet individually valid* cognition. It is neither a material nor a historically universal cognition like the old absolutism of worlds of goods, which historicism rightly brought to an end, believed. This cognition is not absolute and purely 'formal' (Kant), nor is it only 'in fact' relative to time and groups or 'subjectively' valid, as relativist historicism believed. The latter naively presupposed the absoluteness of historical cognition and being.[133]

Thus a new path for metaphysics has also been opened through this approach.

But the novel atmosphere belonging to the *'cosmopolitanism of cultures',* created by the sociology of knowledge, leads us also to expect changes in the *relationship between metaphysics and religion. We expect a new understanding* and *synthesis*—slow as they may be—of the Western, predominantly religious-ecclesiastic mind and the East's predominantly metaphysical and non-ecclesiastic mind, which manifests itself socially in 'sages' and provides self-redemption and self-education through technically guided, spontaneous metaphysical cognitions. There are *two forms of knowledge* that can bring about such mutual understanding between the two greatest cultural units of mankind: on the side of religion, *free 'religious' speculation* and, on the side of spontaneous knowledge, a living *metaphysics based upon psychic techniques* and conjoined with positive science as an *ordered supplement* but simultaneously independent of it.

This process, of course, presupposes a *rediscovery of the true nature of metaphysics,* for which it is today very difficult to win supporters. During the last centuries the very 'idea' of metaphysics has been lost in the debasement of metaphysical knowledge. This loss is *not* due, as Positivism maintains (according to Positivism's predictions the churches must be *already long dead*—much 'sooner' even than metaphysics, because theological thinking, as a phase, must precede metaphysical thinking) to the one-sided development of positive science and its continuous replacement of metaphysics *alone*. Rather, it is due much more to the authoritative churches.[134] In Germany the study of metaphysics at federal universities, which became and *had to* become more and more scientifically specialized, caused great harm to metaphysics after the decline of classical speculation. Metaphysics, and its independence as a discipline, was countered here not only by the *positive-scientific* mind, which represents itself increasingly as the practical-technical mind of the great majority of scholars, but also by the *federal-political ideology and myth-building* of public officials (the Prussian Academy, for example, referred to itself once as the 'body-guard of the *Hohenzollern'*) as well as the ties between churches and their parties throughout the state. For this reason all the more stylistic and effective metaphysicians in the second part of the nineteenth century considered themselves 'lonely thinkers' (Schopenhauer, Nietzsche, E. v. Hartmann)—a fact that is certainly not too surprising when one realizes that almost none of the great philosophers up to Kant had been state-employed university professors.[135] But, *on the basis of the sociology of knowledge,* it is very characteristic of the entire West that in modern Europe, except for a short period between Kant and Hegel when metaphysics flourished, one had to withdraw into 'solitude' and become an 'outsider' in order to be an independent metaphysician.[136] Until recently a social organization has been founded by metaphysical philosophy—apart from loose gnostic sects and societies (Hegelian schools, 'Schopenhauer Societies', the pragmatic circles of Leonardo in Florence)—only where metaphysics has debased itself into a political and ecclesiastical tool. This was the case, for instance, in the 'German Federation of Monists' whose more or less genuinely philosophical undertakings under A. Drew's leadership were unable to overcome E. Haeckel's and W. Ostwald's leftist groups.

The *Stefan George Circle* in Germany, centered around the ingenious poet, is to be mentioned as one erotic-religious, highly aristocratic, gnostic sect born out of the spirit of sharp *opposition to the enmassment [Vermassung] of life*. Its founders came from Rhenish Catholicism with its strongly Latin color. The members of this circle separated the 'pagan' elements, which Roman Catholicism contained much more than Protestantism, from all other components of Catholicism. And through the personal example of their 'Lord and Master' they wished to errect a gnostic metaphysics of self-redemption out of these purified elements and out of the most noble traditions of Latin and German poetry—only in so far as poetry represented to them the germs of and steps toward the work of the 'Master'. But the 'ideas' of this 'circle' fell so short of their master's *personal* image that a philosophical metaphysics could not develop. What ensued was only a specific 'attitude of mind' that truly affected all walks of life, philosophy, and even the foundations of science. We do not yet have a *sociology* of this circle, which E. Troeltsch thought desirable.[137]

156

But we must stress that a sociology of knowledge had been attempted out of the spirit of the Stefan George Circle. It was in the form of a critical reply by E. v. Kahler[138] to Max Weber's intuitionism and nebulous 'mysticisms.' Between these dangerous poles the image of our time, as seen through the sociology of knowledge, takes the form of the Alexandrian-Hellenic Age, during the decline of antiquity. Here, too, a philosophy suddenly appeared along with the new 'specialized scientific disciplines'. Since the time of Plotinus and Proclos it preferred to call itself 'theology', and later it disappeared into mysticism. But from the viewpoint of a properly oriented sociology of knowledge the dissolution today even of science into false gnosticism and dull mysticism (a tendency already present in the Hegelian School) is as much of a danger to our Western [non-technical] culture of knowledge as positivist scientism, the Marxist phantasy of a 'proletarian science', and rising ecclesiastic 'scholasticisms' with their narrow, puny defensive and offensive mechanisms against the currents of time. On the basis of the dynamics of knowledge we have outlined above, all these are strongly *reactionary* phenomena.[139] They are phenomena belonging to the increasing *decline and disintegration of the ordered unity of [non-technical] culture of knowledge* in general. When even Einstein complains (to a friend of mine) that, in regards to 'pure mathematics', a science valued as a model of 'exactness', its own groups and representatives 'do not understand each other anymore'—understandable in light of the formalistic, conventionalistic principle of axiomatics—how much greater must the misunderstandings be in those areas dealing with more subjective judgments? If science is nothing but a 'convenient language' there will be *more* languages than those who speak can understand! If science is primarily 'intuition' there always will be more intuitions than anyone can prove! Only a rigid and thoughtful theory of cognition, *in conjunction with a sociology of knowledge,* can restore order here.

The development of knowledge and politics

A final problematic area for the sociology of knowledge consists of the relationship between the *development of knowledge* and the *development of politics*. It consists of 1 the *outer* competition for power among states, and 2 the changing *forms of constitution* (in their sociological functions)—considered as causes, not in their juridical aspects—as well as the competing and victorious *political parties*.

The development of knowledge and foreign policy

On the basis of my sociological theory regarding the *order of effects that real factors have* upon the *history of mind and ideas,* dealt with in the first part of this treatise, we can expect that such effects and co-determinations will take place predominantly in *highly political* epochs where the flux of law and all legal groups, as well as economy and technology, appear to be within the scope of possible developments that *political* power-relations and their legal expressions by the state leadership will allow.

Of equal objective importance for all *positive knowledge* of nature, peoples, and cultures are, first of all, *conquests and colonizations, politically directed foreign trade,* and, moreover, the systematically controlled *missions* of churches patterned after the state—the 'church' is only the predominant form of religious organization found in a *political* age—in so far as curiosity and thirst for knowledge received new objects from these movements. For instance, the ancient Pythagorean system of astronomy was overthrown by Alexander's conquests because a 'counter-earth' could not be found. Alexander's invasion also brought about the mixture of Greek and oriental ideas and of religious cults, a mixture which characterized later Greece. Friedrich II's Italian campaigns mediated the entry of Arabic science into the West and the spread of Aristotle's chief writings, which became so important in the high Middle Ages. The Turks' conquest of Constantinople indirectly led to the founding of the Florentine Academy and to migrations of Byzantine scholars to Italy. The politically motivated discoveries of Magellan, Columbus, and Vasco da Gama, Napoleon's Egyptian enterprise, British trade colonizations in India and elsewhere, sailing around the globe, missionary work in China, Japan, and India and among primitive peoples, all produced vast amounts of geographical, astronomical, zoological, botanical, and, no less, cultural-historical knowledge—this needs no further elaboration. Certainly the *counter-effect,* for example, of displacing and destroying entire [*non-technical*] cultures of knowledge through such forces seems, all in all, no less great, if we only remember the great example of the displacing of ancient sciences by the Germanic conquests, all the discoveries that fell into deep oblivion for centuries (for example, the 'Copernicanism' of Aristarch of Samos), and all the wealth in knowledge and the *means* for gaining knowledge destroyed in wars, fire, and tumults. For only during such things as war and raids were whole or parts of peoples used to wandering or used to going on a 'journey'. These things have only a 'history'—they really do not have a 'sociology'. All that can be said is that, in general, the expansions

158

of power states in a political era, when there is not yet an ordered, peaceful traffic and trade among peoples living without states, tend to effect mixtures among peoples so that the collective knowledge about the world *increases* with the increasing opportunity for cultural, productive, mutual contacts. The political expansion of power during a political era is, moreover, the strongest force for amalgamating smaller and more dissociated groups into wider and wider clusters of states, enhancing the formation of estates and classes from which the development of *knowledge,* in general, benefits.

But only a partial, dogmatic European view that disregards sociology would assert that the *total* knowledge of mankind had been more furthered than obstructed by the European states' development of worldly powers. The historical fact that remains true is that modern Western positive *specialized sciences* did gain rather than lose by the West's expansion of power, and, in this manner, their methods have *spread* tremendously—but certainly without thereby affecting in any way people's souls and, moreover, their metaphysical and religious views. One must never forget the following: although the contents and results of European, positive, specialized science remain universally valid within the limits of technological objectives, its very origin is *nothing but a European product,* i.e. the result also of an individual and peculiar group of peoples and their history.[140] The unconditional, positive valuation and selection of such a true and correct image of the world, through which the world is controlled and directed, presupposes a whole range of *metaphysical and religious positions*, which themselves stem from specifically *Western* metaphysics and religion. Among such positions are the following: 1 the proposition *'omne ens est bonum'*—which Buddhism, for instance, does not share with the West;[141] 2 the position that it is altogether desireable and valuable to direct and control nature, and that this would not enmesh men into a network of things that would alienate them from cultivation and redemption as their highest goals; and 3 the position that man's metaphysical and eternal destiny is dependent upon his *one* life and his behavior, and he cannot have any effect on earthly things after his death—almost no Asian religion shares this position, with the exception of Judaism and Islam. There are other such positions that bestow the earth and man's one terrestial life with an immense earnestness and an irreplaceable importance. If one ignores such positions, and if one holds that positive science is a 'developmental product' pertaining to all peoples, i.e. a stage of development that, in time, will be reached by all peoples, even *without* European influences, one is a European partisan. This is the case with Comte and

Spencer and also with Marx's fundamentally erroneous theory of capitalism, which, as we saw, thoroughly belongs to our modern Western sciences. One who holds the above position is as much a European partisan as one who considers Christianity, not as an absolute, but still as the most 'perfect' religion out of the whole history of religions (as Troeltsch would have it at the beginning of his scientific work[142]), whereby one naturally and inevitably *presupposes* a Christian-European measure of value (as Troeltsch himself later recognized and stated with such perfect clarity and honesty in his London lectures shortly before his death).

But one sees from the Western and American *missions,* all of which come into question for their active propagations of *metaphysical* and *religious*-ecclesiastical positions, one can by no means hold—in the absence of dogmatic propositions—that such missions ever had any large-scale sociological importance, that they did away with the metaphysics and religions of the cultural units concerned, or even shook or threatened them. This holds true for Christian missions of every sort, which often—against the will of the missionaries themselves—were mere instruments of commerce and political expansion. In Fontane's words: 'They say Christ but mean Kattun'! But this is also true with regard to Asian and recent Buddhist communities in Europe and America. Such phenomena may be historically important—in a *sociology of knowledge* they are of very little importance. Every form of political power, and similarly every mission with particular objectives, is completely insufficient to spread religious and metaphysical knowledge except occasionally and for short periods of time.[143]

A much more significant role must be attributed, from the perspective of a sociology of knowledge, to *world-trade* and industrial expansion, in so far as they originated from economic motivations and only later took political forms, and they generally did not strive for politically dependent markets. They enlarge positive *science* through *technical* and industrial agents, which only secondarily stimulate needs for their respective sciences. One example, recently given by Hans Driesch, is the American schools (schools of medicine) and universities in China.

The *metaphysical* dialogue among the irreplaceable great spiritual individuals belonging to the *cultural fields,* however, cannot be effected by political force, expedient missions, nor economic penetration joined by capitalization and industrialization of the economy in question. Rather, such a dialogue can come about only through a 'sublime and great discussion' (Schopenhauer) that transcends time and space and that the best representatives of the various cultural fields lead on metaphysical subjects—a discussion which is carried on in the already characte-rized atmosphere of the *new 'cosmopolitanism of cultural fields'*. This dialogue has already begun to a hitherto unknown extent, but until now it has been unknown to the world and has had not the least to do with the internationalization of science and technology—which, in comparison with such metaphysical dia-logue, assumes the metaphysical position of *one* of the discussion participants, namely, that of 'Euro-America'. Little importance is to be attributed to 'religious congresses', as they have been copied, artificially and in watered-down versions, from 'philosophical congresses', especially in America, and from very fruitful and effective scientific international congresses, inasmuch as these congresses act more as opportunities for personal expression.[144] But also 'philosophical congresses' are of only little significance. These congresses cannot yet show the great fruits that positive-scientific congresses are able to bring because they lack a common axiomatic and methodological basis, the uniform terminology needed in the exact sciences, and common conventions for the measurement of all sorts of quantities, and the 'division of labor' [*arbeitsteilige Betrieb*] has been essentially impossible here. What in philosophy is only *one* main *object* of investigation remains an unchecked *presupposition* in the positive sciences. Only years of 'sym-philosophizing' upon the mutual bases for insight into the connections among essences can continue here.

The development of knowledge and domestic politics ('logic of classes': 'sociological theory of idols')

The *inner* political destinies of groups combined into states, empires, etc., affects the development of human knowledge much more than foreign policy.[145]

Above all is the colossal *process of liberating work* from thousands of ties originating in politics and war through political struggles between estates, classes, and parties—the development from *'status'* to *'contractus'*, as H. Spencer called it. The larger phases of this struggle, always fought by the *lower classes,* and its formation into *political and social 'democracies'* have, from the perspective of a sociology of knowledge, a threefold relevance to various *types of knowledge*: 1 a regression that frees metaphysics from the aristocratic mind so as to uproot it as a social *institution* of doctrines and knowledge, or reform it into closed systems of individual, *'lonely thinkers'*; 2 increasing dogmatism, juridical-ecclesiasticism, and administration of religions according to the principle, *'C'est la médiocrité qui fonde l'autorité'*, and, on the other side, the saving of upper-class minorities from this process of petrification in the form of conscious aristocratic religion, viz. in the form of the 'sect', and 3 increasing progress of positive-scientific and technological minds, whose interconnections we have shown above.

Indeed, the victory of the Jewish conception of the Godhead by *Christianity,* as a religion predominantly of *lower classes,* is the living germ for all subsequent Western development in all three of the just-mentioned factors. This conception brought with it a positively creative God of 'Work', who 'made' the world in seven days, and a new evaluation of work, which first pertained only to an attitude of the mind. This means that Christianity as a church limits metaphysics by a *'praeambula fidei'.* Structured after the Roman Empire, this 'Church' dogmatized religion, following the deification of its founder, in an ontological sense, by means of a Christ-*cult.* And the new assessment of work in the attitudes and ideologies of the lower classes, victorious over the older upper classes, provides also the primary stimulation for the abolition of slavery and all other forms of forced labor through the complete *religious-metaphysical equality* of slave and master, man and woman, fetus and grown-up man (no abortions), child and adult. The more Christianity became institutionalized the more it practiced a policy of *quantitatively* increasing population and thus established new technical and scientific stimuli.[146] All of this appears in contrast to antiquity and especially Asian cultures, where such developments are unknown. The twofold ordinance, 'Work, but do not enjoy', which spread from Christian orders into the layman's world, is the origin of the systematic *tendency to collect* riches, the first form of the capitalist will to acquisition.[147] It is also in these respects that Christianity presents itself fully within the style of *Europeanism*—at least in its Western-Roman forms, which gradually separated from Byzantium and Rome. Christianity, in this new form, thereby also laid the bases for the common destiny of the Germanic and Romance peoples (in L. v. Ranke's sense) in contrast to the Orient and the development of Russia until Peter, which had been determined, according to a sociology of knowledge, by Byzantium and the Greco-Hellenic fathers, and which lacked the aforementioned three factors.[148]

In both Byzantium and Russia the metaphysical and freely speculative mind remains considerably *freer.* In contrast to the Roman Church, monkhood remains here less preoccupied with a 'common good', more contemplative, and *above* ecclesiastic authority and world-clericism; it is not subjected to ecclesiastic authority and offices. Instead of a Pope and his doctrinal authority, we find in the East the tradition of a 'holy assembly', which, following the teachings of Vincent of Lerin, only *recognizes* the *'quod semper et ubique creditur'*, viz. that which contains the 'holy tradition', and which does not decide *ex sese* on dogma. But, on the other hand, the positive-scientific and technological mind has developed very little here because Roman political activism had been discarded while the Hellenic *contemplative, aesthetic* intellectualism has remained until now as a prevalent trait of the Christian envelopment of the East.[149]

The *fundamentally different structures of the sociology of knowledge* in the Germanic-Romance world and in the East, including Russia, have been created for reasons of a *political* sort— not of a simple religious sort. Since Peter the Great, Russia has not received 'European science and technology' in any way essentially differently than Japan, China, and India did. Even the capitalist economy—in strong contrast to what Karl Marx says—would never have developed on Russian soil had it not been imposed *from outside* by Swedish, Polish, Baltic-German, Jewish, and other power groups and later by the compulsive competition of the rising world economy.

The historical phases of the *liberation of work* need not be compared here with the progress of positive science, for this has already been done repeatedly. Without doubt science is *not* the agent responsible for the liberation of work. Rather, liberation of work is the driving force behind the progress of positive science.

Also well-known is the inner connection between exclusive religions of *grace* (which Calvin most clearly represented, but whom M. Weber overemphasized)—*religious aristocratism*—and *political and ecclesiastical democracy* (as opposed to religious democracy as a means to salvation 'equally' effective for all— *political-ecclesiastical* aristocratism—and the *hierarchy of estates* in the Roman Church), on the one hand, and the gradual *victory of the technical and positive-scientific mind over all metaphysics* and remaining magic techniques. It is everywhere the *same psycho-energetic* mass process—just seen from different angles. This connection compares not only to the victory of territorial principalities and territorial states over imperial powers, but has its primary causes in the alliance of those political powers with the rising city-bourgeoisie, in so far as the expansion of the new religious and scientific movements and doctrines is concerned. Neither a purely logical development in religion, metaphysics, or science, nor a development determined primarily by economic factors can account for this. The modern religious doctrinaires of the Reformation would have been left alone and ineffective without territorial principalities. At best they would have formed only

163

small and wholly transient sects. In the same way the bourgeoisie as a new class would not have been able to do anything without territorial principalities.

But the heart of the question belonging specifically to the sociology of knowledge is the following: Why *did not metaphysics arise wholly anew* after the dreadful ties of the metaphysical mind to the old Church dissolved, as in predominantly Protestant northern Europe? And why was the victory of bourgeois democracy everywhere until the time of d'Alembert's French Encyclopedia also a *victory of the positive sciences and technology?*[150] Or, too, why was the domination of the estates [*Stände*] during the feudal era by means of political powers, blood ties, and tradition, as well as wealth and unfree labor, *connected* nevertheless with a relatively strong (compared to later times) *intellectual-contemplative structure of knowledge,* the knowledge belonging to the extensive, powerful 'estates' of priests, monasteries, and monks? And why was this domination connected with a biomorphic and *conceptually realistic metaphysics* that suppressed and inhibited positive science, a metaphysics which, even if only a *'praeambula fidei',* still had an institutional character—and in no way a system bound to the person as have been all modern metaphysics of the relatively 'lonely thinkers', for example, Descartes, Malebranche, Spinoza, Leibniz, Kant, etc.?

The answer to these questions is the following: a feudal class of leaders that accumulates its wealth not through its own work but through the work of *others* and through *political* privileges, *likewise* can and will maintain, with its own peculiar 'largesse' and through the products of unfree labor, intellectual and contemplative classes that are *economically unproductive.* This happens especially when the feudal class gains wide control over ecclesiastic offices and posts of honor, and when monasteries of the old orders, such as the mostly highly feudal Benedictines, bear an extensively *political* character[151]—in short, when *church and state have organically grown together.* Quite different are the connections between a bourgeoisie that itself works and the territorial powers that grew until the Age of Absolutism. Since these new classes of leaders produced their own wealth, and since the principalities were eager to collect taxes and were greatly interested in abolishing economically unproductive, 'dependent' forms of work—in no way interested in the economically inferior monkhood—the contemplative and *metaphysical attitude of mind increasingly was deprived of its necessary economic basis.* When Bacon said that 'purposes' and all metaphysics of 'forms and qualities' are unproductive and 'devoted to God like nuns', he unconsciously expressed, more as a simile, an *essential interconnection relevant to*

164

the sociology of knowledge. In fact, it is not theoretical insight that separated metaphysics of objective teleology and of 'forms and qualities' from 'modern science'. Rather, this occurs through an *a priori,* insightful interconnection: man can establish purposes for controlling the universe only when there is *no objective teleological* order in it. He can form the universe to his liking only in so far as there are no *ontic* 'forms': he can control the universe only in so far as it contains no constant qualities—which one can merely observe and at best name—but only quantities and measurable 'motions'. Man gains power over the universe only in so far as temporally consecutive events are univocally prede-termined by preceding ones. It is the *'unproductiveness'* of metaphysics of purposes, forms, and qualities (*'qualitates occultae'*)—*not its theoretical mistakes,* which naturally can also very well occur—and it is the *economic* unproductiveness of contemplative classes of metaphysicians—not primarily their proven religious-ethical or epistemological inferiority—that has brought about the collapse of Western institutional metaphysics, as part of a biomorphic world-image, and the intellectual overthrow of contemplators. And such unproductiveness also pressed meta-physics, on the one hand, into the closed, personal 'system' (as a form) and pressed the metaphysician, on the other hand, into the societal way of life belonging to the 'lonely thinker', in the form of the modern 'school'. Hence the causes for this process are again eminently *political.* The moral contempt for 'lazy monks' (seculari-zation of ecclesiastical property), often clothed in ethics and religion, is as much a derived 'ideology of interests' as is the presumedly pure theoretical insight that there are not any objective purposes, forms, or qualities in nature. The gradual dissolution of the estate hierarchy [*Standesordnungen*], brought about first by the mundane *professional* groups, then in the nineteenth century by high capitalism through the growing formation of *classes* by virtue of the repeated victories of the English and American democracies 'from above' (English revolutions) and of Romance democracies 'from below' (French revolutions), and, furthermore, by the transformation of the era of 'power-wealth' into the era of 'wealth-power', *had* to result in a victory for *positive science* and technology and the increasing authority of scientific researchers and scholars. Thus, all the great European revolutions added new dignity to positive science.

It was not science, as Comte held, that suppressed in-stitutionalized metaphysics of forms and essences. Rather, it was largely *politics* that did this. Hence, there is a deep sociological reason for the fact that the revolutionary lower classes of the 'fourth estate' and their leaders tend to replace religious and metaphysical principles with 'science' and, in contrast to the one-sided *rational* scientism of the enlightened bourgeoisie, to make *pragmatic, technological* scientism their guiding idea, long before the Pragmatism of Boole, W. James, and others. One solid proof of this is the very clear conviction that leaders of proletarian socialism hold regarding the sociological condition of metaphysics, on the one hand, and positive inductive science, on the other—in contrast to bourgeois liberalism. The '*feue dame-métaphysique*', Bakunin proclaims, is aristocratic and authoritarian. 'La philosophie rationelle [i.e. positive science in the Comtean sense] est une science toute-democratique. Elle s'organise de bas en haut[!] librement et a pour fondement unique l'experience'. (*Oeuvres*, 68.[152]) Any claim to *a priori* knowledge that is not dependent upon experimental *quantities* but can be gained by *one* exemplary instance, is for Bakunin a knowledge that is '*selon la méthode des États centralisés*', because laws should be prescribed from absolute principles derived from the many facts of experience.[153]

> Behind the question of whether there is in our head a noble metaphysical spirit or only a common and plain human understanding there lies hidden the question of social interests: whether power and law belong to a privileged nobles or to the common people.

The conviction that the inductive method alone is justified (and consequently the denial of any knowledge of essences) is *essentially* and without doubt connected with the *majority* principle based upon the volitional development of groups. Moreover, when one considers that, as we showed above, metaphysics cannot be dealt with in terms of a division of labor [*arbeitsteilig*], that metaphysics is essentially conditioned by persons and individuals, as well as by nations and cultural units, that it can be dealt with only through cosmopolitan, not international, cooperation, and that it can reveal growth but not progress, it is legitimate and fully understandable that beliefs in such things as scientism, exclusively inductive methods, the necessity of a division of labor, progress, and internationalism *hang necessarily together* within the whole of proletarian socialism's ideology of interests. But it is primarily also the *technological pragmatism of work* that makes the proletarian 'faith in science' into a special 'ideology' of human cognition. Man is here in his *essence* the '*homo faber*': he is a being capable of making tools and signs. 'If society has a technical need this bears more on science than it does on ten universities' (Engels). 'It is the need to make work more productive that leads to science and culture [!]'.[154] It was Labriola[155] who pursued most extensively the idea that we examined before but found to be too simplistic:

esso [i.e. the materialist conception of history] parte dalla *praxis* cioè dallo sviluppo della operosità, e come è la *teoria dell'uomo che lavora,* cosi considera la scienze stessa come un lavoro Porta infine a compimento il senso implicito alle scienze empiriche; che noi, cioè, con l'esperimento ci riavviciniamo al fare delle cose, e raggiungiamo la persuasione *che le cose stesse sono un fare,* ossia un prodursi . . .

A very interesting passage, anticipating the whole of modern pragmatism, was found in Proudhon by W. Sombart:[156]

L'idée avec ses categories surgit de l'action et doit revenir à l'action à peine de dechéance pour l'agent. Cela signifie que toute connaissance, dite a priori, y compris la métaphysique est *sortie du travail pour servir d'instrument au travail,* contrairement à ce qu'enseignant l'orgueil philosophique et le spiritualisme religieux, accrédités par la politique de tous les sièdes.

Among the motives that lead the proletariat to absolutize positive science and to abolish not only religion but also metaphysics—the index *librorum prohibitorum* of Soviet Russia contains, for example, all philosophers from Thales through J. G. Fichte—W. Sombart, in one of his very elucidating investigations, mentions the following:[157]

1) Science, in its results, addresses 'all people': it claims 'universality'. This concept is not taken in the high, Kantian sense of a universal reason, but rather in a much more concrete, naturalistic sense and is tantamount to general understandability. Insights furnished by science correspond to the requirements, already known to us, of 'proletarian' thinking: to be 'plain and home-made'. Social democracy will 'not recognize anything above scientific human understanding'. But social democracy holds 'that our intellect is nothing but a home-made, formal, and mechanical faculty' (Dietzgen, *Philosophie,* pp. 37, 42 [*Philosophical Essays,* pp. 223, 260]).
2) Thinking is not its own master in experimental science. Rather, it is subject to sovereign people. It is as though the 'masses' decide what facts are true. It is, so to speak, by a vote that a result is achieved: 'thoughts should be grounded in sense data and experience' (*op. cit.* p. 50 [*Philosophical Essays,* p. 234]).
3) Science fulfills an important requirement of democracy in so far as distrust is its foundation and it is subject to public criticism at any time. 'I do not believe you; prove it to me'. At any time the authority of a doctrine—the facts—can be abolished through an appeal to the people.
4) Science corresponds to the ideal of proletarianism in so far as

it recognizes the principle of egalitarianism [*Egalitätsprinzip*]. 'For science a speck of dust is as important as the stars in the skies'. 'A division between what is of dignity and what is not, is not permissible'. '[T]he entire infinite plurality of entities (consists) of the same unitary and empirical stuff'. 'Everything is under one hat. Difference exists only in form; essentially everything is of one and the same type' (Dietzgen, *Religion,* pp. 30, 47, and elsewhere [*Philosophical Essays*, pp. 128, 152]).

5) Science is rebelious. This has long been recognized. Already Buckle said that wherever the 'Baconian spirit' has taken root a revolution will grow: first in the seventeenth century in England, then in the eighteenth century in France. Proletarian writers seem to consider this quality of science to be of special value. They hope this quality will bring about the destruction of the existing order. 'The revolutionary consequence of inductive systems has smelled out reactionary malice'. 'I maintain that the principle of induction will bring about the most wonderful anti-religious and anti-national consequences' (ibid., pp. 44–5 [*Philosophical Essays*, pp. 148–50]).

We can thoroughly support the correctness of these five motives so much more than we have already indicated in this treatise. For they also correspond exactly to the *sociological origins* of science and metaphysics. One can see from our theory of this origin that both scientific rationalism and intellectualism (which regards all technique as only an application of pure theory), on the one hand, and proletarian worker-pragmatism, on the other, are *wrong*—that they represent nothing but *ideologies based upon interests*: the one, those of the liberal bourgeoisie, and the other, those of the proletariat. Science is plainly the child of the *marriage* between *pure philosophy* and the technical *work-experience* of the corresponding classes.[158] Only philosophy is *a*practical, 'pure' theory. It should thereby be self-evident that philosophy will not cease to be a 'perpetual concern of mankind' (Kant) when it does not agree sociologically with the perspectival interests of a historical, passing class.

But, however, methodologically it does not make sense that intellectual representatives of *classes* accuse each other, in all these and other matters, of representing only an ideology of either the dominating or suppressed class. It makes no sense to argue: 'You must first become a proletarian (or a bourgeois, respectively) so that you can understand what I mean and see the truth of my position.' If there were no realm within the human mind that could raise itself *above* all class ideologies and their perspectival interests, all possible cognitions of truth would have to be deception. All cognition would then be *nothing but a function of the outcome of class struggles*—exactly as the economic theory of history asserts for ethical laws of value-preference, for good and evil. Even the various types of logic and cognition would then only be a function of class attitudes or a function of opting for one such class. On the other hand, it is also a known fact that class attitude *widely determines* both the *ethos* and the *type of thinking*—not just the objects and contents of thinking and cognition. 'Absolutism', not seeing this, is just as precarious as pure class relativism. We already have indicated how to overcome this apparent contradiction. It lies in this: *categorial systems* of intuition, thinking, and valuation, which form themselves in history by functionalizing the comprehension of essences, are determined not according to their validity and possible origins but through *selection and choice, as well as* by classes. Thus it is true that very formal types of thinking and perception can be different among classes—but only with reference to laws governing *great numbers* of cases, because every individual, *in principle, can overcome* his class attitude.

I offer the following examples of such *formal types of thinking that are determined by classes*. I will briefly sketch them and their sociological relevance:

1. Value-prospectivism with respect to time-consciousness ↔ lower class: value-retrospectivism ↔ upper class.
2. Reflection upon becoming ↔ lower class; reflection upon being ↔ upper class.
3. Mechanical world-view ↔ lower class; teleological world-view ↔ upper class.
4. Realism (world given predominantly as 'resistance') ↔ lower class; idealism (world predominantly a 'realm of ideas') ↔ upper class.
5. Materialism ↔ lower class; spiritualism ↔ upper class.
6. Induction, empiricism ↔ lower class; *a priori* knowledge, rationalism ↔ upper class.
7. Pragmatism ↔ lower class; intellectualism ↔ upper class.
8. Optimistic view of the future and pessimistic retrospection ↔ lower class; pessimistic view of the future and optimistic retrospection ('the good old days') ↔ upper class.
9. Thinking that looks for contradictions, or 'dialectical' thinking ↔ lower class; thinking that seeks identity ↔ upper class.
10. Thinking preoccupied with theories about milieu ↔ lower class; nativistic thinking ↔ upper class.

Obviously the opposite terms listed here are not to be construed as merely *philosophical theories* bearing the same titles. Rather, they represent the very functions of *living types of thinking* and

169

living forms of intuition—not reflective knowledge about these forms. They are *class-conditioned, sub-conscious inclinations* for looking at the world in one form or another. They are not class 'prejudices'. They are more than this: they are *formal laws for the formation* of prejudices. And certainly these formal laws, as the laws of prevailing inclinations that form prejudices, are rooted solely in class levels—apart from one's individuality, occupation, degree of knowledge, race, nationality, etc. Were these formal laws completely known to us and could they be completely elucidated in their *necessary* origins from out of class levels, they would represent a new chapter in the sociology of knowledge, to which I refer as a *'sociological doctrine of the idols'* of thinking, intuition, and valuation, an analogy to Bacon's theory of the idols (theory of deception) of outer perception and an analogy to my own theory of the idols of inner perception.[159] These sociologically conditioned 'idols' are *more* than errors. They pertain to both *what* presents itself to a member of a class illustrative of worldly stuff and as the *objective forms* in which it *is* presented to him (without any special attention and without conscious reflection). For this reason they are much stronger, more stubborn, and more obstinate than deceptions occurring in memory and judgment after the world has appeared in intuition. Plain rationalism, which the sociology of knowledge does not influence, assumes only the latter to be important. The world *itself* presents *different formal reliefs* to the upper and lower classes and to both of them in so far as they themselves are aware of their 'rising' or 'sinking'. These idols become *traditional* [*traditional*] within the classes—sucked in, as it were, with the mother's milk. To this extent the economic theory of knowledge is certainly correct. But errors arise when: first, one *equates* these class-conditioned systems of idols with the being and becoming forms of things; second, one *equates* them with the objective forms of thought, intuition, and valuation and judges them to be analogous to these categorial class interests and perspectives; and third, one not only regards such systems as *inclinations* of thinking and intuitional *beginnings*—which certainly they are—but also holds that, out of causal necessity, all individuals, belonging to a class, *must* follow these inclinations and drives in their super-automatic, conscious, mental activities of cognition. Class prejudices, and also the formal laws of their formation, can, *in principle,* be *overcome* by any individual of a class. They can be put out of action by anyone—no matter what his class—the more they are recognized in their sociological lawfulness through the sociological doctrine of idols.

It is a primary practical and educational value of a *sociology of knowledge of classes* to clarify and *objectify* for anyone the automatically self-instituting *idols* and the forms they take in his own class.

One can show very well—when one establishes the rough division between upper and lower classes—why these classes 'had to' look at the world and think in the opposite terms mentioned above:

1 The lower class must always tend to accuse and denounce [*anschwärzen*] past history because it put this class into its place. It is inclined to deduce, as much as possible, past 'culture', which is relatively inaccessible to it, from naturalistic drive factors. But, on the other hand—with a normal 'messianic' focus—it places 'its' *summum bonum* in the *future* by hoping for and awaiting a miracle from God in times of faith (eschatology), believing that the highest good is a question of what the class 'ought' to be, as do utopian socialists, or viewing the highest good as a 'leap into the freedom' of a classless society, as does Marxist socialism.[160] Marxism is just a rationalized form of the ancient Judaic messianism and a secularized form of the hope of God's kingdom—in this regard Marxism is a typical ideology of the lower class. An upper class, on the other hand, tends toward opposite attitudes, especially when it is at its peaks: gratefully and reverently it looks towards the *past*, not seeing what history *owes* humanity—and dreadful is its view of the future. Who can deny that in Gobineau's theory of history and various race ideologists, as well as in O. Spengler, we find elements of the ideology of an upper class that feels itself endangered. Both the historian and sociologist have to 'reckon' with this perspectival view of the world and history based upon class interests, just as they must reckon with the stable masses, and they themselves must avoid falling victim to it.

2 It seems equally plausible to me that the lower class tends to reflect upon *becoming* while the upper class tends to reflect upon *being*. Because at any point in history there are both things relatively stable and things newly becoming—becoming which later is completed as well as that which is not completed because other factors kept it from and trampled it out of 'real' history—the upper class always has the tendency to deduce what is newly becoming from what *has become*; the lower class always tends to deduce what has become from what *is becoming*, i.e. from the 'dialectical' clash of dynamic possibilities. To the first type of thinking history is a static 'realm of the past', which resembles a 'hall of fame for great men and works'. To the second form of thinking history is a never static stream of becoming, which only now and then deposits structures that disappear and sink into this stream as soon as the

forces that created them cease. Scientific history has to free itself from *both* deceiving schemes, and it has to integrate the categorial perspectives of interests into a theory of historical causal factors, similar to those the first part of this treatise attempted to give.

3 That the lower class tends to view all world events mechanically has its deep and necessary root in the fact that every need to question, 'Why?,' introducing itself stealthily (in sharp contrast to conscious, rational, spontaneous questions about causes and effects) results *increasingly* amidst changes judged to be of immediate, 'presumably' *negative* value, rather then amidst changes judged to be of positive value. All automatic questions of *'Why?,'* are born from *care* and from the practical need to direct things by actively taking them apart, moving them, and rearranging them. But every automatic (pre-conscious) consideration of *purposes* and every 'meaningful' impression of the world is born out of *'well'*-directed changes in which one need not interfere, whose efficient causes one does not automatically 'question', and which lead one to be 'thankful' for them with respect to an intelligent 'higher power'.[161] *Both* categories first are seen in the results of human actions and then are transferred into nature. But those in command see their own category with a stress on the idea of *ends,* which enters into all acts—those who must obey see it with a stress on drive impulse (or 'motive'), which is also applied to acts. But both tend to transfer their *one-sided* categorial ideal onto things and onto the becoming of the world in an equally one-sided manner. The privileged tend to experience the given social state of affairs as the consequence of a *stable, meaningful, teleological objective world order.* But the tendency towards *realistic* ways of thinking is very clearly characteristic of the lower class, because every experience of reality is based upon the experience of *resistance* against the activity of willing and attention—and this experience again must have a quite different weight among classes of manual workers than it has among the privileged, i.e. those classes that direct work mentally. Henri Bergson and, more recently, A. Grünbaum[162] have shown that the materialistic world-view is only an extension of the relative natural world-view belonging to the civilized, conditioned by act and work impulses— and resulting from the need to comprehend and to split up extended matter.

The same can be established for the other pairs of opposite terms mentioned above and no less for those pertaining to ethos, which we did not include.

Such considerations, which naturally belong to all classes,[163] become nonsensical only when the nonsense of a 'bourgeois' and 'proletarian' science is supposed to have a foundation, possibly with even a special *'logic'*—the 'scientific' attitude begins wherever one *does not follow* tendencies of thinking conditioned by classes. It is a fundamental error to hold that one 'cannot' do this, to hold that, even in this sense, social existence *necessarily* determines social forms of consciousness. For the automatic drive-conditioned forms of understanding the world, ahistorically atuning themselves to the world, determine equivocally neither our judgments nor our will.

In short, class-conditioned types of thinking have absolutely nothing to do with the aforementioned transformations of categorial structures of environment, to which we referred as primitive, biomorphic, and formal-mechanical types of thinking, and which pertain only to *developmental phases* belonging to groups of men, displayed over vast periods of time. These latter are of a wholly different order of magnitude because a *prevailing* division of classes is found *only* in predominantly 'societal' phases, the third of these phases. Therefore, it is only in a societal phase that there appear class-conditioned trends of thought as forms of the disintegration of the still unitary thinking of the life-community.

Let us now return, after this digression, to the *sociological reasons for the fall of metaphysics as an 'institution'*. We can then ask the question:

How does a metaphysically oriented man *live*—according to the motto, *'primum vivere, deinde philosophari'*—in the changed conditions mentioned above, a man who became simultaneously free of the Church and, in the same process, sociologically and economically homeless? There remain several possibilities available to him: 1 He is a pensioner of the new capitalist economy of which he is just a spectator (the types like Schopenhauer, Maine de Biran, and the Stefan George Circle). 2 He has by chance 'patrons' providing his food. 3 He 'works' either in his main profession or on side jobs (Spinoza, who cut optical glasses; Albert Lange, who was secretary to the Chamber of Commerce). 4 He is a 'statesman' or a politician in some sense (the model for nearly all great English, strongly politicizing 'philosophers'; also our Leibniz). 5 He is an official at a university—not qua metaphysician but qua researcher or 'teacher of philosophy'. (Kant, for example, made a distinction between his being a free metaphysician and a university professor. He felt so strongly about this that he dogmatically lectured on Wolff's ontology, whereas, as a 'citizen of a cosmopolitan republic of scholars', he had refuted it in his *Critique of Pure Reason*.) 6 He pursues positive science as a main occupation, or he is in some other way a 'useful member' in society (for example, Fechner and

173

Lotze). 7 As a state professor of metaphysics, at least in an objective sense, he even unwillingly serves an interest of the state *by virtue of the content* of his metaphysics, in that he bestows on the state, willfully or not, a metaphysical blessing. (Most typically this is seen in the prevalence of Hegelianism, which, at times, bore an institutional character in Prussia.) 8 He is a free writer (for example, Carlyle, Emerson, and the later Nietzsche), whereby philosophy generally takes on, to be sure, a remarkably 'literary' character.

In contrast to metaphysics, positive *science*—which was, during the ages of institutional metaphysics, only an occasional matter for dilettantes, amateurs, adventurers, inventors, astrologers, and alchemists, and only a more or less secondary occupation—became, in the age of advancing democracy, an *institution and a chief occupation,* and it entered into a systematic, rational relationship with technology and industry, crystalizing itself socially. At the state universities of territorial principalities and absolute states this happened chiefly in the following manner: positive science, serving neither the State nor the Church, was first brought together in a so-called 'lower' faculty, which stood in contrast to the two 'higher' faculties of theology and jurisprudence. They were referred to as 'higher' because, during this age, in which the practical had primacy over the theoretical, this faculty was expected to train State and Church officials.[164] Later in the nineteenth century the long existing social valuation of faculties became *reversed*: the humanities [*philosophische Fakultät*] became the *soul* proper of the university—but gradually became, in the process of things, more and more specialized. The theological faculty had to struggle hard for its academic existence. In France it disappeared from the state university after the nullification of the concordat (Combes). Finally, at the end of the nineteenth century, the so-called faculty of political science, better termed the 'faculty of economics', then emerged as a recent separation from the humanities.[165] It gains more and more significance during the growing economic age—and recently has the highest student enrollment.

Thus the necessary 'connection between democracy and inductive method' does not put political democracy on the bandwagon of positive science, as one has held—modern science is from its very foundation *both* inductive and deductive (deductive already as 'mathematical science'), and every scientific discipline becomes all the more rigorous the more it is deductive. Rather, the *relationship of political democracy to the liberating process of work* and the relationship of highly qualified, free labor to *technology,* which demands, as it becomes more highly developed, more and

174

more qualified and skilled workers, *explains,* above all, this *interconnection between democracy and science.* The coolie, and what resembles him, *is not able* to handle the modern machine. For this reason the intensity of well-paid workers, working relatively short hours, increases with their economic productivity [*Fruchtbarkeit*] (Lujo Brentano). The other connection, that increasing democracy demands a higher level of knowledge and education among peoples, is only very secondary. This does not directly pertain to higher forms of knowledge, but rather only to average school education. Instead, the reverse is the case: democracy—in so far as it becomes also a *conformist democracy of education and culture* and, above all, genetically one 'from below', as is predominantly the case with French, Italian, and Spanish democracies (Romance democracies, in general, in contrast to English, highly political democracy)—does not raise but considerably lowers the highest level of science and even philosophy. The truncated sociological 'cone of knowledge'—if I may use this picture to depict the *distance* between the knowledge of the lower classes and that belonging to groups of the highest level, and, simultaneously, the *distribution* of knowledge in the succession of classes—has different forms in various nations. The height of the cone diminishes with the widening of its base, and relative uniformity in knowledge is paid for by lowering the height of every higher level. In contrast to the wholly different sense of 'democracy' as 'national' [*volkstümlich*], science is essentially 'aristocratic', viz. not national. And conversely, it is *philosophy* and metaphysics that are highly aristocratic in their origin, but which can become much more national than science, because in their first stages they rest (at least in principle) upon every man's accessibility to essential research. As total knowledge, philosophy satisfies the need for *cultivation*[166] much more than highly specialized branches of science, whose understandability decreases with increasing specialization.

The sociological form of *democracy 'from below',* which has steadily increased in recent decades even in the history of English democracy—originally the purest form of democracy with the law of cultivation 'from above'—is generally *more hostile* than friendly to higher forms of knowledge. Historically it was the democracies of *liberal* origins that fostered positive science and developed it for all. Unthinking emotional democracies of the *great masses* become the greatest *enemies* of rational positive science even when they effectively express themselves with respect to the state in a parliamentary fashion, inappropriate to them; when, above all, they write the doctrine of so-called 'immediate action' upon their banners; and, generally, wherever they appear in

175

history. On the other side, they fall prey all the sooner to vague myths, which one might call prospective *'class myths'*. This is proven by the eschatological myths, ranging from those of the German farmers' wars to the still existing 'myth' of revolutionary syndicalism[167] and Russian *Bolshevism's myth* of a 'general world strike', 'world revolution', and Russia's special 'mission' to do these things and 'liberate the world', a myth which is nourished by strong Marxist, eastern Jewish Russian orthodox, and pan-Slavic sources. Bolshevism tolerates science only to the extent that it can be of *technical-capitalistic* service.[168] But Western *metaphysics* and philosophy are suppressed by all means of censorship and indexing and with such consistency and rigidity as only the medieval Church, from time to time, had attempted to apply to them! The *Fascist* movement likewise developed the foggiest metaphysical 'myth' of all, which, in its biological, activist center, is absolutely *hostile to knowledge* and *irrational*.[169] The 'popular' movements only could have grown out of a soil that the older democracies were preparing 'from below'. But they dig their own mother's grave wherever they are successful. For these movements came about in part through extensions of the right to vote to women and adolescents—and partly through the opposition of the increasingly inert party mechanisms of parliamentary democracy, which pushed itself into the middle of the people, or masses, and the state. For this reason all these movements have fundamentally common *caesaristic, dictatorial, anti-parliamentary* aims. Certainly these growing movements do not yet have the power to destroy Western science, but the leaping flames of 'agitation' begin to lick its edifice.

On the other hand, these movements are altogether the most remarkable signs of a strong *metaphysical need*. If this need is not sufficiently fulfilled by the new development of a better and *methodic, more rational metaphysics,* conjoined with the positive sciences—and a new European age of relative metaphysics—the edifice of science probably will be destroyed completely. The beginnings of such a new age are contained in all of these above-mentioned movements, at least more so than they are in the weak attempts of 'neo-Romanticism', with which they are curiously united, for example, in the 'youth movements' of the disappointed middle classes of all nations. One cannot doubt that these so-called 'signs of the fall of democracy', especially parliamentary democracy (which, as a constitutional form, has its historical foundational presuppositions in the hyper-scientific theories of reason belonging to the post-absolutist Age of Enlightenment), must also be regarded, if more than transitory, as the greatest danger to the existence and progress of positive *science*. Such phenomena confront us today with such importunity that a person like Lloyd George, full of anxiety, is inquiring about their 'origins', and they appear to justify, at least at first glance, Spengler's perspectives on periods of dictatorship. In any case, they signify the *end* of positivistic scientism as a way of thinking that is, in principle, hostile to metaphysics. Parliamentary democracy's tendency towards self-overcoming, therefore, curiously coincides with the self-overcoming, characterized earlier, of apparent and substitute metaphysics of a materialistic and semi-materialistic nature—the mechanical view of nature—through the completely *formalized* natural sciences. And it also coincides with the self-overcoming of historicism, inimical to metaphysics, through historical *perspectivism*.[170]

Likewise, interesting structures of identity present themselves when we consider the cultural-historical relationship between *societal doctrines* and *political forms of life* that have existed among Western peoples since the collapse of the absolute states.

In terms of public law, no constitution in itself can be generally more favorable to science and the cultivation of knowledge than any other. Only qualitative *identities of style* stand out clearly—for example, between logical deduction from a very few premises as fundamental laws and the centrality of the state and culture, as in France, between the English constitution and prevailing pragmatic induction, and between many equally abstract theories and regional 'preservation' of older local political rights (England). These identities have nothing to do with the enhancement or obstruction of the development of science. They furnish only the *methods* for various *national physiognomies*. *Science,* like philosophy, has both grown and declined equally under the institutions of absolute monarchy, limited monarchy (for example, enlightened despotism), parliamentary monarchy, and parliamentary republicanism. Only theocratic constitutions and those based on mass-rule and Caesarism are, in their nature, deeply *hostile* to it. They exclude the 'educated middle class', which—as Aristotle already stated—has always been the bearer of science and philosophy.[171] But parliamentary democracy, as a sociological phenomenon, has been deeply connected with the spirit of science in the era dominated by liberalism through a number of *common* presuppositions and demands. One of these presuppositions was the general belief that *free discussion* and the play of thesis against thesis, opinion against opinion, lead, in science as well as in the state, to truth and to what is politically 'correct' and, furthermore, can bring about true 'convictions'. 'Freedom will lead you to truth', even though in a principally endless process—that is the *common* belief of science and liberalism.[172] It stands diametrically opposed to the other theory, which invokes the deciding *authorities* also in the question of truth and is based on the competing theory—that of the Gospel—according to which 'the' truth (in an ontological sense) 'makes free', or at least requires a rule of 'experts', as seen already with Socrates in his struggle against Athenian democracy. The absolute, constant, 'eternal truths of reason', belonging to the Age of Enlightenment prior to the 'liberal' epoch, were only the last thin traces of such 'substantial' truth, which during the Middle Ages was still so rich and meaningful. This belief was shattered *simultaneously* by the relativist thinking of *positivist* science and by parliamentary democracy of the liberal age. Even for Kant, science—and through it its object—becomes not an arbitrary but rather a freely determined work of the human mind through 'laws of thought functions', and remnants of the old ontology of reason disintegrate.[173] The long-undermined, static metaphysics of reason, belonging to an absolute truth-capital, collapses as does the belief in an 'absolute' material natural law,[174] upon which the older democracies demanded all their new 'freedoms' and in large part succeeded. The belief in endless discussion as a method of finding what is correct appears in the place of absolute natural law. According to the common belief in this level of knowledge *and* parliamentary democracy (as a political form), natural laws, like legal laws, are certainly in no way materially absolute, as though 'God' were both supreme legislator and guarantor—as was still the case in the epochs of absolutism. But they still are found in every free discussion of opinions (pre-extant, therefore, to acts of cognition) by virtue of the laws of meaning governing discussion that proceeds from rational persuasion. And when such natural and legal laws are 'found', they first are *treated* as laws of the state and *'formulated'* as natural principles! Analogously one thinks of particular 'powers' that actualized the 'natural laws', i.e. in both cases the executive is *subordinated* to the legislature, force and power to the 'law'.[175] Thus—as W. Wundt[176] once summarized this development, pointedly and wittily—first 'God' gave the laws, then 'nature'; then the researcher who finds them assumes responsibility for both, and so they are named after him!

This form of expression may be an exaggeration, but the spirit of the *new epoch* is correctly characterized by it. The new epoch slowly undermines this belief in the localizability of what is right and true by balancing point and counter-point in *political* as well as *scientific* life. In the realm of politics there generally occurs increasing *disintegration* of the old, *genuine political party system,* which rests upon the notion that 'party' is formed not on the basis of specific and expressed interests but simply through some logical or traditional conviction regarding the 'common weal'—a disintegration brought about by all special interest groups, particularly economic ones, which took away the 'good conscience' of the parties and their leaders. Marxist social democracy is the first historical party to justify itself consciously with the material interests of the proletariat. It thereby justifies its 'party existence' ethically and historico-mythically through a historico-philosophical detour: it assigns to the proletariat not only a self-redeeming but a world-redeeming function, because, after the intermediate period of the 'proletarian dictatorship', the class-state will be abolished, and thus the 'leap into freedom' will be successful *for all.* Only by means of this doctrine did it temporarily regain its good party conscience until the reformist epoch. In science, however, the replacement of scientific liberalism appears as *the spirit*—it is not dependent upon special theories of philosophy—*of conventionalism and Pragmatism,* which simply 'tries' to posit its 'presuppositions' and justify them through their success in order to guarantee the logical unity of a 'world-view' or even its own practical 'fruitfulness'. 'Natural laws' become more and more 'laws of large numbers' within this type of thinking. In both cases the result of this new type of thinking is 'fragmentation', leading to the dangers of 'no longer being able to understand one another' and of increasing opportunism among the predominant directions of interest. However, if these dangers are recognized then the *call for metaphysics* can be heard in the sphere of *knowledge*—unfortunately, more often a call for authoritarian ties to an *old* substantial truth, which is offered like merchandise from all sides and generally sold very cheaply to a submissive and desperate conscience. But in the *political* realm one can hear *at the same time* a call for the 'abolition of an antiquated parliamentarism' in favor of a *'dictatorship'* from either the right or the left, and other such things. Thus, liberal scientism and parliamentary democratism have slowly come almost to a halt with these common principles, and occasionally have been replaced by significant literary—non-political—expressions of despair, calls for 'decision', dictatorship, and authority.

With this development also a change in *cultural politics* [*kulturpolitisch*] must come about. Parliamentary democratism means that in the domestic cultural politics of the state all important offices and positions (in the universities and gymnasiums) are to be filled on the basis of parity. Parliamentary democratism encourages, furthermore, the desire for presuppositionless 'theories of *Weltanschauung*' without positing a specific one: there is growing, systematic anxiety especially for theses that valuate and posit. From the view of the *sociology of knowledge,* these two demands are replaced, during the decline of the liberal principle, by the 'federation' [*Bund*], which presumes itself to be in possession again of 'absolute' truth and establishes, outside the civil and ecclesiastical learning institutions, assertions and dogmas all the more daringly the less it can sustain its basis *rationally*. Likewise, even in *politics* such 'federations' of a fascist or communist nature recruit for themselves armed men outside the standing army. Groups that intend to become so 'federated' are everywhere composed of *weak men,* mostly men with a tremendous drive towards submission. No longer do they seek truth and justice, which already is cynically disdained as an 'idea', but rather they seek a 'master' who dictates to them what to do and not do![177] Also, this development has ended in a state of affairs that can only be overcome by a relatively *metaphysical age,* which—in close conjunction with *science,* and not with the mere 'literature' of a 'federation'—could renew the belief in the power of *human reason.* Of course, formal parliamentarism of mere '*Weltanschauung* doctrine' does not suffice here, nor does its connection with 'awaiting' the prophet or a 'prophetic philosophy'—which categorically does not exist—or other 'irrational' sources of cognition, especially 'seers'.[178] Marxism, undermined 1,000 times, and so-called 'scientific socialism' suffice even less. Such a doctrine is nothing but a *utopia* supported by deceptive arguments, which sets itself up as a 'necessary development'—and, in so far as it does contain some truth, is only a significant theory of universal historical development, and as a metaphysics, which it unfortunately is, can only comically affect genuine metaphysics.

Before I examine yet one last and particular set of political developments in regard to its effect upon the world of knowledge— namely, the situation of Europe and the world arising from the World War—one question is to be posed:

Do the *great nations* and world powers better serve the progress of knowledge, or do the *small nations*? The question has often been posed but has been generally answered unsatisfactorily. One thing is certain and has been known for a long time: cultures of knowledge, especially those of positive science, are dependent, to high degrees, upon territories and peoples that possess a plurality of political powers moving back and forth and also represent, in respect to politics, the *individualities* of peoples and tribes. Already Guizot recognized within the incomparable *complexity of Europe*— in contrast to the relatively uniform and colossal Asian empires—a first condition for Europe's liberalism, viz. its relative humanitarianism and active spirit of freedom, in general. The *balance* between the tendency of the temperate climate in northern Europe to compel one to work and that in southern Europe to give enjoyment of the world more elbow-room, is to be added to this, as is the concentrated geo-political arrangement of Europe. The many different city cultures of Greece—in contrast to Rome, whose intellectual achievements certainly did not grow in its later periods—and the rich individual tribal groups and manifold political adversaries in Germany—in contrast to an increasingly united France since Richelieu and in contrast to the British 'Empire', whose spiritual energy has become absorbed by practical considerations—are relative *advantages* for the progress of sciences and especially for different *types* of knowledge. Opposition from religious denominations also increases the *freedom* of science—much as such opposition limits the possibility of unity in *metaphysics*. The plurality of class-distinctions, the multiplicity of country and city estates, and the back-and-forth movement of their struggles, are all equally an advantage for the development of the sciences—to the extent that they must suffocate all tranquil research—but not very significant to metaphysics, which requires quieter and broader possibilities to spread through a relatively uniform humanity. Also war, where it is neither war of extermination nor tends to pull whole peoples down into the proletariat, has itself given steady and strong stimulation to the positive sciences, because of the need for war technology. On the other hand, war is adverse to the metaphysical mind as well as to religion, for which reason the vast pacifist empires of Asia provide a fertile soil for the development of religious and metaphysical knowledge. These homogeneous kingdoms, by contrast, give to human understanding an easier image of eternity, produce a feeling of *duration*, and make dispositions alive for the ideation of essences of all fortuitous being. They intertwine the mind and the heart much less in the 'here-and-now relationships' of things and processes, and let come into bold relief much more easily the great *essential and constant problems of existence* and life—the questions: What is 'life'? 'death'? 'youth'? 'suffering'? etc., *in general*—as the life of society itself takes on a relatively constant character. The small states proper, especially the so-called 'neutral' ones, generally have been, when differentiated enough and more sharply in terms of classes, *more favorably disposed* toward strictly *theoretical* culture of knowledge, at least in the epochs of great, world imperialist states, than the great, and especially the world, powers. And this is so for two reasons: first, the neutral nations have a more objective relationship to all other nations; they take all the good things in philosophy and science from the greater states so that they avoid much better the dangers of national isolation and myth formation. What did Jakob Burckhardt owe to his residence in Basel?[179] Second, they are inclined to be more *contemplative and theoretical* because they are further removed from the struggle and

181

hurried tempo of life. We have known since the time of Gustav Schmoller how extremely *few* great researchers have come from cities (Paris, Berlin, London), much as they are to be found in the great cities in their later years—a condition that was mostly unfavorable to their work. It was because of this that countries like Holland, Denmark, Switzerland, Spain, etc., contributed so much to the sciences during Europe's imperial epochs. Because the small states lack the strong technical stimuli, the abundance of materials, and also the wealth that the great, world powers all have, *positive science* is relatively *less* developed among them; but their *metaphysical and philosophical* sense is proportionally *stronger*.

The World War and the sociological structure of knowledge in Europe: specific European problems

With this I come to my last question: What is the specific *effect of the World War on the sociological structure of knowledge in Europe?* The question does not pertain to suppressions and divisions of peoples in the assessment and consideration of their knowledge—divisions which will soon be normal again with the disappearance of the war psychosis. The principle of science's internationality is too potent and is rooted too deeply in man's powerful interests to be placed in question earnestly and for long, even during the Great War. I ask rather: What will be the total effect of the War on the *relationship between positive and technical knowledge, on the one hand,* and *metaphysical tendencies of knowledge,* on the other?

There can be only one answer, at least for someone with any appreciable knowledge of this state of affairs: *never* again will continental Europe regain its *absolute* position as engineer controlling world civilization, a position which it had during the last era prior to the War, when the political and economic constellations of world history were *exceptionally* more favorable. Even England will not have such a position, because the only possible way for it to realize this, i.e. through its 'splendid isolation', has become impossible for many reasons. Meanwhile, not only have the old trans-oceanic, agrarian countries, Russia, and even Eastern cultures under Japan's leadership, learned from Europe the methods and arts for building industries based upon technical and positive science—they have also progressed in this so considerably by themselves that the time is not far away when they can say to Europe: 'The Moor has served his purpose, and the Moor can now go!' The continuation of Europe's birth-rate, as it was from the beginning of the nineteenth century to the World War, will be absolutely impossible—as also will be the enormous *consequences* and *co-causes* of the pace of technology and industrialization and the pace of positive-scientific research. All this will be impossible because of the prevailing tendency towards decreasing [*abnehmenden*] returns from work, a tendency which encounters only episodic counter-forces.[180] Surely America above all has assumed world leadership for continuing, at the same pace, technology and positive science—America, which, within the sphere of Eurasian civilization, has thus far won the great, cruel game of world conflicts. But the increasing mixture of blood in America and the increasing decline of modern America's Anglo-Saxon leadership, its recently rising socialism and communism, its strong drive-based revolutionary cultural currents, directed against Anglo-Puritan tradition,[181] its prodigious relationship with China and the great Eastern cultures—in which it not only *gives* but also *takes* (as is often entirely forgotten)—all of this will eventually give rise to a leading type of man who also bears a *relatively* more *contemplative* and warmer character.[182] I do not wish here to touch on the degree and dangers of American-Japanese tensions.

On the other hand, because there are some few but profound commonalities that exist between the German mind and the Russian character—namely, 'to live alternately between two zones of being,'[183] a metaphysical-religious one and an earthly, practical one—through the outcome of the War, through the downfall of Czarism, and in view of the new, strong needs of Russia for German aid in her unceasing industrialization, a new type of *East-West cultural interpenetration* will arise. Within this cultural interpenetration I do not mean to include vague literary theories or political 'ideas' and 'programs' that are half Russian and half German. Rather, I mean an *oncoming* and eventual *sociological process of culture and knowledge,* which is yet to be comprehended as a whole. This problem has little to do with an arbitrary, political 'orientation' towards the East or the West, or with whether there will be in the future a permanent end to *the* history to which Leopold v. Ranke referred as that of the 'Germanic-Romance peoples'. In any case, an *easing of tensions,* if not for the West generally then at least for America and England, is to be expected from a vigorous economic and technological trade with Russia, which gains significance for the sociology of knowledge in the act of giving and receiving. For the Anglo-Saxon fear that the 'negligent debtor'—if one allows him to work so that he can pay his debts—will again become for America and England the old 'danger' to world economic competition, will decrease when the technological and economical flow of the traffic is led into directions where potential frictions would be relatively fewer.

But *for a sociology of knowledge* all of these factors point to the *same thing* that we observed in other developments: they point to

183

the fact that hereafter in Europe more room and more spiritual energy will *become free* for long-neglected *scholarly, philosophical and metaphysical tasks*. This will occur *even without a planned* slow-down in the rate of economic and technological development—which does not exist as a 'danger' to scientific and technological progress (because of the decrease in the abnormally great stimuli [*Antriebe*], resting upon foregone world situations, for a now impossible rate of population growth). These have been lodged all too much in the German mind and its predispositions and too deeply rooted in it to be destroyed completely by the excessive realism of the post-Bismarckian period and the quixotic nature of Positivism, unknown in such degrees even to Western peoples and England at that time. Actually, it is not positive science and technology but Positivism, scientism, and technicism that will recede throughout Europe, and probably to a considerable extent throughout the entire world, in favor of a tendency toward theory or philosophy. Positivism, scientism, and technicism relate to scientific technology as does nationalism to good national feelings. And they are, as we saw, highly dangerous in the long run to science and technology because they will let technology drown in industry and let science drown in technology. Europe, which prepared all too much to encompass the earth with its civilization in so short a time—Europe, this all too loud and all too chubby-faced boy—needs to find a limit—indirectly, yet self-imposed (because its methods spread all too quickly)—to its hyper-activeness in order to reach a degree of contemplation and restfulness so that it will also rediscover in *metaphysics* a new promise, temper the hyper-pragmatization and politicization of its churches in favor of more flexible but more ensouled religious unifications—using for its example the East but also its own great pre-Reformationist and pre-Tridentinist past of universal religiosity—and *give up* its anarchistic political methods, which culminated in power-coalitions based upon the struggle for *non*-European markets and led to such widespread *self-destruction*. In the future Europe will have to *think first of itself* and only then of the Persian Gulf, Kiautschau, Morocco, Tripolis, and whatever places—not vice versa. It will have to think first about the *minimum common metaphysical convictions* that will make *possible* a fruitful cooperation of its sciences and prevent their degeneration into Positivism, romanticism, or proletarianism—and only then must it consider industrial evaluations of their results. I do not mean to say, 'It ought to be so'! This *will* probably be the case because all Europe's developments toward the logical meaning of ideal and real factors, which co-determine knowledge, converge in this one goal.

184

But we foresee this development of things with some probability so that it would not be surprising if the new situation that arose from the Dawes report [*Dawesgutachten*], born—at least in part—out of the once again renewed spirit of expertise science [*Wissenschaft*], does not express itself in an *enterprise* and in a *lasting institution of a sort related to the sociology of knowledge* [*wissenssoziologischer Art*]. All great researchers and intellectual leaders who, no matter what their *Weltanschauung* and political conviction may be, consciously advocate the old power-politics on behalf of this new political methodology and exposure, resting upon the increased international productivity of economic work, must themselves be clear of the fact—as they are in France, as I personally was able to determine recently—that such a political methodology, should it be more than the momentary image of a passing election and should it gain *permanence,* also requires a *new* intellectual atmosphere conducive to the sociology of knowledge, and it requires a new location and an institution from which this atmosphere could radiate in all directions. One such institution would be a *'European university',* like that toward which the international intellectual organization linked to the League of Nations is striving with a fundamentally correct basic attitude.

This is not the place to outline specifically the present state of practical negotiations and submit them to criticism. Here it should only be stated that the very *idea* of such a university and the firm will to realize it *must never become lost.* Apart from important personal understandings among the philosophic and scientific *leaderships* of nations concerning cooperation of their nations in all aspects of philosophy and science, the first obligation of such a university would be not what I previously referred to as a 'new exchange of the *Weltanschauungs* belonging to global cultural units', but rather to attend to *specific European tasks.* In matters of the humanities, the common root of European philosophy, the arts, science, religion in history, and the little-known interweavings, absorptions, and influences among the minds of nations, must receive special attention. In respect to state and economy, one question that would have to be central is that which J. M. Keynes formulated, in his preface to Harold Wright's book on *Population,* as the 'most interesting world problem'—among the problems, at least, to which time will give us an answer—namely, 'whether economic progress will continue after a short interval of recovery and restoration, or whether the glorious times of the nineteenth century were a passing *episode'.* The answer toward which Keynes and I tend in regard to this question does not need to be given. Whatever it is, though, the very examination of this question on the basis of population theory and history, politics, and the history of law and the state, absolutely requires an institution that raises the fundamentally *new* position of the European continent in international relations at last to clear awareness and more sober, realistic judgment, as well as counteracting, sharply and clearly, the foolish dreams of historical inertial efficacy and the dullness of purely attitudinal and emotional politics, which still settles like fog over large circles of European nations and spreads a thick haze across their mental vision. As Wright points out:

> As long as national jealousy dictates the actions of statesmen, while the same statesmen summon all to increase once again the number of citizens in the interest of war, as long as the individual classes within every single economy continue to reduce the outcome of production through dispute over its distribution, as long as the *tragic circle* endures to the extent that when population increases and productivity of labor decreases both peoples and classes find more and more reason for this dispute.

As long as this continues there is no chance for Europe to regain any bearable place in the affairs of the world. 'There are two means by which one can meet this impending danger: first, by increasing productivity and, second, through the limitation of births. Both are inevitable if our future should become bearable'.

It seems to me that one way to obtain new stimuli for fruitful *cooperation* among the humanities and social sciences, which both methodologically and in their contents became more restricted to national interests during the nineteenth century, is the following: channel the aforementioned and similar visions of a European university—understood as a *dynamic center of pan-European enlightenment*—into *national* institutions of knowledge and universities, whereby the reputable faculty of such a university would disseminate at home what they learned there by teaching, and whereby, at the same time, the national universities would also credit the students for the semesters they spent studying at the new European university.

It need not be mentioned again that, in addition, the problems of a serious and strict theoretical *sociology of knowledge* could at such an institution receive advancement and clarification corresponding to their importance and significance, which in our country have so long been overlooked.

Notes

Introduction

1 For example, David Riesman, *The Lonely Crowd: A Study of the Changing American Character* (New Haven: Yale University Press, 1950); and Philip E. Slater, *The Pursuit of Loneliness: American Culture at the Breaking Point,* rev. ed. (Boston: Beacon Press, 1976).

2 See, e.g. the descriptions of the modern experience of work in Studs Terkel, *Working* (New York: Pantheon Books, 1974).

3 Slater, p. 177.

4 *Man's Place in Nature* (1928), trans. Hans Meyerhoff (New York: Noonday Press, 1961), p. 4.

5 *The Decline of the West,* trans. Charles Frances Atkinson, 2 vols (New York: Alfred A. Knopf, 1928).

6 *The Crisis of European Science and Transcendental Phenomenology: An Introduction to Phenomenological Philosophy,* trans. David Carr (Evanston: Northwestern University Press, 1970); and *Phenomenology and the Crisis of Philosophy,* trans. Quentin Lauer (New York: Harper & Row, 1965).

7 For example, *The Question Concerning Technology and Other Essays,* trans. William Lovitt (New York: Garland, 1977); and 'Letter on Humanism', trans. Edgar Lohner, in *Philosophy in the Twentieth Century,* ed. William Barrett and Henry D. Aiken (New York: Random House, 1962), III, pp. 271–302.

8 e.g. *The Revolt of the Masses* (New York: Norton, 1932); and *Man and Crisis,* trans. Mildred Adams (New York: W. W. Norton, 1958).

9 e.g. *The Meaning of History* (1936), trans. George Reavey (Cleveland: World Publishing, 1962), esp. chs VIII and IX, 'The End of the Renaissance and the Crisis of Humanism: The Advent of the Machine' and 'The Disintegration of the Human Image'; and *The Fall of Man in the Modern World,* trans. Donald A. Lowrie (Ann Arbor: University of Michigan Press, 1961). Although not directly concerned with the theme of 'crisis', *The Destiny of Man,* trans. Natalie Duddington (New York: Harper & Row, 1960), most clearly illustrates Scheler's profound influence upon Berdyaev.

187

10 As quoted by Thomas J. Sheehan, Introduction to Scheler 'Reality and Resistance: On *Being and Time,* Section 43,' *Listening* 12, no. 3 (Fall 1977): 61.

11 See Peter Berger's and Thomas Luckmann's judgment on the significance of this work in *The Social Construction of Reality: A Treatise in the Sociology of Knowledge* (Garden City, N.Y.: Doubleday, 1966), pp. 4–9.

12 *Formalism in Ethics and Non-Formal Ethics of Values: A New Attempt toward the Foundation of an Ethical Personalism,* trans. Manfred S. Frings and Roger L. Funk (Evanston: Northwestern University Press, 1973).

13 Ed. Lewis Coser, trans. William Holdheim (New York: The Free Press of Glencoe, 1961).

14 Trans. Peter Heath (London: Routledge & Kegan Paul; New Haven: Yale University Press, 1954).

15 e.g. *Introduction to Positive Philosophy,* trans. Frederick Ferre (Indianapolis: Bobbs-Merrill, 1970), pp. 4–8.

16 *Phenomenology and the Crisis of Philosophy,* esp. pp. 181–6.

17 e.g. Carl G. Hempel, *Aspects of Scientific Explanation and Other Essays in the Philosophy of Science* (New York: The Free Press; London: Collier-Macmillan, 1965), p. 245.

18 *Phenomenology and the Crisis of Philosophy,* p. 185.

19 *The Will to Believe and Other Essays in Popular Philosophy* (New York: Dover, 1956), p. 7.

20 As quoted by Lewis Mumford, *The Myth of the Machine: The Pentagon of Power* (New York: Harcourt Brace Javanovich, 1970), p. 434.

21 As quoted by Henry James, in *The Letters of William James,* ed. Henry James (Boston: Atlantic Monthly Press, 1920), II, 2.

22 *Speculum Mentis, or The Map of Knowledge* (London: Oxford University Press, 1924), p. 277.

23 pp. 5–7.

24 e.g. B. F. Skinner, *Beyond Freedom and Dignity* (New York: Bantam, 1972), pp. 189–91.

25 John Dewey noted, for example, that modern capitalism continues to justify itself upon the principles of freedom (viz. 'free market', 'free economy', etc.) but everywhere treats workers and consumers as though their behaviour is determined (viz. not free). *Individualism—Old and New* (New York: Capricorn Books, 1929), pp. 12–13.

26 *The Nature of Sympathy.*

27 *Community and Society (Gemeinschaft und Gesellschaft)* (1887), trans. Charles P. Loomis (New York: Harper & Row, 1963).

28 Ibid., p. 35.

29 p. 166.

30 *Natural Law and the Structure of Matter,* Address, delivered on the hill of Pnyx, Athens, 3 June 1964 (London: Rebel Press, 1970), p. 45.

31 Herbert Spiegelberg, 'The Phenomenology of Essences: Max Scheler (1874-1928)', *The Phenomenological Movement: A Historical Introduction* (The Hague: Martinus Nijhoff, 1960), I, pp. 228–70; and David Lachterman, 'Translator's Introduction' to Scheler, *Selected Philosophical Essays* (Evanston: Northwestern University Press, 1973), pp. xix-xxii.

32 e.g. Aron Gurwitsch, *Studies in Phenomenology and Psychology* (Evanston: Northwestern University Press, 1966), pp. 110–11.

33 'Phenomenology and the Theory of Cognition', *Selected Philosophical Essays*, p. 137. This is a relatively early writing (1913-14) and hence offers what is still very much a phenomenology of consciousness and not the phenomenology of vital drive found in Scheler's later thinking.

34 *Erkenntnislehre und Metaphysik,* ed. Manfred S. Frings, vol. 11 of the *Gesammelte Werke* (Bern: Francke Verlag, 1979). Such a view, long dismissed by biologists, has recently been given support by Max Delbrück, 1969 recipient of the Nobel Prize in Physiology and Medicine. See his article 'Mind from Matter?,' *The American Scholar* 47 (Summer 1978): 339–53.

35 'Idealism and Realism', *Selected Philosophical Essays,* p. 344.

36 *Erkenntnis und Arbeit,* in *Die Wissensformen und die Gesellschaft,* ed. Maria Scheler, vol. 8 of the *Gesammelte Werke* (1960), p. 372.

37 Fragment 44.

38 'Reality and Resistance: On *Being and Time,* Section 43,' trans. Thomas Sheehan, *Listening* 12, no. 3 (Fall 1977): 61–73. Frings, *Person und Dasein: Zur Frage der Ontologie des Wertseins* (The Hague: Martinus Nijhoff, 1969) is the most extensive study comparing Scheler and Heidegger. See also Frings, 'Heidegger and Scheler', *Philosophy Today* 12 (Spring 1968): 21–30.

39 'Idealism and Realism'.

40 Scheler, 'The Idea of Peace and Pacifism', trans. Manfred S. Frings, *Journal of the British Society for Phenomenology* 7 (October 1976): 154–66; 8 (January 1977): 36–50.

41 'The Meaning of Suffering', trans. Daniel Liderbach, S. J., in *Max Scheler (1874-1928) Centennial Essays,* ed. Manfred S. Frings (The Hague: Martinus Nijhoff, 1974), p. 121.

42 *Fundamentals of Concept Formation in Empirical Science,* vol. II, no. 7, *International Encyclopedia of Unified Science* (Chicago and London: University of Chicago Press, 1952), p. 7.

43 For additional discussion of Scheler's phenomenological sociology, see Ernest Ranly, C.PP.S., *Scheler's Phenomenology of Community* (The Hague: Martinus Nijhoff, 1966); Alfred Schutz, *The Problem of Social Reality,* vol. 1 of the *Collected Papers,* ed. Maurice Natanson (The Hague: Martinus Nijhoff, 1967), esp. 'Scheler's Theory of Intersubjectivity and the General Thesis of the Alter Ego,' pp. 150–79; and Frings, *Zur Phänomelogie der Lebensgemeinschaft,* Beihefte zur Zeitschrift für philosophische Forschung, vol. 24 (Meisenheim an Glan: Verlag Anton Hain, 1971).

44 'Ordo Amoris', *Philosophical Essays,* p. 117. That all intentional acts are *value* intentionalities is another point on which Scheler's phenomenology is critical of Husserl's. Husserl, though, seems to acknowledge this point in several places; for example, in the *Idee der Phänomenologie,* ed. W. Biemel (The Hague: Martinus Nijhoff, 1958), p. 14, he says: 'Naturally the universal phenomenology of reason also has to solve the parallel problems of the correlation of valuing and value, etc.' And in *Ideas: General Introduction to Pure Phenomenology,* trans. W. R. Boyce Gibson

(London: Collier-Macmillan, 1962), p. 93:

> this world is not there for me as a mere *world of facts and affairs*, but, with the same immediacy, as a *world of values*, a *world of goods*, a *practical world*. Without further effort on my part I find the things before me furnished not only with the qualities that befit their positive nature, but with value-characters such as beautiful or ugly, agreeable or disagreeable, pleasant or unpleasant, and so forth [emphasis in the original].

45 'Idealism and Realism', *Selected Philosophical Essays*, p. 354.

46 *Formalism in Ethics*, pp. 90–100.

47 'Ordo Amoris', p. 100.

48 Ibid., p. 98.

49 For example, Lewis A. Coser, *The Functions of Social Conflict* (New York: The Free Press, 1956), p. 36; Joseph R. Gusfield, *Symbolic Crusade: Status Politics and the American Temperance Movement* (Urbana: University of Illinois Press, 1963); Carl Nordstrom, Edgar Z. Friedenberg, and Hilary A. Gold, *Society's Children: A Study of Ressentiment in the Secondary School* (New York: Random House, 1967); and Svend Ranulf, *Moral Indignation and Middle Class Psychology* (Copenhagen: Munksgaard, 1938).

50 *Genealogy of Morals*, pt. I, sec. 14, as quoted by Scheler, *Ressentiment*, p. 45.

51 *Ressentiment*, pp. 45–6.

52 Ibid., p. 53.

53 Ibid., pp. 58–9.

54 Ibid., p. 154.

55 Ibid., p. 162.

56 Ibid., pp. 172, 174.

57 'Soziologie des Erkennens', *Die Zukunft* 67 (May 1909): 236–46.

58 1 (1921): 28 ff.

59 *The German Ideology* (1845-46) (New York: International Publishers, 1963), esp. pp. 27–43.

60 *The Essence of Philosophy* (1907), trans. Stephan A. Emery and William T. Emery, University of North Carolina Studies in the Germanic Languages and Literatures, no. 13 (Chapel Hill: University of North Carolina Press, 1954).

61 e.g. *The Protestant Ethic and the Spirit of Capitalism*, trans. Talcott Parsons (London: George Allen & Unwin, 1930).

62 *Sociology and Philosophy*, trans. D. F. Pocock (New York: Free Press, 1953).

63 Peirce's insights into the sociology of knowledge are found throughout his *Collected Papers* but primarily in vol. VI, *Pragmatism and Pragmaticism*, ed. Charles Hartshorne and Paul Weiss (Cambridge, Mass.: Belknap Press of Harvard University Press, 1960), especially 'The Fixation of Belief', 5.358–387. See also John E. Smith, 'Community and Reality', in *Perspectives on Peirce: Critical Essays on Charles Sanders Peirce*, ed. Richard J. Bernstein (New Haven and London: Yale University Press, 1965), pp. 92–119, reprinted in Smith, *Themes in American Philosophy: Purpose, Experience, and Community* (New York and London: Harper &

Row, 1970), pp. 80–108; and R. Jackson Wilson, 'Charles Sanders Peirce: The Community of Inquiry', *In Quest of Community: Social Philosophy in the United States, 1860-1920* (London and New York: Oxford University Press, 1970), pp. 32–59. The late Irish social philosopher, John O'Malley, was exploring the implications of Peirce's semiotics for the sociology of knowledge at the time of his death in 1976. See his *Sociology of Meaning* (London: Chaucer, 1970), an important contribution to the sociology of knowledge.

64 Ranly, p. 71; J. Macquet, *The Sociology of Knowledge,* trans. John F. Locke (Boston: Beacon Press, 1951), pp. 9, 19–28; and Karl Mannheim, *Essays on the Sociology of Knowledge*, ed. Paul Kecskemeti (London: Routledge & Kegan Paul, 1952).

65 *Wissensformen und die Gesellschaft*, p. 12.

66 May 2, 1909, James Papers, Houghton Library, Harvard University, MS, 450, quoted by permission of the Houghton Library.

67 In writing to Husserl requesting a letter of recommendation Scheler suggested: 'Because the gentlemen do not want to have a neo-Hegelian also a word about my relation to Bergson and the new American realists, who are fighting over there against Hegelianism'. August 4, 1913, Max Scheler Archives, Bayerische Staatsbibliothek, Munich.

68 (1910) in *Memories and Studies* (New York: Greenwood Press, 1968), pp. 265–96.

69 Herbert Spiegelberg observes:

Husserl knew practically nothing about Peirce, and . . . Peirce knew about Husserl only the wrong things . . . [But] There is, to be sure, a very different story in the case of Max Scheler. True, even Scheler knew of Peirce only through James' *Pragmatism* [?!]. But in his extended discussion of pragmatism, on which he had been working since 1910 [1909], it was Peirce who served as its main representative. In fact, he took pragmatism of the Peircean variety so much more seriously than Husserl that, in his book on epistemology and sociology ['Der philo-sophische Pragmatismus', in *Die Wissensformen und die Gesellschaft* (Leipsig: Der Neue Geist, 1926), pp. 259–323], he devoted a lengthy chapter to an examination of its claims. Also, while rejecting pragmatism as a correct interpretation and account of our primary relation to the world and likewise of the nature of positive science, Scheler's interest in Peirce (whose name he misspells consistently as Pierce [?]) rather than in James [!?] would seem to be another example of Scheler's uncanny flair for what was philosophically significant, long before others had discovered it ['Husserl and Peirce's Phenomenologies: Coincidence or Interaction', *Philosophy and Phenomenological Research* 17 (December 1956): 183–84].

C. Wright Mills noted that 'Besides the French and German traditions . . . the literature of American pragmatism is replete with unexploited suggestions for the sociology of knowledge'. And he pointed out that Scheler alone had picked up these suggestions in his *Erkenntnis und Arbeit*. 'Bibliographical Appendix' to *Contemporary Social Theory*, ed. Harry Elmer Barnes, Howard Becker, and Frances Bennett Becker (New York and London: D. Appleton-Century, 1940), p. 892.

70 Review of *Versuche zu einer Soziologie des Wissens,* ed. Max Scheler, *The American Journal of Sociology* 31 (1925-26): 262, 264. See also Small's review of *Kölner. Vierteljahrshefte für Sozialwissenschaften,* ed. Max Scheler, *et al., The American Journal of Sociology* 27 (July 1921): 92–94. Cf. Mead, *Mind, Self and Society* (University of Chicago Press, 1934), and *The Philosophy of the Act,* ed. Charles W. Morris (University of Chicago Press, 1938).

71 'American Neglect of a Philosophy of Culture', *The Philosophical Review* 35 (September 1926): 434–46; 'The "Formal Problems" of Scheler's Sociology of Knowledge', *The Philosophical Review* 36 (March 1927): 101–20; 'The Doctrine of "Illusion" and "Error" in Scheler's Phenomenology', *Journal of Philosophy* 24 (1927); 624–33; 'Max Scheler 1874-1928', *The Philosophical Review* 38 (1929): 547–88.

72 e.g. *The Problems of Social Reality.*

73 Howard Becker Papers, University of Wisconsin, Madison, Box 2, Folder III, 1–3; 'Some Forms of Sympathy: A Phenomenological Analysis', *Journal of Abnormal and Social Psychology* 26 (1931): 58–68; Review of *Wesen und Formen der Sympathie, American Journal of Sociology* 33 (1927-28): 637–42; Becker, and Harry Elmer Barnes, *Social Thought from Lore to Science* (Washington: Harren Press, 1952), esp. 'Phenomenology and Scheler' and 'The Forms of Knowledge and Society', pp. 906–13, *et passim*; Becker, and Helmut Otto Dahlke, 'Max Scheler's Sociology of Knowledge', *Philosophy and Phenomenological Research* 2 (March 1942): 309–22. Also, Dahlke, 'The Sociology of Knowledge', in *Contemporary Social Theory,* pp. 64–89.

74 e.g. 'The Roots of Social Knowledge', *American Journal of Sociology* 32 (July 1926): 59–79, although Cooley's analysis here is restricted to knowledge that produces effects. Also see *Social Organization: A Study of the Larger Mind* (New York: C. Scribner, 1909), and *Human Nature and Social Order,* rev. ed. (New York: Charles Scribner, 1922).

75 e.g. 'Sociology and the Social Sciences: The Social Organism and the Collective Mind', *American Journal of Sociology* 26 (January 1921): 401–24; 27 (July 1921): 1–21; (September 1921): 169–83, reprinted in *Introduction to the Science of Sociology* (University of Chicago Press. 1921), pp. 187–241.

76 e.g. 'Is There a Social Mind?,' *American Journal of Sociology* (March 1922): 561–72; (May 1922): 721–36.

77 e.g. *Experience and Nature* (Chicago and London: Open Court, 1925); *The Quest for Certainty* (New York: Putnam, 1929); *Philosophy and Civilization* (New York: Minton, Balch, 1931); and *Logic: The Theory of Inquiry* (New York: H. Holt, 1938).

78 C. Wright Mills, who studied Scheler's sociology of knowledge while a student of Becker, made some preliminary studies of the implications of American pragmatism for the sociology of knowledge. 'Methodological Consequences of the Sociology of Knowledge', *The American Journal of Sociology* 46 (November 1940): 316–30, explores the pragmatisms of Peirce, Dewey, and Mead. He notes, too, how numerous American sociologists immediately rejected the notion that sociological factors could influence ideas and the cognition of truth. See also Mills, 'Language,

Logic, and Culture', *American Sociological Review* 4 (1939): 670–80.
79 'Scheler's Theory of Sympathy and Love', *Philosophy and Phenomenological Research* 2 (March 1942): 273–91.
80 Wilfried Hartmann, 'Max Scheler and the English-Speaking World', *Philosophy Today* 12 (Spring 1968): 31–41, provides a detailed response to McGill and others who have made similar charges (e.g. Marvin Farber) and identifies other factors that have undermined interest in Scheler among English-speaking peoples.
81 In this regard, too, Scheler's thinking parallels that of American philosophers such as Josiah Royce, Ralph Barton Perry, and Wilbur Marshall Urban, who, like Scheler, made value prior to knowledge. Scheler would have been in full agreement with Royce's claim that:

> The question, 'How ought I to conceive the real?' is logically prior to the question. 'What is the real itself?' ... the ought is prior in nature to the real; or the proposition, I ought to think so, is prior to the proposition, this is so (*Lectures on Modern Idealism,* ed. J. Lowenberg (New Haven: Yale University Press, 1923), p. 237).

And he would have agreed too with Urban that 'because meaning lies above all being, and because meaning is inseparable from value, that the value-centric predicament cannot be escaped'. *The Intelligible World* (New York: Macmillan, 1929), p. 64. And again, 'We cannot detach meanings and values from mind without becoming unintelligible'. 'Philosophy of Spirit: Idealism and the Philosophy of Value', in *Contemporary Idealism in America* (New York: Macmillan, 1932), p. 106. See also Perry, *General Theory of Value: Its Meaning and Basic Principles Construed in Terms of Interest* (Cambridge, Mass.: Harvard University Press, 1967).
82 'The Forms of Knowledge and Culture', *Philosophical Perspectives,* trans. Oscar A. Haac (Boston: Beacon Press, 1958), pp. 13–49.
83 Ibid., p. 134, fn 26.
84 Ibid., p. 47.
85 Ibid., p. 42.
86 Knowledge of salvation also tends to become non-communicable but for very different reasons. Because it is knowledge that seeks the ultimate source and absolute unity of all things, knowledge of salvation sees language as a barrier to be overcome; words can only fragment that unity. Thus, knowledge of salvation is expressed in simple phrases, such as 'All is One', single words, such as 'Om', and often silence.
87 'The Forms of Knowledge and Culture', p. 43.
88 e.g. Alfred Jules Ayer, *Language, Truth and Logic* (New York: Dover Publications, 1952).
89 'Man in the Era of Adjustment', *Philosophical Perspectives*, pp. 94–126.
90 Thus a genuine feminist movement, according to Scheler, is not one whereby women merely seek access to the prevailing male values and institutions (e.g. equal rights and opportunities) but a radical overthrow of those male values and institutions and a liberation of long repressed female values. 'The Meaning of the Feminist Movement', trans. Manfred S. Frings, *The Philosophical Forum* 9 (Fall 1977): 42–54.

Chapter 1 Cultural sociology

1 We therefore reject Max Weber's restriction of sociology to the understandable subjective and objective 'meaning content' (objective mind). If anyone ever had a conviction about the divine or about the course of his people's history or about the structure of the stars in the heavens 'because' he belonged to the privileged class, or to an oppressed class, or because he was a Prussian officer or a Chinese coolie, or because his blood represented this or that racial mixture, neither this man nor any other need *know'* or even surmise that this is the case. In the last analysis we agree with the statement of Karl Marx that it is the *being* of man (though not, of course, merely his economic or 'material' being, as Marx implies) toward which his whole possible *'consciousness'*, 'knowledge', and the limits of his understanding and experience are directed.

2 A major part of our pure sociology, the theory of the *essential forms* of grouping, is given in our *Der Formalismus in der Ethik und die materiale Wertehik* (1913-1916), section VI, B 4, ad 4 [5th ed., ed. Maria Scheler, vol. 2 of the *Gesammelte Werke* (Bern: Franke Verlag, 1966), pp. 509 ff.; *Formalism in Ethics and Non-Formal Ethics of Value: A New Attempt toward the Foundation of an Ethical Personalism,* trans. Manfred S. Frings and Roger L. Funk (Evanston: Northwestern University Press, 1973), pp. 519 ff.].

3 I shall develop both theories in detail in my *Philosophische Anthropologie* [ed. Manfred S. Frings, vol. 12 of the *Gesammelte Werke* (forthcoming)]. That a theory of the development of human drives and an energetics of drives is the foundation of the whole sociology of real factors, has been most clearly seen in recent times by W. McDougall.

4 A much more thorough grounding of this law will come with the concluding volume of our series *Schriften zur Soziologie und Weltanschauungslehre* [4 vols (1923-4); 2nd ed. (in one vol.), ed. Maria Scheler, vol. 6 of the *Gesammelte Werke* (1963)], entitled *Probleme der Geschichtsphilosophie.* [Scheler never completed this volume. Manuscripts for it, along with other writings on the philosophy of history, will appear as vol. 13 of the *Gesammelte Werke,* ed. Manfred S. Frings.]

5 The *lowering* of the value-level of everything spiritual, such as a particular religion or a form of art, through its increased *propagation* and its growing among the masses, is therefore an inescapable law of the human realization of meaning and value.

6 The law of the few pioneers and the many imitators was first explained by G. Tarde in the book *Les Lois de l'imitation* (1895) [*The Laws of Imitation,* trans. Elsie Clews Parson (New York: Holt, 1903)].

7 I need not say that the laws of *meaning* have nothing to do with the pairs of opposites, 'true-false', 'good-evil', 'beautiful-ugly', 'holy-profane', and analogous value-opposites.

8 Here I am steering clear of the metaphysical 'meaning' of this fate.

9 A noteworthy division of the kinds of 'objective mind' has been given by Hans Freyer in his book *Zur Theorie des objecktiven Geistes,* (1923).

10 Besides the essential laws of the foundations of acts of a static kind, there are also developmental phase-laws with a logical importance scarcely recognized, which have nothing to do with the so-called phase-rules of a

majority of actual development series (rules obtained by comparing these series), nor with mere lines of direction, lines of *singular* factual development, like the development of *one* earthly humanity or of *this* Prussian state, it being meaningless to speak of a law in the latter case. A 'direction' can be disclosed by a temporal phase-comparison of a group (a major direction, a secondary one, a cul-de-sac, a tangent, etc.), but it is never a law. The developmental phase-law, on the other hand, is an *essential law* of the transition from stage to stage, in such a way that the peculiar factual beginning and ending of the development remains variable. It controls all *possible* factual development.

11 That is, the history of the formation, growth, decline, and structural changes of mind *itself,* not of its accomplishments and its works.

12 This theory, rejected here, of the unity of 'rational human nature' is assumed throughout by 'Humanism', which in turn is *only* European (as E. Troeltsch states in his *Historismus*) [*Der Historismus und seine Probleme,* vol. I, *Das logische Problem der Geschichtsphilosophie,* vol. 3 of the *Gesammelte Schriften* (Tübingen: J. C. B. Mohr (P. Siebeck), 1922)]. It was taken over from the Church's teaching, eliminating only original sin and inherited guilt.

13 I have dealt with the 'functionalizing' of the objective knowledge of essences at length in 'Probleme der Religion', in my book *Vom Ewigen im Menschen* (1921) [4th ed., ed. Maria Scheler, vol. 5 of the *Gesammelte Werke* (1954), pp. 100–353; 'Problems of Religion', in *On the Eternal in Man,* trans. Bernard Noble (London: Student Christian Movement Press, 1960; New York: Harper, 1961), pp. 105–356].

14 See E. Troeltsch, *Der Historismus und seine Überwindung*; also his lectures in England edited by Friederich v. Hügel, pp. 76 ff. [*Christian Thought: Its History and Application*, Lectures Written for Delivery in England during March 1923, ed. Baron F. von Hügel (University of London Press, 1923), pp. 24 ff.; 2nd ed. (New York: Meridian Books, 1957), pp. 53 ff.]

15 Strict proof for the above statements and the justification for the term 'idea' of man, in contrast to the empirical concept, 'man-animal', I will supply in my *Anthropologie.*

16 O. Bumke, *Kultur und Entartung,* 2nd ed. (Berlin, 1922).

17 Here also I must refer to the *Philosophischen Anthropologie* which is to appear soon and on which I have worked for years. References to this problem were already given in my study 'Zur Idee des Menschen' (1915), in *Von Umsturz der Werte* [4th ed., ed. Maria Scheler, vol. 3 of the *Gesammelte Werke* (1955), pp. 171–95; 'On the Idea of Man (1915)', trans. Clyde Nabe, *Journal of the British Society for Phenomenology* 9 (October 1978): 184–98].

18 See my book *Der Formalismus in der Ethik und die materiale Wertethik,* especially the chapter concerning the relativity in values and valuation, section V, 5 [*Formalism in Ethics,* pp. 275–95].

19 See my article on Comte's law of three stages. Über die positivistische Geschichtsphilosophie des Wissens', in *Schriften zur Soziologie und Weltanschauungslehre* (*Moralia*).

20 This holds with considerable generality for all primitive discoveries and tools, such as primitive ground-working instruments (shoe, plowshare) or primitive ways of making fire (fire bore, etc.). They are *at once* tools and

NOTES TO PAGES 44–51

cultic forms of expression of an inner experience. The idea of human generation and the concept of the earth as a fructifying mother are always the principal modes of these discoveries.

21 W. Dilthey, *Einleitung in die Geisteswissenschaften* (1883) [in vol. 1 of the *Gesammelte Schriften* (Leipzig: B. G. Teubner, 1924)]; also, *Die geistige Welt*, I and II (*Gesammelte Schriften*, vol. 5, ed. George Misch, Leipzig, 1924). In his admirable introduction, Misch points out that Dilthey departed more and more from the viewpoint of his early period, strongly influenced by Positivism, that metaphysics was a poetry of concepts (*op. cit.,* pp. XXXVII, LXI ff.). However, even in 'Das Wesen der Philosophie' [originally in *Systematische Philosophie* (Berlin: B. G. Teubner, 1907), pp. 1–27] we still read, 'hereafter, metaphysics, as a universally valid science, is forever destroyed' (*Gesammelte Schriften,* vol. 5, p. 371) [*The Essence of Philosophy,* trans. Stephen A. Emery and William T. Emery, University of North Carolina Studies in the Germanic Languages and Literatures, no. 13 (Chapel Hill: University of North Carolina Press, 1954), p. 32].

22 Thus, for example, H. Scholz in his *Religionsphilosophie,* 2nd ed. (Berlin, 1923).

23 See the distinguished work by F. Tönnies, *Kritik der Öffentlichen Meinung* (Berlin, 1922).

24 On the essence and source of national ideologies see *Schriften zur Soziologie und Weltanschauungslehre* (*Nation*), and also my study on 'cant' ['Zur Psychologie des englischen Ethos und des cant'] in the supplement to my book *Der Genius des Krieges und der deutsche Krieg* (1915) [in *Politische-pädagogische Schriften,* vol. 4 of the *Gesammelte Werke* (forthcoming)].

25 See E. Troeltsch, *Soziallehren der christlichen Kirchen und Gruppen* (1912) [*The Social Teaching of the Christian Churches,* 2 vols. trans. Olive Wyon (London: George Allen & Unwin, 1931)].

26 I have presented a precise characterization of these essential forms of human groups in the book *Der Formalismus in der Ethik und die materiale Wertethik,* section VI, B, ad 4. The divisions made there are expanded by Edith Stein in *Beiträge zur philosophischen Begründung der Psychologie und der Geisteswissenschaften,* in the *Jahrbuch für Philosophie und phänomenologische Forschung,* vol. 5 [(1922); 2nd ed. (Tubingen: Max Niemeyer, 1970)]. Th. Litt has a similar aim in his work *Individuum und Gemeinschaft,* 2nd ed. (Leipzig, 1924).

27 For the exact course of this dispute consult even today K. Prantl, *Geschichte der Logik im Abendlande* [4 vols] (Leipzig, 1855-70).

28 See the concluding chapter, 'Probleme der Religion', in my book *Vom Ewingen im Menschen.* In a very lopsided way, such monopolies and privileges of the period of youth are taken as metaphysical knowledge by Bachofen, whose method is criticized very learnedly even by C. A. Bernoulli in his great work, *J. J. Bachofen und das Natursymbol* (1925); they are taken even more radically by L. Klages (cf. Bernoulli) in *Mensch und Erde* (1920), *Von Wesen des Bewusstseins* (1921), and *Von kosmologischen Eros* (1922). In this theory, spawned by Romanticism (Savigny), the whole history of man's knowledge is a progressive 'decadence', in as

lopsided a view as that of Positivism, which makes that history a steady progress.

29 'Direction' is the primary, 'guidance', the secondary function of mind. Direction *holds out a value-idea,* while guidance is the *repression or release of the instinctive impulses* whose assigned *movements* bring the idea to *realization.* Direction conditions.the *kind* of control.

30 As assumed, for example, by the economic view of history.

31 I believe I can show elsewhere that on this fundamental point concerning the basic relationship between the history of mind and the history of real factors in general, such otherwise widely divergent scholars as W. Dilthey (see *Die Einbildungskraft des Dichters,* 1887), E. Troeltsch (see the introduction to *Die Soziallehren der christlichen Kirchen und Gruppen,* 1912 [*The Social Teaching of the Christian Churches,* vol. I, pp. 23–37]), and M. Weber (see his preliminary writings on the sociology of religion, 1915-1919) are in *essential* agreement with the above. [Scheler is probably referring here to Weber's essays published posthumously as *Gesammelte Aufsätze zur Religionssoziologie,* 3 vols (Tübingen: J. C. B. Mohr [P. Siebeck], 1920-1); *The Protestant Ethic and the Spirit of Capitalism* (a section of vol. I), trans. Talcott Parsons (London: George Allen & Unwin, 1930); 'The Protestant sects and the spirit of Capitalism', 'The social psychology of the world religions', and 'Religious rejections of the world and their directions' (also sections of vol. I), in *From Max Weber: Essays in Sociology,* trans. and ed. H. H. Gerth and C. Wright Mills (New York: Oxford University Press, 1946), pp. 267–359; *The Religion of China: Confucianism and Taoism* (the remainder of vol. I), trans. and ed. Hans H. Gerth (New York: Free Press, 1951); *The Religion of India: The Sociology of Hinduism and Buddhism* (vol. II), trans. and ed. Hans H. Gerth and Don Martindale (New York: Free Press; London: Collier-Macmillan 1958); *Ancient Judaism* (vol. III), trans. Hans H. Gerth and Don Martindale (New York: Free Press, 1952)].

32 This occurs in my *Philosophischen Anthropologie* along with the fourth volume of my series on sociology and the theory of *Weltanschauung* (*Probleme der Geschichtsphilosophie*).

33 W. Wundt, *Völkerpsychologie,* vol. VIII, 'Die politischen Gesellschaft' [1917]. The recent work of Fr. Oppenheimer, *System der Soziologie,* vol. I (Jena, 1922), is also very much to the point. More critical is A. Vierkandt in *Gesellschaftlehre* (Stuttgart, 1922), pp. 320 ff. For ourselves we do not accept the view of Vierkandt that the state could 'also' have arisen purely by association—not only as a dominative organization.

34 See my treatise on capitalism (1914) in *Vom Umsturz der Werte,* where I first demonstrated the significance of the contrast between wealth born of power and political power born of wealth.

35 The theory of this order of the development of drives forms an important part of our forthcoming *Philosophischen Anthropologie.*

36 See Fritz Graebner, *Das Weltbild der Primitiven* (Munich, 1924), a book which explains in an unusually clear way the contrast between patriarchal and matriarchal cultures, affecting the whole *Weltanschauung,* technology, and character of law. He also pursues brilliantly the idea that the high cultures represent mixtures of these two cultures and always have

the tendency to equalize this inner contrast through a political monarchy of a more or less despotic form.

37 G. Schmoller, *Die soziale Frage,* vol. I (Munich, 1918).

38 See the examples cited by Graebner, *op. cit.,* pp. 48 ff.

39 A good historical treatment of the rise of the theory of class conflict is given by W. Sombart in his article 'Die Idee des Klassenkampfes', *Weltwirtschaftliches Archiv* 21, no. 1 (1925) [:22–36].

40 See Max Weber's economic sociology (*Wirtschaft und Gesellschaft* (Tubingen, 1922), in which he points out the political nature of the Customs Union and its antagonisms to the economically determined tendencies of the industry of Rhenish Westphalia and Silesia and to East Prussian agriculture. [*Economy and Society: An Outline of Interpretive Sociology,* 3 vols, trans. Guenther Roth, Claus Wittich, *et al.* (New York: Bedminster Press, 1968).]

41 What is meant here are not the causes of the war in the historical sense of a single causality that includes the free-will acts of ruling persons, but only the sociological cause of the *tensions* that the war presupposes, therefore the causes of the *'potentiality'* of war. Between France, the leading factor in the creation of the power coalition hostile to the Central Powers, and the Central Powers themselves, there existed no outstanding *economic* tensions. (The question of 'guilt', which concerns only the spiritual personal repression or non-repression of the given tensions, continues in any case; it is not touched at all by a sociological explanation of the possibility of war.) Even if we assume, however, that with the eventual new structure of Europe, economy and its interweaving of interests had gained a victory over power politics and its spirit, still there would have continued between this new Europe, in which economy as a history-making factor had first achieved its complete victory over the power politics of the states, and the *non*-European world, even Russia, the essentially and primarily *power* political relationship of the past. In a third case, a possible confrontation with Japan by the nations of America and Australia, blocking the expansion of the fecund Japanese people, the opposition of *race and blood*, and the cultural differences between the Whites and the Yellows founded therein, would overshadow all other conflicts of whatever kind, and a victory by Japan, as the *new* 'pioneer' of Western civilization, would resurrect the *oldest* motive for the birth of political power structures and would again raise racial conflict as the primary causal factor in history.

42 For proof I must refer to my *Philosophischen Anthropologie,* the sections on 'Trieblehre' [Theory of drives] and 'Theorie des Altes und des Tod' [Theory of aging and death]. For the order of the origin of the basic drives, see Paul Schilder's *Medizinische Psychologie [für Artzte und Psychologen]* (Berlin, 1924) [*Medical Psychology,* trans. David Rapaport (New York: International Universities Press, 1953)], which contains about the best treatment we have in German.

43 We cannot show more precisely here that there is a connection between this point and metahistory, or the metaphysics of history.

44 That we in no way need to be concerned about the spiritual culture of the coming distinctly and purely economic age, that the industrial wealth

of the segments that control the basic production and energy supply for the whole economy could extensively replace the present state and what the state has done for spiritual culture, in fact without subjecting the spiritual culture to the service of the interests of political governing classes in the same degree as the state, having its origin in power politics, was accustomed to doing—for this I think North America is already a significant example, not only in itself but also in what Americans have achieved outside their country (China). This is also an important model for our European industry, which in this respect is still but little enlightened. In this regard the disadvantages of industrialism and capitalism were only temporary phenomena, and it is precisely a sharply delineated economism that will offset these disadvantages.

Chapter 2 Formal problems

1 The Age of Enlightenment saw in a one-sided way only knowledge as the condition for society. It was an important realization of the nineteenth and twentieth centuries to see that there is also a societal condition for knowledge.

2 The detailed epistemological reason for this proposition is found in my book *Wesen und Formen der Sympathie* (1923), part C [6th ed., ed. Manfred S. Frings, vol. 7 of the *Gesammelte Werke* (1973), pp. 209 ff.; *The Nature of Sympathy*, trans. Peter Heath (London: Routledge & Kegan Paul; New York: Yale University Press, 1954), pp. 213 ff.)].

3 See also *Wesen und Formen der Sympathie,* part A, II [*The Nature of Sympathy*, pp. 8 ff.], where all these problems become thoroughly clarified.

4 See also *Wesen und Formen der Sympathie* (1923), p. 143 [vol. 7 of the *Gesammelte Werke,* p. 130; *The Nature of Sympathy,* p. 122].

5 That cooperation is 'productive' is, when correctly understood, an important insight of O. Spann, [*Kurzgefasstes*] *System der Gesellschaftslehre* (Berlin, 1914) [later ed. entitled *Gesellschaftslehre*; 4th ed., ed. Horst Kitzmantel, vol. 4 of the *Gesamtausgabe* (Graz: Akademische Druck- und Verlagsanstalt, 1969)].

6 An example of a radical sort is the withholding of the holy writings of Indian religion and metaphysics from the lowest caste of the Sudras. One might also think of the withdrawing (although only to a very limited extent) of the freedom to read the Holy Scriptures by the medieval Church from the laity, a policy similar to secret diplomacy.

7 I must refer to the complete foundation for these laws of order contained in volume I of my metaphysics, which will soon appear [*Erkenntnislehre und Metaphysik,* ed. Manfred S. Frings, vol. II of the *Gesammelte Werke* (1979)].

8 I use the term *co*-conditioned. We must reject 'sociologism' (in analogy to psychologism). Sociologism fails to distinguish forms of thinking and intuition from 'forms of being', nor does it distinguish the successively reflexive *knowledge* of both forms from those forms *themselves*. It also reduces forms of being (like Kant) to forms of thinking and intuition, but (in contrast to Kant) it reduces subjective forms again to forms of work and speech of 'society'. This theory of origins corresponds to a conventionalism in logic and theory of knowledge first taught by Th.

Hobbes ('True and false exist only in human speech') and later held by H. Poincaré. Sociologism makes a '*fable convenue*' not only out of history but out of *the scientific world-view as a whole*. De Bonald was mistaken in this in that he believed social consensus to be a criterion of truth when he sought all knowledge in the 'tradition of language' and reduced language itself to primal revelation. His theory is only an ecclesiastical-orthodox analogy to positivist 'sociologism', for example, that of Durkheim. Such erroneous paths in sociology can be avoided if we reduce all functional *forms* of thought to *functionalized comprehensions of essences* in the *things themselves,* and if we see only in the respective *selections* within these functionalizations a product of *society* and its *perspectives of interests* as opposed to a 'pure' realm of meanings. That in this case there *can* also be a 'pre-logical level' of human society, as Lévy-Bruhl justifiably assumes, I showed briefly in my 'Remarks' ['Zu W. Jerusalems "Bermerkungen"'] to W. Jerusalem's essay ['Bemerkungen zu Max Schelers Aufsatz "Die positivistische Geschichtsphilosophie des Wissens und die Aufgaben einer Soziologie der Erkenntnis"'] in the *Kölner Vierteljahrsheften für Sozialwissenschaften* I, no. 3 (1921) [pp. 35–9 and 28–34, respectively]. [Scheler's remarks are reprinted in vol. 6 of the *Gesammelte Werke*, pp. 327–30. And Scheler's essay on which Jerusalem commented appeared in vol. I, no. 1 of the same journal, pp. 22–31, and later, in a revised form, as Über die positivistische Geschichtsphilosophic des Wissens (Dreistadiengesetz),' *Moralia* (1924), in *Schriften zur Soziologie und Weltanschauungslehre,* vol. 6 of the *Gesammelte Werke,* pp. 27–35; 'On the positivistic philosophy of the history of knowledge and its law of three stages', trans. Rainer Koehne, in *The Sociology of Knowledge: A Reader,* ed. James E. Curtis and John W. Petras (New York: Praeger; London: Duckworth, 1970), pp. 161–9.]

9 Concerning these divisions on the basis of patriarchal totemistic culture, see Graebner's previously mentioned work, *Das Weltbild der Primitiven* [Munich, 1924]; and Lévy-Bruhl, *Das Denken der Naturvölker* [trans. from the French by Wilhelm Jerusalem] (Vienna, 1921) [*Les Fonctions mentales dans les societés intérieures* (Paris: F. Alcan, 1910); *How Natives Think,* trans. Lilian A. Clare (London: George Allen & Unwin, 1926).].

10 See the end of my essay 'Die Idole der Selbsterkenntnis' (1911), contained in *Vom Umsturz der Werte* ['The idols of self-knowledge', in *Selected Philosophical Essays,* trans. David R. Lachterman (Evanston: Northwestern University Press, 1973), pp. 3–97]. Thus the powers of the soul presumed by Plato correspond exactly to the 'estates' of his state—in line with his proposition that the state is 'the great human'.

11 M. Weber, C. Schmitt, in his remarkable book *Politische Theologie* (1922), and O. Spengler, in some of the *profound insights* of his well-known work, have begun to develop these problems also for the well-delineated areas of society. Concerning the structural identities between *political monarchies* in high cultures and *monotheism,* see Graebner, *op. cit.,* pp. 109 ff., 'Gottesglaube und Staatsgedanke'.

I have shown such structural identities in Greek city particularism and Greek polytheism (and in the Platonic pluralistic conception of 'ideas'). I have shown this also in the stoic theory where the world becomes *one* large common being (cosmopolitics), one large 'empire', in which increasing universalism and individualism condition one another; in the high Middle Ages' conception of the world as a 'realm of levels' of profound forms, and in the feudal estate structure of that society; in the images of world and soul belonging to Cartesianism and what follows it (Malebranche); in the absolute principalities; in Calvinism and the new concept of sovereignty (in both cases intermediary powers and *'causae secundae'* are eliminated in favor of the *'causae primae'*); in the essential relationships between Deism (God as engineer and machinist), the theory of free trade, political liberalism, associative psychology, and statics ('balance of power') in the methods of foreign policy; in the social individualism of the Age of Enlightenment and Leibniz's system of monads; in the conception of organic nature as a 'struggle of life' and in practical-ethical utilitarianism and economic competition and class struggle (Karl Marx, Malthus, Darwin); in Kant's theory where it is held that understanding produces first an order for nature and the moral world from out of a chaos of sensations and drives, and in the development of the Prussian state (see my essay *Die Ursachen des Deutschenhasses* [(1917, 1919), in *Politisch-pädagogische Schriften*, vol. 4 of the *Gesammelte Werke* (forthcoming)]); and for the relationship between the sociological foundation of Czarism and the religious thinking of orthodoxy. See also, in my book *Wesen und Formen der Sympathie,* the elaborations on the structural resemblances that the systems of theism, materialism, and monism have with *constitutional forms* of the state. See, too, C. Schmitt, *op. cit.*

12 See also my book *Wesen und Formen der Sympathie* (1923), pp. 277 ff. [vol. 7 of the *Gesammelte Werke, pp.* 232 ff.; *The Nature of Sympathy,* pp. 238 ff.], and Graebner, *op. cit.,* p. 132: 'Attributes play a much greater role in primitive thought, whereas substances play a much smaller role than they do with us today. The animal and human organism is most strongly grasped as substance'. In addition, L. Lévy-Bruhl in his book, translated by Jerusalem, *Das Denken der Naturvölker* (Vienna, 1921), as well as his new foundational book, *La Mentalité primitive* (Paris, 1922) [*Primitive Mentality,* trans. Lilian A. Clare (London: George Allen & Unwin; New York: Macmillan, 1923)]; see also Jerusalem's essay ['Die soziologische Bedingtheit des Denkens und der Denkform'] in the collection of essays entitled *Versuche zu einer Soziologie des Wissens* (Munich, 1924), edited by myself. It would be a serious error to think that these analogies pertain only to primitive anthropomorphisms; they also exist in *high* cultures.

13 See in this regard my article 'Weltanschauungslehre, Soziologie und Weltanschauungssetzung', in *Schriften zur Soziologie und Weltanschauungslehre.*

14 See my examples in the article cited above.

15 The biggest categorial difference would have to lie between matriarchal and patriarchal cultures. In this regard see Graebner, *op. cit.*

16 See, in *Der Genius der Kriegs* (1915), the chapter 'Die geistige Einheit Europas'.

17 Let me refer here to the most important ones (I will deal in detail with such parallel coordinations in my *Philosophischen Anthropologie*):

    1 between the developmental stages of man's psychic functions until

the age of two, i.e. the 'becoming human', and psychic functions and accomplishments of the highest adult mammals (Edinger);

2 between the image of the human soul as changed by pathological symptoms and those animal psyches in which the said function does not yet exist (for example, the absence of functions of the frontal lobe in higher apes);

3 between normal psychic behavior among primitive groups and pathological (or exceptional) psychic adult behavior within high levels of civilization (see Schilder, Storch, *et al.*);

4 between psychic life of primitives and the human child (see W. Stern, E. Jaensch, Bühler, Koffka, Lévy-Bruhl);

5 between the elimination of higher centers in the genesis of the human mass soul among higher civilizations and the animal soul, or animal societies (see Scheler, *Wesen und Formen der Sympathie*);

6 between the instant formation of the mass psyche within civilization and the enduring psychic direction of the primitive 'horde' (see also Freud's *Massenpsychologie und Ich-Analyse* [(1921); *Group Psychology and the Analysis of the Ego,* trans. James Strachey, International Psycho-Analytical Library, no. 6 (London: Boni & Liveright, 1922)]);

7 between the mass psyche and pathological or exceptional consciousness (hysteria, depersonalization, hypnosis; see S. Freud, *op. cit.*, and P. Schilder, *Über das Wesen der Hypnose* [1922]);

8 between the behavior of the masses and that of children;

9 between normal child behavior and the pathological or abnormal behavior of adults ('retardations' and infantilism);

10 between the formation and disintegration of psychic functions in individual stages of life and parallel stages in aging peoples and civilizations (see my work 'Altern der Kulturen', in *Kölner Vierteljahrsschrift für Sozialwissenschaft* [never published]);

11 between child-like and female psychic life (the child-like 'constitution' of the female psycho-physical organism), moreover between differential sex psychology and patriarchal and matriarchal cultures; and

12 between the mentality and the degree of cultivation within the lower classes and the degree of cultivation of an 'elite' that lived three or more generations before ('theory of levels' of knowledge and class structure).

18 See in this regard Graebner, *op. cit.*, ch. IV, 'Weltanschauungen und Sprachen'.

19 See F. Tönnies's profoundly penetrating investigation into the history of philosophical terminology [*Philosophische Terminologie in psychologisch-soziologischer Ansicht*] (1906) [originally published as 'Philosophical Terminology' (Welby Prize Essay, 1898), trans. Mrs Bosanquet, *Mind* 8 (1899): 289–332, 467–91; 9 (1900): 46–61].

20 The groupings, technologies, and authorities with which the 'Word of the Holy Spirit' within the religious communities of Christian cultural fields are connected, for example, Papacy, church council, parish, and the *'spiritus sanctus internus'* of Luther, perhaps created the most important religious-*sociological* character of these communities.

21 See *La Mentalité primitive*, p. 520: 'L'espace y est plutôt senti que

conçu; ses directions sont lourdes de qualités, et chacune des ses régions, comme on l'a vu (*op. cit.,* pp. 231–9), participe de tout ce qui s'y trouve habituellement'. [*Primitive Mentality,* p. 445: 'In it space is felt rather than imagined; its directions are weighted with qualities, and each of its regions, as we have already seen (*vide supra,* ch. VII, pp. 208–15), participates in all that is usually found there'.]

22 Concerning the lack of sense for the *'causae secundae'* among primitives, see Lévy-Bruhl, *op. cit.,* especially the end.

23 Concerning the arguments for 'insight' among animals, see W. Köhler, *Intelligenzprüfungen bei Menschenaffen,* 2nd ed. (Berlin, 1921) [*The Mentality of Apes,* trans. Ella Winter (London: Kegan Paul Trench, Trubner; New York: Harcourt, Brace, 1925)]; see also the partly critical, very fine elaborations by K. Bühler, *Die geistige Entwicklung des Kindes,* 3rd ed. (1923) [*The Mental Development of Children: A Summary of Modern Psychological Theory,* trans. Oscar Oeser (London: Kegan Paul, Trench, Trubner; New York: Harcourt, Brace, 1930)]; K. Koffka, *Die Grundlagen der der psychischen Entwicklung* (1921) [*The Growth of the Mind: An Introduction to Child-Psychology,* trans. Robert Morris Ogden (London: Kegan Paul, Trench, Trubner; New York: Harcourt, Brace, 1924)]; O. Selz, *Über die Gesetze des geordneten Denkverlaufs* (1913/1922); and G. Kafka, 'Tierpsychologie', in vol. I of the *Handbuches der vergleichenden Psychologie* (1922).

24 E. Jaensch, [*Über*] *Der Aufbau der Wahrnehmungswelt* [*und ihre Struktur im Jugendalter*] (1923).

25 Concerning this *essential* difference between man and animals in general, which is not to be confused with the *empirical* difference, i.e. the anatomical, physiological, and psychological difference between primitives and higher apes, see my forthcoming *Philosophischen Anthropologie*; also, as a propaedeutic for this see my already quoted essay 'Zur Idee des Menschen', in the book *Vom Umsturz der Werte.*

26 See my aforementioned work on A. Comte's law of the three stages.

Chapter 3 Material problems

1 Concerning the definition of 'folk-religion', see the introduction to the book by A. Dieterich, *Mutter Erde,* 2nd ed. (Leipzig, 1905). Concerning the division among religions in general and the structure of the history of religions, see the rewarding essay by J. Wach, *Religionswissenschaft* (Leipzig, 1924).

2 In this regard see Fritz Graebner, *op. cit.* [*Das Weltbild der Primitiven* (Munich, 1924)].

3 Concerning Greek religion, see Bachofen, *Das Mutterecht* (1861) [vols 2 and 3 of the *Gesammelte Werke* (Basel: B. Schwabe, 1948)]; also C. A. Bernoulli's rich new (aforementioned) work on Bachofen [*J. J. Bachofen und das Natursymbol* (1925)], which, however, requires a sharp critique.

4 Very relevant in this regard is E. LeRoy, *Dogme et critique* (Paris, 1907).
   E. Troeltsch has so thoroughly investigated the various forms of religious communities in Christian-Western culture (church, sect, and mystical

community are his main concepts) that we need not discuss them further here.

5 Max Weber, in his *Religionssoziologie*, has provided us with a large number of examples concerning the reciprocal relationship between class structure and the religious object-world; still more examples can be found. The sociology of religion must avoid a causal interpretation of these corresponding relationships, whether they be made in terms of an economic or any other conception of history. [Scheler is referring here either to Weber's *Gesammelte Aufsätze zur Religionssoziologie*, 3 vols (Tübingen: J. C. B. Mohr [P. Siebeck], 1920–1), or to his 'Religionssoziologie: Typen der religiösen Vergemeinschaftung', bk. II, ch. IV of *Wirtschaft und Gesellschaft* (Tübingen: J. C. B. Mohr [Paul Siebeck], 1922), part III of the series *Grundriss der Sozialökonomik*. In the fourth edition (1956) this essay appears as part II, ch. V, pp. 245–381, and bears the title 'Typen der religiösen Vergemeinschaftung (Religionssoziologie)'. 'Religious groups (the sociology of religion)', trans. Ephraim Fischoff, in *Economy and Society*, vol. II, pp. 399–634; also published separately as *The Sociology of Religion* (Boston: Beacon Press, 1963).]

6 See also A. v. Harnack's excellent work on the gnostic Marcion, *Marcion: Das Evangelium vom Fremden Gott* (Leipzig, 1921).

7 Similarly, Positivism temporarily became, at the time of [Emile] Combes [1835–1921], a philosophy of the *state* both in Brazil and in France, as did Hegel's philosophy in Prussia under the ministry of Altenstein. In Soviet Russia, Marxism is the state philosophy.

8 R. Eucken, *Geschichte der philosophischen Terminologie* (1879).

9 In this regard, see W. Dilthey, *Die geistige Welt*, vol. 5 of the *Gesammelte Schriften* [Leipzig: B. G. Teubner] (1924), pp. 339 ff. 'Das Wesen der Philosophie' (1907) is a most highly instructive essay for the sociology of knowledge.

10 On these points I must retract a judgment I made in my necrology of E. Troeltsch; see ['Ernst Troeltsch als Soziologe'] *Kölner Vierteljahrshefte für Sozialwissenschaften* III, no. 1 (1923-24): 7–21.

11 Shortly before the downfall of the last Manchu dynasty, which had ruled since 1644, Kung was deified (1907) by an imperial decree. Laotse has been deified in Taoism for 2,000 years. Similarly Buddha, Akbar, and Ali have been deified. See in this volume my essay on the 'Soziologie der Vergottung' [unpublished manuscript].

12 One reads in R. Rolland's book, *Mahatma Gandhi* (German translation, Zurich, 1923) [*Mahatma Gandhi: The Man Who Became One with Universal Being*, trans. Caroline D. Groth (New York and London: Century; London: Swarthmore Press, 1924)], about the anxiety and fear that the great Indian religious revolutionary leader had even before the tendency began here and there in India to deify him. He knew: if he were deified his whole movement would be *practically* and politically *dead*.

13 R. Sohm has shown everything essential here in his admirable works on the origin of ecclesiastical law.

14 In this regard, see my 'Probleme der Religion' in *Vom Ewigen im Menschen* [1921]; also, H. Scholz, *Religionsphilosophie* (1921); R. Otto, *Das Heilige* (1920) [*The Idea of the Holy: An Inquiry into the Non-Rational*

Factor in the Idea of the Divines and Its Relation to the Rational, trans. John W. Harvey (London: Humphrey Milford, Oxford University Press, 1923)]; J. Wach, *Religionswissenschaft* (1924).

15 But how slowly was this biomorphic-theological conception of the heavens abandoned! For Aristotle his *'nous'* and 'spirits of the spheres' are still 'astronomical hypotheses' (see in this regard W. Jaeger's recent work on Aristotle [*Aristoteles: Grundlegung einer Geschichte seiner Entwicklung* (Berlin: Weidmann, 1923); *Aristotle: Fundamentals of the History of His Development,* trans. Richard Robinson (Oxford: Clarendon Press, 1934)]). Even Kepler originally introduced, in his work *De harmonice mundi,* spirits of spheres, which are supposed to act according to his three laws of planetary motion. Newton was the first to displace completely this conception with his own law of masses. But his 'gravity' still retained something thoroughly magical, as Mach pointedly said (see *Geschichte der Mechanik*), despite his explanation that he wished 'to establish no hypotheses', because it retained a timeless, distant effect and conspiration of the masses in absolute, yet demonstrable, space. [Scheler is probably referring here to Mach's *Die Mechanik in ihrer Entwicklung: Historisch-kritisch dargestellt* (Leipzig: F. A. Brockhaus, 1883); *The Science of Mechanics,* trans. T. J. McCormack (Chicago: Open Court; London: Watts, 1893).] One can say that Einstein was the first to eliminate these last remnants of 'magic' from our image of nature through his general theory of relativity.

16 See, above all, his valuable work on Jansenism [*Die Staats- und Sozial-lehren der französischen Jansenisten im 17. Jahrhundert*] (1914); further-more, the contribution in the writings in memory of Max Weber (1925) [Scheler is probably referring to Honigsheim's 'Zur Soziologie der mittelalterlichen Scholastik (Die soziologische Bedeutung der nominalistis-chen Philosophie),' in *Hauptprobleme der Soziologie: Erinnerungsausgabe für Max Weber,* ed. Melchior Palyi (Munich and Leipzig: Verlag von Duncker & Humbolt, 1923) vol. II, pp. 173-238], as well as his contributions to my anthology, *Versuche zu einer Soziologie des Wissens* (Munich, 1924).

17 J. W. Kirijewski [Ivan V. Kirèevskiĭ], *Drei Essays* [translated from Russian to German by Harold von Hoerschelmann] (Munich, 1921).

18 Those knowledgeable in the internal politics of German universities know that professorships tied to the Church strive to fill the chairs of philosophy with experimental psychologists or with researchers who only subsequently seek to synthesize positive-scientific results, i.e. with persons who are harmless to the teachings of the Church. The more the churches and their representatives join in the techniques of guiding and directing their masses and the more pragmatic they become, the closer becomes their cooperation with the world of work, technology, industry, and positive science. For this reason they represent today a ten-times stronger bastion against the mystical tendencies of the times (against the bad tendencies, for example, anthroposophy, as well as the good tendencies) than science.

19 Concerning the 'proofs for God', what the Jesuit P. H. Lennertz says about the contradiction contained in my theory of the cognition of God

['Probleme der Religion'] in respect to the teachings of the Catholic Church, is thoroughly correct. It was—as I had to learn only slowly and painfully—a complete mistake of all 'modernistic' theology to regard the Thomistic philosophy as *separable* from the ecclesiastic dogmatics. For the ontological validity of the principle of causality itself is *dogma* today—and it is not only the 'that' but also the *method* of metaphysics and the cognition of God by causal conclusions. See P. H. Lennertz, *Schelers Konformitätssystem und die Lehre der katholischen Kirche*, (Cologne, 1924).

20 Concerning the primacy of the ideal of the wise man in China as opposed to the Western ideal of the hero, see the interesting remarks by R. Wilhelm in *Chinische Lebensweisheit* (Darmstadt, 1922).

21 See the recent outstanding work (already cited) by Jaeger, *Aristoteles* (Berlin, 1923), on the genesis of the Aristotelean system.

22 In this formal meaning of scholasticism there is, however, also a Protestant 'scholasticism'. It is a twofold one: it is the still strong Aristotelean Scholasticism introduced by Melanchthon, which ends up in Wolffianism, and it is the Protestant scholasticism of the nineteenth century, the Kantian scholasticism, which likewise reveals the above-mentioned mark of 'scholasticism in general'.

23 The present movement of fundamentalism shows that this applies not only to Europe but also to the United States of America. This movement would make it law that nothing may be taught in any state school (and even the universities!) that contradicts the Bible, especially any form of the theory of evolution (!).

24 I have shown already in my above-cited essay, 'Weltanschauungslehre, Soziologie und Weltanschauungssetzung', how much I recognize as necessary a theory of *Weltanschauung* and consider it especially practically applicable for adult education and, on the other side, how much I regard a pure theory of *Weltanschauung* as a precondition for posited philosophy. But this discipline must not attempt to replace metaphysics—just as the science of religious studies must not replace theology.

25 We refer to the dissertation by Paul Landsberg at the University of Cologne, *Wesen und Bedeutung der platonischen Akademie* [: *Eine erkenntnissoziologie Untersuchung*] (Bonn, 1923), which appeared in the series *Schriften zur Philosophie und Soziologie,* edited by myself; moreover, we wish to make reference to Landberg's remarks in 'Zur Erkennt nissoziologie der aristotelischen Schule', in my anthology, *Versuche zu einer Soziologie des Wissens* (Munich, 1924).

26 So judges even W. Wundt in his book *Die Nationen und ihre Philosophie* (1915).

27 A series of such constructions are found in suitable form in the book by N. Hartmann, *Grundzüge einer Metaphysik der Erkenntnis* (1921); see also W. Dilthey, 'Das Wesen der Philosophie', *op. cit.*

28 A scholastic translation of the Aritotelean proposition: 'The human soul is in a certain way everything'. Giordano Bruno, Nicolaus Cusanus, and Leibniz take up this idea at the beginning of modern philosophy; Goethe's works are permeated by it. For a new understanding of it see my book *Der Formalismus in der Ethik,* section VI, A 3, d [*Formalism in Ethics,* pp. 396–8].

29 For this reason, W. Ostwald not unfittingly calls the hypo-theses of positive science proto-theses.

30 See in this regard my speech 'Die Formen des Wissens und die Bildung', delivered on the occasion of the tenth anniversary of the Lessing-Hochschule of Berlin (Bonn, 1925). [In *Philosophische Weltanschauung* (1929), in *Späte Schriften*, ed. Manfred S. Frings, vol. 9 of the *Gesammelte Werke* (1976), pp. 85–119; 'The Forms of Knowledge and Culture', in *Philosophical Perspectives,* trans. Oscar A. Haac (Boston: Beacon Press, 1958), pp. 13–49.]

31 Concerning the effect of the philosophy of the seventeenth, eighteenth, and nineteenth centuries on 'public opinion', see Tönnies's deep and significant work.

32 A special investigation by the sociology of knowledge would be needed for the peculiar Pythagorean school, and its strictly Doric, conservative style, with the idea of number and order as its focal point.

33 In this regard see my book on the *Wesen und Formen der Sympathie* (1923).

34 The introduction to my *Philosophischen Anthropologie* will contain a history of man's self-understanding and his relation to sub-human nature and the deity. Is this self-understanding and consciousness of self-value ever increasing throughout the vast stretches of history, a history revealing how an entity only slowly gains a consciousness of its true dignity—or is it only a history of megalomania? We will look into this question.

35 A certain exception is made by Th. Gomperz in his *Griechische Denker* [3 vols] (1893-1909) [*Greek Thinkers: A History of Ancient Philosophy,* 4 vols, trans. L. Magnus and G. G. Berry (London: J. Murray; New York: Scribner, 1901–12)]—it is only that his judgment is everywhere one sidedly positivistic.

36 Descartes said that he wanted to write also for the Turks. H. Bergson stresses with justification the easily understandable, universal style of the great French philosophers in his study 'La Philosophie française' [*Revue de Paris* 3 (May-June 1915): 236–56, and in *La Science française* (Paris: Larousse, 1915), I, 15–37; published as *La Philosophie* (Paris: Larousse, 1915); contained in *Écrits et paroles*, ed. R. M. Mossé-Bastide, Bibliothèque de philosophie Contemporaine (Paris; Presses Universitaires de France, 1957-9), vol. II, pp. 413–36, and in *Mélanges: L'idée de lieu chez Aristote, Durée et simultanéité, correspondance, pièces diverses, documents,* ed. André Robinet (Paris: Presses Universitaires de France, 1972), pp. 1,157–89].

37 In Germany the statesman is almost completely unphilosophical, and the philosopher is almost completely a-practical. The academies are purely scientific and most of the time avoid philosophers (Kant). An organization like the Académie française, where scholars, philosophers, poets, politicians, military people, etc., meet, is impossible in Germany.

38 I do not enter here into a discussion on the national peculiarities of the structures of knowledge. See my essay 'Das Nationale im Denken Frankreichs' (1915), in *Schriften zur Soziologie und Weltanschauungslehre,* and my study on the English 'cant' in the appendix of my book *Der Genius des Kriegs und der deutsche Krieg* (1915); furthermore, see P. Duhem, *Ziel*

und Struktur der physicalischen Theorin (German translation, Leipzig, 1908, with a preface by E. Mach) [*La Théorie physique: son objet et sa structure*. Bibliothèque de philosophie expérimentale, vol. II (Paris: Chevalier & Rivière, 1906); *The Aim and Structure of Physical Theory*, trans. Philip Wiener (Princeton University Press, 1954)], as well as W. Sombart, *Der proletarische Sozialismus* [10th rev. ed. of *Sozialismus und soziale Bewegung*], vol. I [*Die Lehre*], 1924 [*Socialism and the Social Movement*, trans. of 6th German ed. by M. Epstein (London: J. M. Dent; New York: E. P. Dutton, 1909)].

39 Schopenhauer first spoke of metaphysics as 'a sublime conversation among all geniuses of all times and peoples, enduring beyond space and time'.

40 It develops always in contrast to the matriarchal, animistic cultures turned 'inward'.

41 I refer here to the valuable studies in my book *Der Formalismus in der Ethik* [*und die materiale Wertethik* (1913-16)]; furthermore, to the treatise *Erkenntnis und Arbeit* in the present volume [*Die Wissensformen und die Gesellschaft*]. See also what follows. Many good points on the conditions of feelings and drives for perceiving, remembering, and thinking can also be found in R. Müller-Freienfels, *Grundzünge einer Lebenspsychologie,* vols I and II (Leipzig, 1923-5), and P. Schilder, *Medizinishche Psychologie* (Berlin, 1924).

42 See Muckle's instructive work on Count Saint-Simon, in which this point is made very sharply. [Scheler is referring here probably to Muckle's *Henri de Saint-Simon: Die Persönlichkeit und ihr Werk* (Jena: G. Fischer, 1908), or to his *Saint-Simon und die Geschichtstheorie: Ein Beitrag zu einer Dogmenschichte der historischen Materialismus* (Jena: G. Fischer, 1906).]

43 Concerning the reason for a lack of historical sense and for the deficiencies of historiography, in our sense, in the Asian high cultures, see E. Troeltsch, *Der Historismus und seine Probleme* [Tubingen: J. C. B. Mohr (P. Siebeck), 1922]; furthermore, see the many good observations by O. Spengler.

44 R. Jhering, *Der Geist des romanischen Rechts* [*auf den verschieden en Stufen seiner Entwicklung*] (Leipzig, 1852-65), and *Der Zweck im Recht* [2 vols], (Leipzig, 1877-83) [*Law as a Means to an End,* trans. of vol. 1 by Isaac Husik (Boston: Boston Book Company, 1913)].

45 W. Windelband, *Geschichte der Philosophie* (Freiburg, 1892), pp. 298 ff. [(later ed. published as *Lehrbuch der Geschichte der Philosophie*); 15th ed., ed. Heinz Heimsoeth (Tübingen: J. C. B. Mohr [Paul Siebeck], 1957), pp. 323 ff.; *A History of Philosophie, with Especial Reference to the Formation and Development of Its Problems and Conceptions,* trans. of 2nd German ed. by James H. Tufts (New York and London: Macmillan, 1901), pp. 378 ff.].

46 In this regard see E. Troeltsch, *Gesammelte Schriften*, vol. 4 [*Aufsätze zur Geistesgeschichte und Religionssoziologie*], ed. H. Baron (1925), pp. 202 ff. and 297 ff., on Protestantismus' ['Luther, der Protestantismus und die moderne Welt'] and 'Das Wesen des modernen Geistes'.

47 The section 'Psychologie des Alterns' in my forthcoming *Philosophischen Anthropologie* will furnish a thorough foundation for this law, for the individual as well as for cultural groups.

48 See Dilthey's treatises concerning the rise of the Age of Enlightenment in the epoch of the absolute state. [Scheler is referring here to Dilthey's essays 'Die deutsche Aufklärung im Staat und in der Akademie Friedrichs des Grossen', in the *Deutschen Rundschau* 107 (April-May 1901): 21–58, 210–35, incorporated with other related manuscripts into 'Friedrich der Grosse und die deutsche Aufklärung', in *Studien zur Geschichte des deutschen Geistes,* ed. Paul Ritter, vol. 3 of the *Gesammelte Schriften* (1927), pp. 81–205.]

49 Fr. Strich's book *Deutsche Klassik und Romantik [oder Vollendung und Unendlichkeit: Eine Vergleich]* (Munich, 1922), which in its method is oriented around Wölfflin's *Grundbegriffen [Kunstgeschichtliche Grundbegriffe: Das Problem der Stilentwicklung in der neueren Kunst* (Munich: F. Bruckmann, 1915); *Principles of Art History: The Problem of the Development of Style in Later Art,* trans. M. D. Hottinger (London: G. Bell, 1932)], pointedly shows that there is a well-defined type of what is classic and what is romantic, despite the various colorations and historical causes of the positive types of romantic feeling and thinking. But we know very little about the typical *sociological reasons* for the rise of such movements.

50 The American socialist Upton Sinclair in his poignant and perhaps exaggerated book *The Goose-Step* (1924) (translated under the title *Der Parademarsch* [Berlin 1924] gives a very commendable description of such conditions in universities of the United States—a development which will also occur here in Europe.

51 See the fine introduction to this process of becoming by K. Joël, *Der Ursprung der Naturphilosophie aus dem Geiste der Mystik* (Jena, 1906); also see the respective chapters in my book *Wesen und Formen der Sympathie* [(Bonn, 1923), vol. 7 of the *Gesammelte Werke*].

52 In this regard see also my book *Wesen und Formen der Sympathie,* pp. 127 ff. [vol. 7 of the *Gesammelte Werke,* pp. 103–4; *The Nature of Sympathy,* pp. 93–4]; also, E. Lucka, *Die drei Stufen der Erotik* (Berlin, 1917) [*Eros: The Development of the Sex Relation through the Ages,* trans. Ellie Schleussner (New York and London: G. P. Putnam, 1915); *The Evolution of Love,* trans. Ellie Schleussner (London: George Allen & Unwin, 1922)]; and W. Sombart, *Luxus und Kapitalismus* (Leipzig, 1922) [*Luxury and Capitalism,* trans. W. R. Dittmar (Ann Arbor: University of Michigan Press, 1967)].

53 See also Jakob Burckhardt, *Die Kultur der Renaissance in Italien* [1860] in regard to the new feeling of nature [vol. 3 of the *Gesammelte Werke* (Berlin: Rütten & Loenig, 1955); *The Civilisation of the Period of the Renaissance in Italy,* trans. of 3rd German ed. (1877-8) by S. G. C. Middlemore (London: Kegan Paul, 1878), later ed. published as *The Civilisation of the Renaissance*].

54 See the essays by P. Honigsheim in the Max Weber commemorative essays (1923) and in my previously mentioned anthology, *Versuche zu einer Soziologie des Wissens* (1924).

55 'Die Revolution in der Wissenschaft' (1921), in *Aufsätzen zur Geistesgeschichte und Religionsgeschichte* (Tübingen, 1925) [vol. 4 of the *Gesammelte Schriften* (1968), pp. 653–77].

56 E. Mach, *Erkenntnis und Irrtum* (1905).

57 See the article 'Was ist Materie?' in *Naturwissenschaften* 12, nos 28, 29, 30 (1924) [: 561–8, 585–93, 604–11, in the *Gesammelte Abhandlungen*, ed. K. Chandrasekharan (Heidelberg: Springer-Verlag, 1968), II, 486–510]; see also Weyl's pointed judgment on the pioneership of philosophy in the history of physics.

58 M. Dvořák, *Kungstgeschichte als Geistesgeschichte* [: *Studien zur abendländischen Kunstentwicklung*] (Munich, 1924), and H. Schmalenbach. *Leibniz* (Munich, 1921).

59 J. Nadler has shown in his *Die berliner Romantik, 1800-1819* (Berlin, 1921) that it is probable that German romanticism stems from east German colonial tribes.

60 *Wesen und Formen der Sympathie,* part C [*The Nature of Sympathy,* part III].

61 Also, W. Sombart in his book *Luxus und Kapitalismus* (Leipzig, 1922).

62 See also A. Grünbaum in his forthcoming book, *Herrschen und Lieben als Grundmotive der philosophischen Weltanschauungen* (Bonn, 1925). [Scheler wrote the foreword to this work.]

63 How many restrictions Comte bestowed on science on the basis of his narrow sensualism, restrictions which science has ever since broken through! He contested, for example, the existence of a psychology based in self-observation, the cognition of the chemistry of stars, the mechanistic theory of heat, the possibility of a theory of evolution, and the solvability of the problems of the infinity of space, time, matter, etc.

64 This limitation of the goal of cognition remains unknown to most of our great researchers. Only Giovanni Battista Vico established the principle: 'We know only in nature what we can also produce'. (See also E. Cassirer, *Das Erkenntnisproblem in der Philosophie und Wissenschaft der neueren Zeit* (1906-20).) In this he was before his time.

65 E. Cassirer, *Substanzbegriff und Funktionsbegriff* (1910) [in *Substance and Function, and Einstein's Theory of Relativity,* trans. William Curtis Swabey and Marie Collins Swabey (Chicago and London: Open Court 1923)].

66 O. Spengler, *Der Untergang des Abendlandes*, vol. II, p. 367 [*The Decline of the West,* trans. Charles Francis Atkinson, vol. II, *Perspectives of World-History* (New York: Alfred A. Knopf, 1928), pp. 300–1].

67 This is a deductive conclusion by Spengler on the basis of his new periodization, in which the year 1000 is the beginning of the 'Faustian Age'.

68 C. Bouglé, *Leçons de sociologie sur l'évolution des valeurs* (Paris, 1922).

69 E. Radl, *Geschichte der biologischen Theorien in der Neuzeit,* 2nd ed., 1913, especially vol. II [*The History of Biological Theories,* trans. and ed. E. J. Hatfield (London: Humphrey Milford, Oxford University Press, 1930)].

70 Concerning the unanimous agreement of all Marxist socialists, including the leaders of the Soviet Union, on the technical origin of natural science and its exclusively technical meaning, see W. Sombart, *Der proletarische Sozialismus,* vol. I.

71 See the following treatise, *Erkenntnis und Arbeit,* in this volume [*Die Wissensformen und die Gesellschaft*].

72 I refer to the technological, not the specifically economic, aspects of this thesis. See also in this regard my *Schriften zur Soziologie und Weltanschauungslehre*, especially the essay 'Arbeit und Weltanschauung' (1920) [vol. 6 of the *Gesammelte Werke*, pp. 273–89].

73 For example, Henri Bergson, Edouard Le Roy, and the Italian, Benedetto Croce.

74 Moritz Schlick is at present the most sharp-sighted representative of this strongly nominalistic theory of science, which reduces all cognition to finding one element within a complex and to a univocal designation of what can be found; see his *Allgemeine Erkenntnislehre* (Berlin, 1918).

75 See the excellent description by H. Heimsoeth, *Die sechs grossen Themen der abendlandischen Metaphysik und der Ausgang des Mittelalters* (Berlin, 1922), ch. VI. 'Erkenntnis und Wille'; also, E. Przywara, *Religionsbegrundung: Max Scheler—J. H. Newman* (Freiburg, 1923).

76 See in this regard E. R. Jaensch, *Einige allegemainere Fragen der Psychologie und Biologie [des Denkens, Erläutert an der Lehre vom Vergleich]* (Leipzig, 1920). Many excellent points are also made by R. Müller-Freienfels, *Grundzüge einer Lebenspsychologie*, vol. I (Leipzig, 1924).

77 Only in this fashion does the curious contradiction that scholastic philosophy, most strongly guided by feelings and 'prejudices' of faith, is in its intention strictly 'intellectualistic', explain itself.

78 In a similar way the Spanish word *'hidalgo'* (nobleman) = *hijo de algo*, 'son of something'.

79 Concerning the philosophical value of this theory, see *Der Formalismus,* 1st–3rd eds, pp. 165 ff. [4th ed., vol. 2 of the *Gesammelte Werke* (1954), pp. 181 ff.; 5th ed., pp. 175 ff.; *Formalism in Ethics*, pp. 165 ff.].

80 In this regard see vol. I of my forthcoming metaphysics.

81 The schemata of the Christian conception of history, as they have been formulated for the Middle Ages by Otto von Freising, completely break down through this process.

82 Concerning the meaning of this explanation of nature, see the treatise *Erkenntnis und Arbeit*, in this volume [*Die Wissensformen und die Gesellschaft*].

83 In this regard see in *Vom Umstrurz der Werte* my treatise *Das Ressentiment im Aufbau der Moralen,* ch. V, 2, 'Die Subjektivierung der Werte' ['The Subjectivization of Values', in *Ressentiment,* ed. Lewis A. Coser, trans. William W. Holdheim (New York: Free Press, 1961), pp. 144–9]; see also my ethics, section V, on the 'concept of value', ch. 3 [*Formalism in Ethics*, pp. 265–70].

84 The English national economist Petty was the first to reject the theory of *'justum pretium'*.

85 See W. Köhler, *Die physischen Gestalten in Ruhe und im stationären Zustand* (Braunscheig, 1920); also, the forms of laws of quantum theory.

86 Although in an insufficient way, even H. Münsterberg knew this in his *Philosophie der Werte [: Grundzüge einer Weltanschauung]* (Leipzig, 1908). See my elucidation of this question in my ethics [ch. IV; *Formalism in Ethics,* ch. 4]. To think of the world as value-free is a task that man posits to himself for the sake of value: the vital values of *mastery* and power over things.

87 Concerning the essential form of this type of communality, see my *Ethik*, ch. VI, B 4, ad 4 [*Formalism in Ethics*, pp. 519–61].

88 See my essay 'Versuche einer Philosophie des Lebens' (1913), in *Vom Umsturz der Werte*.

89 Concerning the epistemological aspects of this, see the treatise *Erkenntnis und Arbeit* in this volume [*Die Wissensformen und die Gesellschaft*].

90 Concerning these phases and the origin of capitalism, see W. Sombart, *Der moderne Kapitalismus* (2nd ed., 1916-27)—a work which also contains much of importance for the sociology of knowledge.

91 See the essay by Max Planck, 'Die Stellung der neueren Physik zur mechanischen Naturanschauung' [1919], in *Physicalische Rundblicke* [*: Gesammelte Reden und Aufsätze*] (Leipzig, 1922) [pp. 38–63: 'The place of modern physics in the mechanical view of nature', in *A Survey of Physics: A Collection of Lectures and Essays*, trans. R. Jones and D. H. Williams (New York: E. P. Dutton, 1923), pp. 27–44, later ed. entitled *A Survey of Physical Theory*]; also, Walther Nernst, *Zum Gültigkeitsbereich der Naturgesetze* [*: Rede zum Antritt des Rektorates der Friedrich-Wilhelms-Universität in Berlin gehalten in der Aula am 15. Oktober 1921*] (Berlin rectoral address, 1921), as well as W. Köhler, *Physische Gestalten*. See, too, the following treatise, *Erkenntnis und Arbeit*, in the present volume [*Die Wissensformen und die Gesellschaft*].

92 Thus the fundamental theory of functions has been most strongly stimulated by problems of physics, whereas non-Euclidean geometry (Riemann) was initially a purely speculative work, becoming only recently also important in physics.

93 In this regard see Alois Riehl, *Der philosophische Kritizismus und seine Bedeutung für die positive Wissenschaft*, vol. 2 [part I, *Die Sinnlichen und logischen Grundlagen der Erkenntnis*] (1879) [later ed. entitled *Der philosophische Kritizismus, Geschichte und System*].

94 Bouglé, *op. cit.*, pp. 22 ff.; also, O. Spann, *Kurzgefaßtes System der Gesellschaftslehre* (1914), p. 62 [vol. 4 of the *Gesamtausgabe*, p. 349]. Especially characteristic is the invention of the telegraph in Göttingen by Gauss and Weber, who had not the slightest idea of the industrial applicability of their wire, which connected the observatory with the institute of physics.

95 See in this regard J. v. Liebig's beautiful work, *Über Francis Bacon von Verulam und die Methode der Naturforschung* (Munich, 1863).

96 Pierre Duhem, *Ziel und Struktur der physikalischen Theorien* (translated into German by E. Mach) (Leipzig, 1908). See the profound book *Philosophie der Naturwissenschaft* [*: Versuch eines einheitlichen Verstandnisses der Methoden und Ergebnisse ⟨anorganischen⟩ Naturwissenschaft*] by Theodor Haering (Munich, 1923).

97 Empirical, inductive intellectualism (J. S. Mill, for example) and rational, realistic intellectualism and criticism make no difference here; they are equally in error.

98 Striving toward acquisition and striving toward acquiring are two qualitatively different things and should not be confused! It is only the latter that is the psychological trait of capitalism; the former we find in the

whole world. Concerning the psychological trait of the capitalist entrepreneur, see the in many ways new and important work by J.· Schumpeter, *Theorie der wirtschaftlichen Entwicklung* (Leipzig, 1912) [*The Theory of Economic Development: An Inquiry into Profits, Capital, Credit, Interest, and the Business Cycle,* trans. Redvers Opie, Harvard Economic Studies, no. 46 (Cambridge, Mass.: Harvard University Press, 1934)], especially the psychological foundation of his 'dynamic' theory of capital interests.

99 For it is on the contrary what is truly one's own that one seeks to hide under the traditions of earlier times within Scholasticism.

100 See in my book *Wesen und Formen der Sympathie,* part C, on the reality of the *alter ego* [*The Nature of Sympathy,* part III].

101 Adam Smith is also the father of the false theory of class formation through acquired riches; see *The Wealth of Nations.*

102 See W. Sombart's article on the origin of double-entry bookkeeping in Italy and its relation to modern science, *Archiv für* [*Socialwissenschaft und*] *Sozialpolitik* (1923). [No article by Sombart appears in this volume of the journal, nor did Sombart ever write for it an article specifically on this subject.]

103 Concerning the significance of the free amateur researcher [*Liebhaber-forscher*] in England in comparison to Germany, see Radl's excellent observations in vol. 2 of his *Geschichte der biologischen Theorien der Neuzeit* (1913).

104 See my work on 'Universität und Volkshochschule' [1921], in this volume [*Die Wissensformen und die Gesellschaft,* vol. 8 of the *Gesammelte Werke,* pp. 383–420].

105 See the preceding footnote.

106 Preliminary works on this are those of the ethnologists, who at any rate show that there is *not* one entirely *rigid order* of techniques through which all people pass (for example, frequent absence of pottery); see Boas, Graebner, and Ehrenreich; concerning later Western conditions, see the chapters dealing with technique in W. Sombart's work, *Der moderne Kapitalismus* (1916), vol. I, ch. 3.

107 Concerning the difference between technique in matriarchal cultures (working with the soil, pottery, weaving) and in patriarchal cultures (working with wood, for example), see Graebner, *op. cit.,* Hahn, Boas, *et al.*

108 See the judgment of Frederick Soddy in *Science and Life* (1920):

> We need only recall the past history of the progress of science to
> be assured that, whether it takes years or centuries, artificial
> transmutation and the rendering available of a supply of energy
> as much beyond that of fuel as the latter is beyond brute energy
> will be eventually effected [pp. 35–6].

109 The will of domination by men over men is, as every good observation teaches, in no way only a means to gain domination over things; rather, this will is something—as Kant correctly teaches in his *Anthropologie* [*in pragmatischer Hinsicht* (1798, 1800); *Anthropology from a Pragmatic Point of View,* rev. B ed. (1800), trans. Mary J. Gregor (The

Hague: Martinus Nijhoff, 1974)]—completely *original* to man and would never completely disappear even in the face of an ideal technique of production.

110 The technological theory of history, which has developed equally in histories of art (Semper's book on style, for example) [Gottfried Semper, *Der Stil in den technischen und tektonischen Kunsten, oder praktische Aesthetik: Ein Handbuch für Techniker, Kunstler, und Kunstfreunde*, 2 vols (Frankfurt: Verlag für Kunst und Wissenschaft, 1860–3)], histories of war (concerning this see Delbrück's refutation of the theory that the technique of firearms would have destroyed the institution of knighthood) [Hans Delbrück, *Geschichte der Kriegskunst im Rahmen der politischen Geschichte*, vol. 3, *Das Mittelalter* (Berlin: Georg Stilke, 1923), p. 668, vol. 4, *Neuzeit* (1920), pp. 55–6, and 'Über die Bedeutung der Erfindungen in der Geschichte', in *Historische und politische Aufsätze* (Berlin: Walter & Apolant, 1887), pp. 131–48], histories of religion (Usener's overestimation of the cult for the formation of religious-object ideas), science (Labriola and pragmatism), and in the ethos (Buckle and Spencer), 'explaining' the progress of developments of style, of military constitutions, of science, as a method, of economy, and of law, is always *equally wrong*. On the other hand, a technological theory of history is still more justified for science than the Marxist wholly unclear 'relations of production', which means for Marx sometimes managerial form, sometimes legal form, sometimes technique, and sometimes class structure.

111 The Indian 'non-resistance movement' (non-resistance, non-violence) against British domination, led by Mahatma Gandhi, shows that large political and economic 'movements' can be enacted in a purely psycho-technical manner. See in this regard Romain Rolland, *Mahatma Gandhi*. In addition see K. Kanakogi (Japanese), *Gandhi, der Geist der indischen Revolution* (Berlin, 1924); note the pointed judgment of Kanakogi on the German 'passive resistance' in the Ruhr region: 'The German people and their leaders do not know what real passive resistance is'.

112 See his recent, sober speach on 'Psychologie und Medizin', in the *Berliner Medizinische Gesellschaft*. A. Kronfeld, in his book *Psychotherapie* [*Charakterlehre, Psychoanalyse, Hypnose, Psychagogik*], 2nd ed. (Berlin, 1925), furnishes a good introduction to current psychotherapeutics.

113 See in this regard the essay by M. Geiger on the Christian Science movement in America [' "Christian Science" in Amerika'] in the *Süddeutsche Monatshefte* [6, vol. 2 (June 1909): 733–57]; see also Holl's work on the same subject. Kraepelin, *et al.*, have often stressed that our age strikingly resembles the Hellenistic age in terms of the increasing number of these psycho-therapeutic circles and sects and in terms of the increased public interest in abnormal and pathological psychic phenomena. The same holds true for the ever-spreading tendencies to make 'occult' phenomena into starting points for a new metaphysics.

114 The first volume of my metaphysics will deal in detail and critically with Husserl's theory on this question.

115 I first explicated in my *Formalismus* the special problems belonging to a sociology of knowledge concerning the '*co*-intuiting and immediate co-thinking of primal phenomena and ideas', viz. of what is *essentially*

unobservable and indefinable (because it must be pre-given already to all 'possible' observations of things and states of affairs and to all 'possible' definitions and axioms). I have also shown in the same work the problem of the 'phenomenological dispute' (in principle unsolvable by criteria). See also P. L. Landberg's dissertation at the University of Cologne. 'Zur Soziologie der platonische Akademie' [published as *Wesen und Bedeutung der platonische Akademie*] (Bonn, 1923).

116 See in this regard my essay 'Vom Wesen der Philosophie [und der moralischen Bedingung des philosophische Erkennens]' (1916), in *Vom Ewigen im Menschen* [pp. 61–99; 'The nature of philosophy and the moral preconditions of philosophical knowledge', in *On the Eternal in Man*, pp. 67–104].

117 A detailed theory of the levels of givenness in perception teaches us that the moment of reality in the experience of resistance is truly *pre*-given to, and not subsequent to or co-given with, the given contents and the whatness of objects in perception, remembrance, etc.—so that the pregivenness of the experience of resistance is the condition, and not the consequence of, perception (as similarly our drive impulses are the condition for all representations). This theory no less shows that the *very same* processes that give the moment of *reality* are also the conditions for the **hic-et-nunc** whatness of objects. To the extent that this moment of resistance has been deactivated the *'essence'*, which is identical in objects and independent of their *hic et nunc, must* remain for the subject. Vol. 1 of my metaphysics will provide more details on this. See the treatise *Erkenntnis und Arbeit*, in this volume [*Die Wissensformen und die Gesellschaft*], chs. V and VI.

118 See in this regard my treatise 'Vom Sinn des Leidens', in *Schriften zur Soziologie und Weltanschauungslehre*, and the relevant sections in my book *Wesen und Formen der Sympathie*.

119 I tend to see the ultimate root of this revolutionary spirit in present-day Europe—to which in part also belongs the inner European revolutionary war, the so-called 'World War'—in the 'revolt of things' themselves against human beings. All other revolutions are derived revolutions.

120 I have already emphasized this thought sharply in my treatise *Das Ressentiment im Aufbau des Moralen* (1912); see also R. Rolland, *Mahatma Gandhi* (German translation, Zurich, 1923).

121 See in this regard the end of this treatise.

122 See the recent valid objections of Bouglé in his book *Leçonsde de sociologie sur l'évolution des valeurs* (Paris, 1922); furthermore, see the instructive essays by E. Lederer on the Japanese economy, which show what constitutive obstructions the rationalization of capitalism have on the Japanese mentality, the Japanese *ethos,* and certainly the drive-conditioned structure of needs among the Japanese (see *Frankfurter Zeitung*, 1924 ['Japan: Politisch-ökonomisch Einbrüche aus dem fernen Oston', *Frankfurter Zeitung*, 1st morning ed., 11 May 1924, pp. 3–4; 14 May 1924, pp. 1–2; 16 May 1924, pp. 1–2]).

123 See H. Weyl's essay, 'Was ist Materie?,' *op. cit.* We do not have to mention here in particular that the ever-increasing insight that extensive

magnitudes (temporal and spatial determinations) and the Gestalt forms of bodies are of no more essential significance than other qualities, and that accordingly the entire appearance of bodies is nothing but *ideal*, i.e. the *objective appearance* of ordered, effective forces has nothing to do with idealism of the mind.

124 See [A. Sommerfeld, 'Die Grundlagen der Quantentheorie und des bohrschen Atommodells'] *Naturwissenschaften* 12, no. 47 [November 21, 1924]: 1,048.

125 'Reue und Wiedergeburt', in *Vom Ewigen im Menschen*, p. 15 [4th and 5th eds, vol. 5 of the *Gesammelte Werke*, p. 34; 'Repentence and rebirth', in *On the Eternal in Man*, p. 41].

126 See the article [E. Spranger,] 'Zur Theorie des Verstehens und zur geisteswissenschaftlichen Psychologie', in the *Volkelt festschrift* [*Festschrift Johannes Volkelt zum 70. Geburtstag dargebracht*] (Munich, 1918).

127 [Th.Litt.] 'Der Perspektivismus der Weltbilder', in *Individuum und Gemeinschaft* [*: Grundegung der Kulturphilosophie*], 2nd ed. (Leipzig, 1922) [1924], p. 48.

128 See his study on 'Historismus', in *Archiv für Sozialwissenschaft* [*und Sozialpolitik*] 52, no. 1 [June 1924]: 26 [K. Mannheim, 'Historicism', in *Essays on the Sociology of Knowledge*, trans. and ed. Paul Kecskemeti (London: Routledge & Kegan Paul, 1952), p. 105].

129 See the noteworthy ch. 11, 'Werte der Geschichte', in his book [W. Stern,] *Wertphilosophie* (vol. 3 of *Person und Sache*) (Leipzig, 1924).

130 [N. Hartmann,] 'Die Pluralität der Subjekte und ihre gegenseitige Repräsentation', ch. 40, d, in *Grundzüge einer Metaphysik der Erkenntnis* (1921), pp. 267 ff. [ch. 44, d, in 5th ed. (Berlin: Walter de Gruyter, 1965), pp. 332–3].

131 Concerning this question I concur with everything Max Weber developed in his justifiably famed address 'Wissenschaft als Beruf' (Munich, 1919) [in *Gesammelte Aufsätze zur Wissenschaftslehre* (Tübingen J. C. B. Mohr, 1922), pp. 524–55; 'Science as a Vocation', in *From Max Weber*, pp. 129–56]. But see also my criticism of the address in my essay 'Weltanschauungslehre, Soziologie und Weltanschauungssetzung' (1922), in *Schriften zur Soziologie und Weltanschauungslehre*. [See also 'Max Webers Ausschaltung der Philosophie (Zur Psychologie und Soziologie der nominalistischen Denkart)', Appendix d to *Probleme einer Soziologie des Wissens, Gesammelte Werke*, vol. 8, pp. 430–8.]

132 See my treatise *Der Formalismus in der Ethik*, section V 6 [*Formalism in Ethics*, pp. 295 ff.], where I began to expand upon the theory of the dimensions of relativity among valuations.

133 The deepest and the best of what has been written on the subject is ch. II of E. Troeltsch's *Historismus*, Über die Maßstäbe zur Beurteilung historischer Dinge [und ihr Verhältnis zu einem gegenwärtigen Kulturideal]'. Troeltsch arrives at the deepest judgment of his standpoint on p. 166: 'Spontaneity, *a priority*, and self certainty *without* timelessness, universal validity, and absoluteness: this is the only possible formula'. I completely agree with this.

134 The indubitable historical fact that the progress of the Western development of thought has led directly not only to a decline of the

churches and the 'theological spirit' but also to the tremendous decline of *metaphysics,* reveals the flagrant mistake of a positivist sociology of knowledge. Refraining from metaphysics *must indeed necessarily* revive anew the authoritarian churches, because the *ens a se* and the *summum bonum* are a genuinely underivable *sphere* of being and consciousness, which must always be filled with some content. If, therefore, man believes he may and can fill this sphere with content without individual, spontaneous research—as Positivism makes valid—a new climactic period of authoritarian churches is inevitable. For these churches will place their dogmas precisely in these empty spheres.

135 During the whole period of the philosophy of Enlightenment, university philosophers were, with few exceptions, neither Catholic-ecclesiastical, Scholastic Aristoteleans nor Protestant-Scholastic Aristo-teleans of the type for which Melanchton was especially responsible. The most famous university philosopher of that time was Christian Wolff, who, however, was likewise not spared the clash with the state (The Göttingen Seven).

136 One now will better understand, on the basis of this tendency of the sociology of knowledge, even the demands for free higher academies of learning contained in my essay 'Universität und Volkshochschule'. I wish to mention briefly here also that I can *not* consider Count Hermann Keyserling's well-intentioned 'Schule der Weisheit' [School of Wisdom] to be such an institution because it renounces all metaphysical content. [See Keyserling's 'Introduction' to *Creative Understanding* (New York and London: Harper 1929), pp. vii-xxiv, for a description of the School.]

137 The best I know in this regard is the fine, subtle work by Christian Geyer, *Die Religion Stefan Georges* [: *Ein Beitrag zur Wiedergeburt unseres Volkes aus dem Geist der Jugend*] (Jugend und Religion [: Eine Reihe zeitgemässer Schriften, no. 5], Greifenverlag, 1924); I cannot elaborate on this further here.

138 See E. v. Kahler's treatise *Der Beruf der Wissenschaft* (Berlin, 1920). Also, A. Salz, *Für die Wissenschaft gegen die Gebildeten unter ihren Verachtern* (Munich, 1921); E. R. Curtius, 'Max Weber über Wissenschaft als Beruf', *Die Arbeitsgemeinschaft* 17 (1920): 197 ff.; E. Troeltsch, 'Die Revolution in der Wissenschaft' (1921), *op. cit.* [in n. 55 above]; Max Scheler, 'Weltanschauungslehre, Soziologie, Weltanschauungssetzung' (1922), *op. cit.*

139 See also the penetrating speech by the Secretary of State, C. H. Becker, on the occasion of the Kant anniversary celebration in Königsberg, *Kant und die Bildungskreise der Gegenwart* (1924), which certainly appears to me to be too much influenced, not in judgment but in the way the author looks at groups, by H. Rickert's book *Die Philosophie des Lebens* (1920). See in this regard my treatise 'Die deutsche Philosophie der Gegenwart', in *Deutsches Leben der Gegenwart*, ed. Ph. Witkop (Berlin, 1922) [in vol. 7 of the *Gesammelte Werke*, pp. 259–326].

140 See in this regard the works on the sociology of religion by Max Weber, which with justification stress this point as wholly fundamental.

141 This proposition is wrong if *'bonum'* means more than valuable. For the *'omne ens'* is, qua *ens,* indifferent to good and bad. Likewise, the axiom

of Buddhism, Schopenhauer, and Hartmann is wrong: *'omne ens est malum'*, or 'it would be better if there were nothing'.

142 See his writing *Die Absolutheit des Christentums und die Religionsgeschichte* (Tübingen, 1901); concerning Troeltsch's London address, subsequently cited, see the footnote on p. 195 [n. 14].

143 Mohammed's 'holy war', as the preparatory form of the faith of the prophet, has had only short-lived success and, therefore, is of no great importance today.

144 It is obvious that absolutely no church of revelation can be based on religious 'discussion'. Consequently, the Roman Church, for example, generally does not send anyone to these congresses.

145 I have repeatedly stressed that, if the 'cultural state' means a state that is creative in matters of spiritual culture, including even matters of knowledge, there is not and cannot be such a thing. The state has in principle only the significance of at best suppressing powers that exclude the becoming and advancement of a culture.

146 See my work 'Bevölkerungsprobleme als Weltanschauungsfragen' (1921), contained in *Schriften zur Soziologie und Weltanschauungslehre*.

147 See in this regard Bruno A. Fuchs, *Der Geist der bügerlich-kapitalistischen Gesellschaft.* [*Eine Untersuchung über seine Grundlagen und Voraussetzungen*] (Munich, 1918) [1914].

148 See my essay 'Über östliches und Westliches Christentum' (1915), contained in *Schriften zur Soziologie und Weltanschauungslehre*.

149 See Th. G. Masaryk, *Zur russischen Geschichts- und Religionsphilosophie: Soziologische Skizzen* (Jena, 1913), where this point has been well developed. [*The Spirit of Russia: Studies in History, Literature and Philosophy*, trans. Eden and Cedar Paul (London: George Allen & Unwin; New York: Macmillan, 1919).] Concerning eastern Christian mysticism, see the excellent book by Aksakow, (Darmstadt, 1924).

150 Concerning the origin of Positivism, see E. Troeltsch, *Der Historismus und seine Probleme* (1922), vol. I, pp. 371 ff.

151 The orders of mendicant friars are not *only* a religious revival of the primal evangelic spirit of voluntary poverty, as opposed to the profane and super-rich monasteries of the older orders. Rather, they become also an *economic necessity* when this condition of power-born wealth no longer suffices to feed the contemplatives and their organizations.

152 See W. Sombart's new book, *Der proletarische Sozialismus* (10th rev. ed. of *Sozialismus und soziale Bewegung*) (Jena, 1924), vol. I, pp. 138 ff., and his ch. 16, 'Die Wissenschaft', basic to a sociology of knowledge of the proletariat and coinciding exactly with the views suggested here.

153 J. Dietzgen, *Sozialdemokratische Philosophie* (1906), p. 25 [in *Sämtliche Schriften* (later ed. entitled *Gesammelte Schriften*), vol. I, *Das Wesen der menschlichen Kopfarbeit, und kleinere Schriften* (Wiesbaden: Verlag der Dietzgenschen Philosophie, 1911), pp. 184–5, and in *Schriften in drei Bänden* (Berlin: Akademie-Verlag, 1961), vol. I, p. 368; 'Social-Democratic Philosophy', in *Some of the Philosophical Essays on Socialism and Science, Religion, Ethics, Critique-of-Reason and the World-at-Large*, trans. M. Beer and Th. Rothstein, ed. Eugene Dietzgen and Joseph Dietzgen, Jr. (Chicago: Charles H. Kerr, 1908), p. 204]. See also the other

instructive propositions of Dietzgen, as they are cited by W. Sombart, *op. cit.*, vol. I, p. 230.

154 Dietzgen, *op. cit.*, p. 7 [*Sämtliche Schriften*, p. 163; *Schriften in drei Bänden*, vol. I, p. 338; 'Social-Democratic philosophy', p. 176].

155 A. Labriola, *Discorrendo di Socialismo* [*e di Filosofia*], vol. I (1898), pp. 79–80. [*Socialism and Philosophy*, trans. of the 3rd Italian ed. by Ernest Untermann (Chicago: C. H. Kerr, 1906), pp. 84–5.]

156 Sombart, *op. cit.*, vol. I, p. 140.

157 Sombart, *op. cit.*, vol. I, p. 234. [References to Dietzgen's *Religion* are to his *Die Religion der Sozialdemokratic* (1870-75), 4th-6th eds 1877-1903: 'The Religion of Social Democracy', in *Some of the Philosophical Essays*, pp. 90–154.]

158 See our earlier elaborations.

159 See my treatise 'Idole der Selbsterkenntnis', in *Vom Umsturz der Werte*.

160 See in this regard W. Sombart, *op. cit.*, vol. I, ch. 24, 'Die mythische Begründung'. See also J. Plenge, *Marx und Hegel* (1911).

161 I will not be able to show here that both objectively and ontologically the categories of *'causa efficiens'* and *'causa finalis'* are *equally human subjective ones* and do not pertain to actual becoming.

162 A. Grünbaum, *op. cit.*

163 Thus, not something specifically for the upper classes, as it appears so often for the practical Marxists.

164 See in this regard Kant's *Der Streit der Fakultäten*.

165 At very modern universities, such as the University of Cologne, the political science faculty leads all other faculties on festive occasions; it has become the 'highest' faculty. Theological faculties are missing entirely in Germany's universities, which are economically sustained by the *cities* (for example, Frankfurt a. M., Hamburg, Cologne).

166 See my address 'Die Formen des Wissens und die Bildung' (Bonn, 1925), especially the introduction.

167 Concerning this and its theoretician G. Sorel, see W. Sombart, *Der proletarische Sozialismus*, vol. I, especially ch. 24, 'Die mythische Bergründung'.

168 See in this regard vol. 2 [*Die Bewegung*] of W. Sombart's work, *Der proletarische Sozialismus* (1924), pp. 481 ff., 'Die geistigen Machtmittel' (of the Soviet Union).

169 See in this regard the judgment of Benedetto Croce in his essay 'Der Liberalismus', in the *Europäische Revue* [1,] no. 2 [May] 1925 [pp. 97–101], ed. Anton Rohan. See also my address cited above.

170 Naive people who consider as *a priori* 'entirely impossible' a decline of the Western culture of knowledge should always be referred anew to the temporary decline of the ancient culture of knowledge, brought about by Christianity and the victories of the Nordic peoples, and, furthermore, to the victory of Bolshevism in Russia. Also, the movement of fundamentalism in the United States, which tends to exclude the theory of evolution from all public schools, is proof for our contention that modern democratization is becoming increasingly *hostile* to science.

171 This is a fact that, where the middle class has collapsed to the extent

that it has at present in Germany, allows us to harbor only dull suppositions concerning the future of the scientific spirit.

172 Details on this can already be found in my book *Der Genius des Krieges und der deutsche Krieg* (1915): see also C. Schmitt, *Geistesgeschichtliche Grundlagen des heutigen Parliamentarismus* (Munich-Leipzig, 1923).

173 Very many good points on this and the metaphysical-religious background of the belief in one absolute, ontically valid reason are to be found in W. Dilthey and in E. Troeltsch's *Historismus*.

174 What alone comes into question here is the assumption of a material natural law, which is, however, only *relative* for one level of human cultural development, bound by *one* ethos, as it has indeed been thrown open to discussion more recently by Joseph Kohler.

175 O. Liebmann has already appropriately shown this parallel in his writing *Zur Analysis der Wirklichkeit* (1876).

176 See in W. Wundt's *Philosophische Studien* the article 'Was sind Naturgesetze?' [Wundt never wrote an article by this title. Scheler is probably referring to Wundt's essay 'Wer ist der Gesetzgeber der Naturgesetze?'. *Philosophische Studien* 3, no. 3 (1886): 493–6.]

177 See the closing works of vol. II of Spengler's *Der Untergang des Abendlandes*.

178 See Max Weber, Radbruch, Jaspers.

179 See Karl Joël's book *Jakob Burckhardt als Geschichtsphilosoph* (1910) At present a large number of excellent researchers (for example, Lorentz, Bohr, Arrhenius, Einstein) have become citizens of neutral states.

180 The book by Harold Wright, *Bevölkerung* (Preface by J. M. Keynes, trans. Melchior Palyi (Berlin, 1924)) admirably presents plenty of facts underlying this judgment. [*Population* (London: Nisbet; New York: Harcourt, Brace, 1923).]

181 Concerning this point see the good description by G. Hübener in his recent essay on American cultural problems ['Zum gegenwärtigen Kulturproblem in den Vereinigten Staaten'] in the *Preußische Jahrbücher* [197, no. 2 (August 1924): 161–82].

182 This has already been correctly stressed, in my opinion, by W. James and also by Tagore in his Tokyo speech on his impressions of America.

183 It appears to me that no one else has clarified this better—with more precaution—than Alfred Weber in his essay 'Deutschland und der Osten', in *Deutschland und die europäische Kulturkris* (Berlin, 1924).

Name index

Subject index

absolute, the, 14, 45, 71, 113, 132
absolutes, 89, 135, 154; in science, 122
absolutism, 88, 167, 169, 216; age(s) of,
    48, 59–60, 178; religious, 85; of
    science, 151, 167; of the state, 44,
    48, 109, 174, 177, 209
abstraction, 5, 11–12, 96, 127, 152
acquiring, acquisition, 133, 162, 212
act(s), activity, 13, 25, 34, 70, 78, 102,
    123, 128, 141, 167, 172, 194; action
    and passion, 124; of person, spirit,
    40, 44–6, 84, 101, 117
adjustment of cultures, 146, see cosmo-
    politanism of cultures
advertising, marketing, 7, 140
aesthetic values, 14, see beauty
agriculture, 122, 132, 138
'alien', the, 68
alienation, 1, 5, 85, 159
America, 25–6, 94, 142, 144–5, 160,
    183, 191, 198–200, 214, 220; philo-
    sophy, 193; universities, 137, 209
anthropomorphism, 117, 150, 201
anticipation, expectation, 38, 72, 116,
    151, 153
antiquity, 52, 62, 83, 86–7, 112, 114–15,
    123, 157–8, 162, 219
a priority, 216
architecture, 114
aristocracy, 161, 163, 166, 175; re-
    ligious, 162–3
'ars demonstrandi' and 'ars inveniendi',
    48, 119
art(s), 21, 35–6, 38–44, 51, 55, 68, 70,
    110, 114, 185, 194, 214; artists, 1,
    18, 110; sociology of, 33; style in,

43, 49, 114, 214; technique in, 49
asceticism, 45, 90, 113, 140, 143
astronomy, 87, 104, 158
atomists, 106
authority(ies), 134, 167, 177, 179, 202;
    absolute historic, 151

beauty, 4, 14, 18, 21, 26, 125, 194
becoming, 9–10, 14–15, 125, 169–72,
    209, 219
being, 40, 95, 112–13, 123, 126, 147,
    153, 169–71, 193; absolute, 96;
    primordial, 155; spheres of, 70–1,
    217; and value, 126; see forms
being-, thing-in-itself (*Ens a se*), 96, 136,
    150–3, 217
belief, 82, 89
biology, 43, 113, 121, 126, 130–1, 158,
    189; mechanistic, 73
biomorphism, 107, 173; biomorphic
    metaphysics, 106, 164; biomorphic,
    organismic world-view, -image, 43,
    48–9, 70, 73, 75, 90, 92, 108, 124,
    130, 138, 165
birth-control, 143–4
blood (as real sociological factor), 41,
    56–7, 62–3, 108, 113, 198; bonds
    of, blood ties, 7, 18, 59, 81, 87, 164;
    classes of, 115
bodies, physical, 100, 148, 150, 215
body, the, 28, 71–2; lived, 71–2, 103;
    object, 72, -soul dualism, 107;
    -subject, 13
Bolshevism, 93, 115, 176, 219
bourgeoisie, 22, 38, 99, 107–8, 111, 118,
    128–9, 142, 147, 163–4, 166, 168;

226

229

Routledge Social Science Series

Routledge & Kegan Paul   London, Henley and Boston

39 Store Street, London WC1E 7DD
Broadway House, Newtown Road,
Henley-on-Thames, Oxon RG9 1EN
9 Park Street, Boston, Mass. 02108

Contents

*Authors wishing to submit manuscripts for any series in
this catalogue should send them to the Social Science Editor,
Routledge & Kegan Paul Ltd, 39 Store Street,
London WC1E 7DD*

●*Books so marked are available in paperback*
All books are in Metric Demy 8vo format (216 × 138mm approx.)

International Library of Sociology

General Editor   John Rex

GENERAL SOCIOLOGY

Barnsley, J. H. The Social Reality of Ethics. *464 pp.*
Brown, Robert. Explanation in Social Science. *208 pp.*
● Rules and Laws in Sociology. *192 pp.*
Bruford, W. H. Chekhov and His Russia. *A Sociological Study. 244 pp.*
Burton, F. and **Carlen, P.** Official Discourse. *On Discourse Analysis, Government Publications, Ideology. About 140 pp.*
Cain, Maureen E. Society and the Policeman's Role. *326 pp.*
●**Fletcher, Colin.** Beneath the Surface. *An Account of Three Styles of Sociological Research. 221 pp.*
Gibson, Quentin. The Logic of Social Enquiry. *240 pp.*
Glucksmann, M. Structuralist Analysis in Contemporary Social Thought. *212 pp.*
Gurvitch, Georges. Sociology of Law. *Foreword by Roscoe Pound. 264 pp.*
Hinkle, R. Founding Theory of American Sociology 1883-1915. *About 350 pp.*
Homans, George C. Sentiments and Activities. *336 pp.*
Johnson, Harry M. Sociology: *a Systematic Introduction. Foreword by Robert K. Merton. 710 pp.*
●**Keat, Russell** and **Urry, John.** Social Theory as Science. *278 pp.*
Mannheim, Karl. Essays on Sociology and Social Psychology. *Edited by Paul Keckskemeti. With Editorial Note by Adolph Lowe. 344 pp.*
Martindale, Don. The Nature and Types of Sociological Theory. *292 pp.*
●**Maus, Heinz.** A Short History of Sociology. *234 pp.*
Myrdal, Gunnar. Value in Social Theory: *A Collection of Essays on Methodology. Edited by Paul Streeten. 332 pp.*
Ogburn, William F. and **Nimkoff, Meyer F.** A Handbook of Sociology. *Preface by Karl Mannheim. 656 pp. 46 figures. 35 tables.*
Parsons, Talcott, and **Smelser, Neil J.** Economy and Society: *A Study in the Integration of Economic and Social Theory. 362 pp.*
Podgórecki, Adam. Practical Social Sciences. *About 200 pp.*
Raffel, S. Matters of Fact. *A Sociological Inquiry. 152 pp.*
●**Rex, John.** (Ed.) Approaches to Sociology. *Contributions by Peter Abell,* Sociology and the Demystification of the Modern World. *282 pp.*
●**Rex, John** (Ed.) Approaches to Sociology. *Contributions by Peter Abell, Frank Bechhofer, Basil Bernstein, Ronald Fletcher, David Frisby, Miriam Glucksmann, Peter Lassman, Herminio Martins, John Rex, Roland Robertson, John Westergaard and Jock Young. 302 pp.*
Rigby, A. Alternative Realities. *352 pp.*
Roche, M. Phenomenology, Language and the Social Sciences. *374 pp.*
Sahay, A. Sociological Analysis. *220 pp.*

3

Strasser, Hermann. The Normative Structure of Sociology. *Conservative and Emancipatory Themes in Social Thought. About 340 pp.*
Strong, P. Ceremonial Order of the Clinic. *About 250 pp.*
Urry, John. Reference Groups and the Theory of Revolution. *244 pp.*
Weinberg, E. Development of Sociology in the Soviet Union. *173 pp.*

FOREIGN CLASSICS OF SOCIOLOGY

● **Gerth, H. H.** and **Mills, C. Wright.** From Max Weber: *Essays in Sociology. 502 pp.*
● **Tönnies, Ferdinand.** Community and Association. *(Gemeinschaft and Gesellschaft.) Translated and Supplemented by Charles P. Loomis. Foreword by Pitirim A. Sorokin. 334 pp.*

SOCIAL STRUCTURE

Andreski, Stanislav. Military Organization and Society. *Foreword by Professor A. R. Radcliffe-Brown. 226 pp. 1 folder.*
Carlton, Eric. Ideology and Social Order. *Foreword by Professor Philip Abrahams. About 320 pp.*
Coontz, Sydney H. Population Theories and the Economic Interpretation. *202 pp.*
Coser, Lewis. The Functions of Social Conflict. *204 pp.*
Dickie-Clark, H. F. Marginal Situation: *A Sociological Study of a Coloured Group. 240 pp. 11 tables.*
Giner, S. and **Archer, M. S.** (Eds.). Contemporary Europe. *Social Structures and Cultural Patterns. 336 pp.*
● **Glaser, Barney** and **Strauss, Anselm L.** Status Passage. *A Formal Theory. 212 pp.*
Glass, D. V. (Ed.) Social Mobility in Britain. *Contributions by J. Berent, T. Bottomore, R. C. Chambers, J. Floud, D. V. Glass, J. R. Hall, H. T. Himmelweit, R. K. Kelsall, F. M. Martin, C. A. Moser, R. Mukherjee, and W. Ziegel. 420 pp.*
Kelsall, R. K. Higher Civil Servants in Britain: *From 1870 to the Present Day. 268 pp. 31 tables.*
● **Lawton, Denis.** Social Class, Language and Education. *192 pp.*
McLeish, John. The Theory of Social Change: *Four Views Considered. 128 pp.*
● **Marsh, David C.** The Changing Social Structure of England and Wales, 1871-1961. *Revised edition. 288 pp.*
Menzies, Ken. Talcott Parsons and the Social Image of Man. *About 208 pp.*
● **Mouzelis, Nicos.** Organization and Bureaucracy. *An Analysis of Modern Theories. 240 pp.*
Ossowski, Stanislaw. Class Structure in the Social Consciousness. *210 pp.*
● **Podgórecki, Adam.** Law and Society. *302 pp.*
Renner, Karl. Institutions of Private Law and Their Social Functions. *Edited, with an Introduction and Notes, by O. Kahn-Freud. Translated by Agnes Schwarzschild. 316 pp.*

Rex, J. and **Tomlinson, S.** Colonial Immigrants in a British City. *A Class Analysis. 368 pp.*

Smooha, S. Israel: Pluralism and Conflict. *472 pp.*

Wesolowski, W. Class, Strata and Power. *Trans. and with Introduction by G. Kolankiewicz. 160 pp.*

Zureik, E. Palestinians in Israel. *A Study in Internal Colonialism. 264 pp.*

SOCIOLOGY AND POLITICS

Acton, T. A. Gypsy Politics and Social Change. *316 pp.*

Burton, F. Politics of Legitimacy. *Struggles in a Belfast Community. 250 pp.*

Etzioni-Halevy, E. Political Manipulation and Administrative Power. *A Comparative Study. About 200 pp.*

● **Hechter, Michael.** Internal Colonialism. *The Celtic Fringe in British National Development, 1536–1966. 380 pp.*

Kornhauser, William. The Politics of Mass Society. *272 pp. 20 tables.*

Korpi, W. The Working Class in Welfare Capitalism. *Work, Unions and Politics in Sweden. 472 pp.*

Kroes, R. Soldiers and Students. *A Study of Right- and Left-wing Students. 174 pp.*

Martin, Roderick. Sociology of Power. *About 272 pp.*

Myrdal, Gunnar. The Political Element in the Development of Economic Theory. *Translated from the German by Paul Streeten. 282 pp.*

Wong, S.-L. Sociology and Socialism in Contemporary China. *160 pp.*

Wootton, Graham. Workers, Unions and the State. *188 pp.*

CRIMINOLOGY

Ancel, Marc. Social Defence: *A Modern Approach to Criminal Problems. Foreword by Leon Radzinowicz. 240 pp.*

Athens, L. Violent Criminal Acts and Actors. *About 150 pp.*

Cain, Maureen E. Society and the Policeman's Role. *326 pp.*

Cloward, Richard A. and **Ohlin, Lloyd E.** Delinquency and Opportunity: *A Theory of Delinquent Gangs. 248 pp.*

Downes, David M. The Delinquent Solution. *A Study in Subcultural Theory. 296 pp.*

Friedlander, Kate. The Psycho-Analytical Approach to Juvenile Delinquency: *Theory, Case Studies, Treatment. 320 pp.*

Gleuck, Sheldon and **Eleanor.** Family Environment and Delinquency. *With the statistical assistance of Rose W. Kneznek. 340 pp.*

Lopez-Rey, Manuel. Crime. *An Analytical Appraisal. 288 pp.*

Mannheim, Hermann. Comparative Criminology: *a Text Book. Two volumes. 442 pp. and 380 pp.*

Morris, Terence. The Criminal Area: *A Study in Social Ecology. Foreword by Hermann Mannheim. 232 pp. 25 tables. 4 maps.*

Podgorecki, A. and **Łos, M.** *Multidimensional Sociology. About 380 pp.*

Rock, Paul. Making People Pay. *338 pp.*

● **Taylor, Ian, Walton, Paul,** and **Young, Jock.** The New Criminology. *For a Social Theory of Deviance. 325 pp.*
● **Taylor, Ian, Walton, Paul** and **Young, Jock.** (Eds) Critical Criminology. *268 pp.*

SOCIAL PSYCHOLOGY

Bagley, Christopher. The Social Psychology of the Epileptic Child. *320 pp.*
Brittan, Arthur. Meanings and Situations. *224 pp.*
Carroll, J. Break-Out from the Crystal Palace. *200 pp.*
● **Fleming, C. M.** Adolescence: Its Social Psychology. *With an Introduction to recent findings from the fields of Anthropology, Physiology, Medicine, Psychometrics and Sociometry. 288 pp.*
● The Social Psychology of Education: *An Introduction and Guide to Its Study. 136 pp.*
Linton, Ralph. The Cultural Background of Personality. *132 pp.*
● **Mayo, Elton.** The Social Problems of an Industrial Civilization. *With an Appendix on the Political Problem. 180 pp.*
Ottaway, A. K. C. Learning Through Group Experience. *176 pp.*
Plummer, Ken. Sexual Stigma. *An Interactionist Account. 254 pp.*
● **Rose, Arnold M.** (Ed.) Human Behaviour and Social Processes: *an Interactionist Approach. Contributions by Arnold M. Rose, Ralph H. Turner, Anselm Strauss, Everett C. Hughes, E. Franklin Frazier, Howard S. Becker et al. 696 pp.*
Smelser, Neil J. Theory of Collective Behaviour. *448 pp.*
Stephenson, Geoffrey M. The Development of Conscience. *128 pp.*
Young, Kimball. Handbook of Social Psychology. *658 pp. 16 figures. 10 tables.*

SOCIOLOGY OF THE FAMILY

Bell, Colin R. Middle Class Families: *Social and Geographical Mobility. 224 pp.*
Burton, Lindy. Vulnerable Children. *272 pp.*
Gavron, Hannah. The Captive Wife: *Conflicts of Household Mothers. 190 pp.*
George, Victor and **Wilding, Paul.** Motherless Families. *248 pp.*
Klein, Josephine. Samples from English Cultures.
   1. Three Preliminary Studies and Aspects of Adult Life in England. *447 pp.*
   2. Child-Rearing Practices and Index. *247 pp.*
Klein, Viola. The Feminine Character. *History of an Ideology. 244 pp.*
McWhinnie, Alexina M. Adopted Children. *How They Grow Up. 304 pp.*
● **Morgan, D. H. J.** Social Theory and the Family. *About 320 pp.*
● **Myrdal, Alva** and **Klein, Viola.** Women's Two Roles: *Home and Work. 238 pp. 27 tables.*

Parsons, Talcott and **Bales, Robert F.** Family: Socialization and Inter-action Process. *In collaboration with James Olds, Morris Zelditch and Philip E. Slater. 456 pp. 50 figures and tables.*

SOCIAL SERVICES

Bastide, Roger. The Sociology of Mental Disorder. *Translated from the French by Jean McNeil. 260 pp.*

Carlebach, Julius. Caring For Children in Trouble. *266 pp.*

George, Victor. Foster Care. *Theory and Practice. 234 pp.*
Social Security: *Beveridge and After. 258 pp.*

George, V. and **Wilding, P.** Motherless Families. *248 pp.*

● **Goetschius, George W.** Working with Community Groups. *256 pp.*

Goetschius, George W. and **Tash, Joan.** Working with Unattached Youth. *416 pp.*

Heywood, Jean S. Children in Care. *The Development of the Service for the Deprived Child. Third revised edition. 284 pp.*

King, Roy D., Ranes, Norma V. and **Tizard, Jack.** Patterns of Residen-tial Care. *356 pp.*

Leigh, John. Young People and Leisure. *256 pp.*

● **Mays, John.** (Ed.) Penelope Hall's Social Services of England and Wales. *About 324 pp.*

Morris, Mary. Voluntary Work and the Welfare State. *300 pp.*

Nokes, P. L. The Professional Task in Welfare Practice. *152 pp.*

Timms, Noel. Psychiatric Social Work in Great Britain (1939-1962). *280 pp.*

● Social Casework: *Principles and Practice. 256 pp.*

SOCIOLOGY OF EDUCATION

Banks, Olive. Parity and Prestige in English Secondary Education: a Study in Educational Sociology. *272 pp.*

● **Blyth, W. A. L.** English Primary Education. *A Sociological Description.* 2. Background. *168 pp.*

Collier, K. G. The Social Purposes of Education: *Personal and Social Values in Education. 268 pp.*

Evans, K. M. Sociometry and Education. *158 pp.*

● **Ford, Julienne.** Social Class and the Comprehensive School. *192 pp.*

Foster, P. J. Education and Social Change in Ghana. *336 pp. 3 maps.*

Fraser, W. R. Education and Society in Modern France. *150 pp.*

Grace, Gerald R. Role Conflict and the Teacher. *150 pp.*

Hans, Nicholas. New Trends in Education in the Eighteenth Century. *278 pp. 19 tables.*

● Comparative Education: *A Study of Educational Factors and Tra-ditions. 360 pp.*

● **Hargreaves, David.** Interpersonal Relations and Education. *432 pp.*

● Social Relations in a Secondary School. *240 pp.*

School Organization and Pupil Involvement. *A Study of Secondary Schools.*

● **Mannheim, Karl** and **Stewart, W.A.C.** An Introduction to the Sociology of Education. *206 pp.*
● **Musgrove, F.** Youth and the Social Order. *176 pp.*
● **Ottaway, A. K. C.** Education and Society: An Introduction to the Sociology of Education. *With an Introduction by W. O. Lester Smith. 212 pp.*
Peers, Robert. Adult Education: *A Comparative Study. Revised edition. 398 pp.*
Stratta, Erica. The Education of Borstal Boys. *A Study of their Educational Experiences prior to, and during, Borstal Training. 256 pp.*
● **Taylor, P. H., Reid, W. A.** and **Holley, B. J.** The English Sixth Form. *A Case Study in Curriculum Research. 198 pp.*

SOCIOLOGY OF CULTURE

Eppel, E. M. and **M.** Adolescents and Morality: *A Study of some Moral Values and Dilemmas of Working Adolescents in the Context of a changing Climate of Opinion. Foreword by W. J. H. Sprott. 268 pp. 39 tables.*
● **Fromm, Erich.** The Fear of Freedom. *286 pp.*
● The Sane Society. *400 pp.*
Johnson, L. The Cultural Critics. *From Matthew Arnold to Raymond Williams. 233 pp.*
Mannheim, Karl. Essays on the Sociology of Culture. *Edited by Ernst Mannheim in co-operation with Paul Kecskemeti. Editorial Note by Adolph Lowe. 280 pp.*
Zijderfeld, A. C. On Clichés. *The Supersedure of Meaning by Function in Modernity. About 132 pp.*

SOCIOLOGY OF RELIGION

Argyle, Michael and **Beit-Hallahmi, Benjamin.** The Social Psychology of Religion. *About 256 pp.*
Glasner, Peter E. The Sociology of Secularisation. *A Critique of a Concept. About 180 pp.*
Hall, J. R. The Ways Out. *Utopian Communal Groups in an Age of Babylon. 280 pp.*
Ranson, S., Hinings, B. and **Bryman, A.** Clergy, Ministers and Priests. *216 pp.*
Stark, Werner. The Sociology of Religion. *A Study of Christendom.*
Volume II. *Sectarian Religion. 368 pp.*
Volume III. *The Universal Church. 464 pp.*
Volume IV. *Types of Religious Man. 352 pp.*
Volume V. *Types of Religious Culture. 464 pp.*
Turner, B. S. Weber and Islam. *216 pp.*
Watt, W. Montgomery. Islam and the Integration of Society. *320 pp.*

SOCIOLOGY OF ART AND LITERATURE

Jarvie, Ian C. Towards a Sociology of the Cinema. *A Comparative Essay on the Structure and Functioning of a Major Entertainment Industry. 405 pp.*

Rust, Frances S. Dance in Society. *An Analysis of the Relationships between the Social Dance and Society in England from the Middle Ages to the Present Day. 256 pp. 8 pp. of plates.*

Schücking, L. L. The Sociology of Literary Taste. *112 pp.*

Wolff, Janet. Hermeneutic Philosophy and the Sociology of Art. *150 pp.*

SOCIOLOGY OF KNOWLEDGE

Diesing, P. Patterns of Discovery in the Social Sciences. *262 pp.*

● **Douglas, J. D.** (Ed.) Understanding Everyday Life. *370 pp.*

Glasner, B. Essential Interactionism. *About 220 pp.*

● **Hamilton, P.** Knowledge and Social Structure. *174 pp.*

Jarvie, I. C. Concepts and Society. *232 pp.*

Mannheim, Karl. Essays on the Sociology of Knowledge. *Edited by Paul Kecskemeti. Editorial Note by Adolph Lowe. 353 pp.*

Remmling, Gunter W. The Sociology of Karl Mannheim. *With a Bibliographical Guide to the Sociology of Knowledge, Ideological Analysis, and Social Planning. 255 pp.*

Remmling, Gunter W. (Ed.) Towards the Sociology of Knowledge. *Origin and Development of a Sociological Thought Style. 463 pp.*

URBAN SOCIOLOGY

Aldridge, M. The British New Towns. *A Programme Without a Policy. About 250 pp.*

Ashworth, William. The Genesis of Modern British Town Planning: *A Study in Economic and Social History of the Nineteenth and Twentieth Centuries. 288 pp.*

Brittan, A. The Privatised World. *196 pp.*

Cullingworth, J. B. Housing Needs and Planning Policy: *A Restatement of the Problems of Housing Need and 'Overspill' in England and Wales. 232 pp. 44 tables. 8 maps.*

Dickinson, Robert E. City and Region: *A Geographical Interpretation. 608 pp. 125 figures.*

The West European City: *A Geographical Interpretation. 600 pp. 129 maps. 29 plates.*

Humphreys, Alexander J. New Dubliners: *Urbanization and the Irish Family. Foreword by George C. Homans. 304 pp.*

Jackson, Brian. Working Class Community: *Some General Notions raised by a Series of Studies in Northern England. 192 pp.*

● **Mann, P. H.** An Approach to Urban Sociology. *240 pp.*

Mellor, J. R. Urban Sociology in an Urbanized Society. *326 pp.*

Morris, R. N. and **Mogey, J.** The Sociology of Housing. *Studies at Berinsfield. 232 pp. 4 pp. plates.*

Rosser, C. and **Harris, C.** The Family and Social Change. *A Study of Family and Kinship in a South Wales Town. 352 pp. 8 maps.*

● **Stacey, Margaret, Batsone, Eric, Bell, Colin** and **Thurcott, Anne.** Power, Persistence and Change. *A Second Study of Banbury. 196 pp.*

RURAL SOCIOLOGY

Mayer, Adrian C. Peasants in the Pacific. *A Study of Fiji Indian Rural Society. 248 pp. 20 plates.*

Williams, W. M. The Sociology of an English Village: *Gosforth. 272 pp. 12 figures. 13 tables.*

SOCIOLOGY OF INDUSTRY AND DISTRIBUTION

Dunkerley, David. The Foreman. *Aspects of Task and Structure. 192 pp.*

Eldridge, J. E. T. Industrial Disputes. *Essays in the Sociology of Industrial Relations. 288 pp.*

Hollowell, Peter G. The Lorry Driver. *272 pp.*

● **Oxaal, I., Barnett, T.** and **Booth, D.** (Eds) Beyond the Sociology of Development. *Economy and Society in Latin America and Africa. 295 pp.*

Smelser, Neil J. Social Change in the Industrial Revolution: *An Application of Theory to the Lancashire Cotton Industry, 1770–1840. 468 pp. 12 figures. 14 tables.*

Watson, T. J. The Personnel Managers. *A Study in the Sociology of Work and Employment. 262 pp.*

ANTHROPOLOGY

Brandel-Syrier, Mia. Reeftown Elite. *A Study of Social Mobility in a Modern African Community on the Reef. 376 pp.*

Dickie-Clark, H. F. The Marginal Situation. *A Sociological Study of a Coloured Group. 236 pp.*

Dube, S. C. Indian Village. *Foreword by Morris Edward Opler. 276 pp. 4 plates.*

India's Changing Villages: *Human Factors in Community Development. 260 pp. 8 plates. 1 map.*

Firth, Raymond. Malay Fishermen. *Their Peasant Economy. 420 pp. 17 pp. plates.*

Gulliver, P. H. Social Control in an African Society: a Study of the Arusha, Agricultural Masai of Northern Tanganyika. *320 pp. 8 plates. 10 figures.*

Family Herds. *288 pp.*

Jarvie, Ian C. The Revolution in Anthropology. *268 pp.*

Little, Kenneth L. Mende of Sierra Leone. *308 pp. and folder.*

Negroes in Britain. *With a New Introduction and Contemporary Study by Leonard Bloom. 320 pp.*

Madan, G. R. Western Sociologists on Indian Society. *Marx, Spencer, Weber, Durkheim, Pareto. 384 pp.*

Mayer, A. C. Peasants in the Pacific. *A Study of Fiji Indian Rural Society. 248 pp.*

Meer, Fatima. Race and Suicide in South Africa. *325 pp.*

Smith, Raymond T. The Negro Family in British Guiana: *Family Structure and Social Status in the Villages. With a Foreword by Meyer Fortes. 314 pp. 8 plates. 1 figure. 4 maps.*

SOCIOLOGY AND PHILOSOPHY

Barnsley, John H. The Social Reality of Ethics. *A Comparative Analysis of Moral Codes. 448 pp.*

Diesing, Paul. Patterns of Discovery in the Social Sciences. *362 pp.*

● **Douglas, Jack D.** (Ed.) Understanding Everyday Life. *Toward the Reconstruction of Sociological Knowledge. Contributions by Alan F. Blum, Aaron W. Cicourel, Norman K. Denzin, Jack D. Douglas, John Heeren, Peter McHugh, Peter K. Manning, Melvin Power, Matthew Speier, Roy Turner, D. Lawrence Wieder, Thomas P. Wilson and Don H. Zimmerman. 370 pp.*

Gorman, Robert A. The Dual Vision. *Alfred Schutz and the Myth of Phenomenological Social Science. About 300 pp.*

Jarvie, Ian C. Concepts and Society. *216 pp.*

Kilminster, R. Praxis and Method. *A Sociological Dialogue with Lukács, Gramsci and the early Frankfurt School. About 304 pp.*

● **Pelz, Werner.** The Scope of Understanding in Sociology. *Towards a More Radical Reorientation in the Social Humanistic Sciences. 283 pp.*

Roche, Maurice. Phenomenology, Language and the Social Sciences. *371 pp.*

Sahay, Arun. Sociological Analysis. *212 pp.*

Slater, P. Origin and Significance of the Frankfurt School. *A Marxist Perspective. About 192 pp.*

Spurling, L. Phenomenology and the Social World. *The Philosophy of Merleau-Ponty and its Relation to the Social Sciences. 222 pp.*

Wilson, H. T. The American Ideology. *Science, Technology and Organization as Modes of Rationality. 368 pp.*

International Library of Anthropology

General Editor Adam Kuper

Ahmed, A. S. Millenium and Charisma Among Pathans. *A Critical Essay in Social Anthropology. 192 pp.*
Pukhtun Economy and Society. *About 360 pp.*

Brown, Paula. The Chimbu. *A Study of Change in the New Guinea Highlands. 151 pp.*
Foner, N. Jamaica Farewell. *200 pp.*
Gudeman, Stephen. Relationships, Residence and the Individual. *A Rural Panamanian Community. 288 pp. 11 plates, 5 figures, 2 maps, 10 tables.*
  The Demise of a Rural Economy. *From Subsistence to Capitalism in a Latin American Village. 160 pp.*
Hamnett, Ian. Chieftainship and Legitimacy. *An Anthropological Study of Executive Law in Lesotho. 163 pp.*
Hanson, F. Allan. Meaning in Culture. *127 pp.*
Humphreys, S. C. Anthropology and the Greeks. *288 pp.*
Karp, I. Fields of Change Among the Iteso of Kenya. *140 pp.*
Lloyd, P. C. Power and Independence. *Urban Africans' Perception of Social Inequality. 264 pp.*
Parry, J. P. Caste and Kinship in Kangra. *352 pp. Illustrated.*
Pettigrew, Joyce. Robber Noblemen. *A Study of the Political System of the Sikh Jats. 284 pp.*
Street, Brian V. The Savage in Literature. *Representations of 'Primitive' Society in English Fiction, 1858–1920. 207 pp.*
Van Den Berghe, Pierre L. Power and Privilege at an African University. *278 pp.*

International Library of Social Policy

General Editor   Kathleen Jones

Bayley, M. Mental Handicap and Community Care. *426 pp.*
Bottoms, A. E. and **McClean, J. D.** Defendants in the Criminal Process. *284 pp.*
Butler, J. R. Family Doctors and Public Policy. *208 pp.*
Davies, Martin. Prisoners of Society. *Attitudes and Aftercare. 204 pp.*
Gittus, Elizabeth. Flats, Families and the Under-Fives. *285 pp.*
Holman, Robert. Trading in Children. *A Study of Private Fostering. 355 pp.*
Jeffs, A. Young People and the Youth Service. *About 180 pp.*
Jones, Howard, and **Cornes, Paul.** Open Prisons. *288 pp.*
Jones, Kathleen. History of the Mental Health Service. *428 pp.*
Jones, Kathleen, with **Brown, John, Cunningham, W. J., Roberts, Julian** and **Williams, Peter.** Opening the Door. *A Study of New Policies for the Mentally Handicapped. 278 pp.*
Karn, Valerie. Retiring to the Seaside. *About 280 pp. 2 maps. Numerous tables.*
King, R. D. and **Elliot, K. W.** Albany: Birth of a Prison—End of an Era. *394 pp.*

Thomas, J. E. The English Prison Officer since 1850: *A Study in Conflict.* *258 pp.*

Walton, R. G. Women in Social Work. *303 pp.*

● **Woodward, J.** To Do the Sick No Harm. *A Study of the British Voluntary Hospital System to 1875. 234 pp.*

International Library of Welfare and Philosophy

General Editors   Noel Timms and David Watson

● **McDermott, F. E.** (Ed.) Self-Determination in Social Work. *A Collection of Essays on Self-determination and Related Concepts by Philosophers and Social Work Theorists. Contributors: F. B. Biestek, S. Bernstein, A. Keith-Lucas, D. Sayer, H. H. Perelman, C. Whittington, R. F. Stalley, F. E. McDermott, I. Berlin, H. J. McCloskey, H. L. A. Hart, J. Wilson, A. I. Melden, S. I. Benn. 254 pp.*

● **Plant, Raymond.** Community and Ideology. *104 pp.*

Ragg, Nicholas M. People Not Cases. *A Philosophical Approach to Social Work. About 250 pp.*

● **Timms, Noel** and **Watson, David.** (Eds) Talking About Welfare. *Readings in Philosophy and Social Policy. Contributors: T. H. Marshall, R. B. Brandt, G. H. von Wright, K. Nielsen, M. Cranston, R. M. Titmuss, R. S. Downie, E. Telfer, D. Donnison, J. Benson, P. Leonard, A. Keith-Lucas, D. Walsh, I. T. Ramsey. 320 pp.*

● (Eds). Philosophy in Social Work. *250 pp.*

● **Weale, A.** Equality and Social Policy. *164 pp.*

Primary Socialization, Language and Education

General Editor   Basil Bernstein

Adlam, Diana S., *with the assistance of Geoffrey Turner and Lesley Lineker.* Code in Context. *About 272 pp.*

Bernstein, Basil. Class, Codes and Control. *3 volumes.*
● 1. *Theoretical Studies Towards a Sociology of Language. 254 pp.*
2. *Applied Studies Towards a Sociology of Language. 377 pp.*
● 3. *Towards a Theory of Educational Transmission. 167 pp.*

Brandis, W. and **Bernstein, B.** Selection and Control. *176 pp.*

Brandis, Walter and **Henderson, Dorothy.** Social Class, Language and Communication. *288 pp.*

Cook-Gumperz, Jenny. Social Control and Socialization. *A Study of Class Differences in the Language of Maternal Control. 290 pp.*

● **Gahagan, D. M** and **G. A.** Talk Reform. *Exploration in Language for Infant School Children. 160 pp.*

Hawkins, P. R. Social Class, the Nominal Group and Verbal Strategies. *About 220 pp.*

Robinson, W. P. and **Rackstraw, Susan D. A.** A Question of Answers. *2 volumes. 192 pp. and 180 pp.*

Turner, Geoffrey J. and **Mohan, Bernard A.** A Linguistic Description and Computer Programme for Children's Speech. *208 pp.*

Reports of the Institute of Community Studies

Baker, J. The Neighbourhood Advice Centre. A Community Project in Camden. *320 pp.*

● **Cartwright, Ann.** Patients and their Doctors. *A Study of General Practice. 304 pp.*

Dench, Geoff. Maltese in London. *A Case-study in the Erosion of Ethnic Consciousness. 302 pp.*

Jackson, Brian and **Marsden, Dennis.** Education and the Working Class: *Some General Themes raised by a Study of 88 Working-class Children in a Northern Industrial City. 268 pp. 2 folders.*

Marris, Peter. The Experience of Higher Education. *232 pp. 27 tables.*
● Loss and Change. *192 pp.*

Marris, Peter and **Rein, Martin.** Dilemmas of Social Reform. *Poverty and Community Action in the United States. 256 pp.*

Marris, Peter and **Somerset, Anthony.** African Businessmen. *A Study of Entrepreneurship and Development in Keyna. 256 pp.*

Mills, Richard. Young Outsiders: *a Study in Alternative Communities. 216 pp.*

Runciman, W. G. Relative Deprivation and Social Justice. *A Study of Attitudes to Social Inequality in Twentieth-Century England. 352 pp.*

Willmott, Peter. Adolescent Boys in East London. *230 pp.*

Willmott, Peter and **Young, Michael.** Family and Class in a London Suburb. *202 pp. 47 tables.*

Young, Michael and **McGeeney, Patrick.** Learning Begins at Home. *A Study of a Junior School and its Parents. 128 pp.*

Young, Michael and **Willmott, Peter.** Family and Kinship in East London. *Foreword by Richard M. Titmuss. 252 pp. 39 tables.*
The Symmetrical Family. *410 pp.*

Reports of the Institute for Social Studies in Medical Care

Cartwright, Ann, Hockey, Lisbeth and **Anderson, John J.** Life Before Death. *310 pp.*

Dunnell, Karen and **Cartwright, Ann.** Medicine Takers, Prescribers and Hoarders. *190 pp.*

Farrell, C. My Mother Said. . . . *A Study of the Way Young People Learned About Sex and Birth Control. 200 pp.*

Medicine, Illness and Society

General Editor   W. M. Williams

Hall, David J. Social Relations & Innovation. *Changing the State of Play in Hospitals. 232 pp.*

Hall, David J., and **Stacey, M.** (Eds) Beyond Separation. *234 pp.*

Robinson, David. The Process of Becoming Ill. *142 pp.*

Stacey, Margaret *et al.* Hospitals, Children and Their Families. *The Report of a Pilot Study. 202 pp.*

Stimson G. V. and **Webb, B.** Going to See the Doctor. *The Consultation Process in General Practice. 155 pp.*

Monographs in Social Theory

General Editor   Arthur Brittan

● **Barnes, B.** Scientific Knowledge and Sociological Theory. *192 pp.*

Bauman, Zygmunt. Culture as Praxis. *204 pp.*

● **Dixon, Keith.** Sociological Theory. *Pretence and Possibility. 142 pp.*

Meltzer, B. N., Petras, J. W. and **Reynolds, L. T.** Symbolic Interactionism. *Genesis, Varieties and Criticisms. 144 pp.*

● **Smith, Anthony D.** The Concept of Social Change. *A Critique of the Functionalist Theory of Social Change. 208 pp.*

Routledge Social Science Journals

The British Journal of Sociology. *Editor – Angus Stewart; Associate Editor – Leslie Sklair. Vol. 1, No. 1 – March 1950 and Quarterly. Roy. 8vo. All back issues available. An international journal publishing original papers in the field of sociology and related areas.*

15

Community Work. *Edited by David Jones and Marjorie Mayo. 1973. Published annually.*

Economy and Society. *Vol. 1, No. 1. February 1972 and Quarterly. Metric Roy. 8vo. A journal for all social scientists covering sociology, philosophy, anthropology, economics and history. All back numbers available.*

Ethnic and Racial Studies. *Editor – John Stone. Vol. 1 – 1978. Published quarterly.*

Religion. Journal of Religion and Religions. *Chairman of Editorial Board, Ninian Smart. Vol. 1, No. 1, Spring 1971. A journal with an inter-disciplinary approach to the study of the phenomena of religion. All back numbers available.*

Sociology of Health and Illness. *A Journal of Medical Sociology. Editor – Alan Davies; Associate Editor – Ray Jobling. Vol. 1, Spring 1979. Published 3 times per annum.*

Year Book of Social Policy in Britain, The. *Edited by Kathleen Jones. 1971. Published annually.*

Social and Psychological Aspects of Medical Practice

Editor Trevor Silverstone

Lader, Malcolm. Psychophysiology of Mental Illness. *280 pp.*

● **Silverstone, Trevor** and **Turner, Paul.** Drug Treatment in Psychiatry. *Revised edition. 256 pp.*

Whiteley, J. S. and **Gordon, J.** Group Approaches in Psychiatry. *256 pp.*

Printed in Great Britain by
Lowe & Brydone Printers Limited, Thetford, Norfolk